AIRBORNE

OSPREY
PUBLISHING

AIRBORNE

THE COMBAT STORY OF
ED SHAMES
OF
EASY COMPANY

IAN GARDNER

FOREWORD BY JAMES C. ROBERTS

DEDICATION

I would like to dedicate this book to the following soldiers: Paul Rogers, Amos Taylor, Roderick Strohl, Forrest Guth and Joseph Madona.

These soldiers made me the soldier I became!

Edward D. Shames

God Almighty! In a few short hours we will be in battle with the enemy. We do not join battle afraid. We do not ask favors or indulgence but ask that, if you will, use us as your instrument for the right and an aid in returning peace to the world. We do not know or seek what our fate will be. We only ask this, that if die we must, that we die as men would die, without complaining, without pleading and safe in the feeling that we have done our best for what we thought was right. Oh Lord! Protect our loved ones and be near us in the fire ahead, and with us now as we each pray to you.

Colonel Wolverton's prayer on the eve of
3rd Battalion's insertion into Normandy
(5th June 1944)

First published in Great Britain in 2015 by Osprey Publishing,
PO Box 883, Oxford, OX1 9PL, UK
PO Box 3985, New York, NY 10185-3985, USA
E-mail: info@ospreypublishing.com

OSPREY PUBLISHING IS PART OF THE OSPREY GROUP

A CIP catalogue record for this book is available from the British Library

Ian Gardner has asserted his right under the Copyright, Designs and Patents
Act, 1988, to be identified as the Author of this Work.

ISBN: 978 1 4728 0485 3
ePub ISBN: 978 1 4728 1343 5
PDF ISBN: 978 1 4728 1342 8

Index by Zoe Ross
Typeset in Bembo
Originated by PDQ Digital Media Solutions, Bungay
Printed in China through Worldprint Ltd.

15 16 17 18 19   10 9 8 7 6 5 4 3 2 1

Front cover (left to right): Paratroopers from the 506th PIR advancing
towards Foy (NARA via Reg Jans); Ed Shames, photographed in his new
uniform after receiving his battlefield commission (Ed Shames); Parachutes
open overhead as waves of paratroops land in Holland during operations by
the 1st Allied Airborne Army. September 1944. (Roger-Viollet / Topfoto)

Osprey Publishing is supporting the Woodland Trust, the UK's leading
woodland conservation charity, by funding the dedication of trees.

www.ospreypublishing.com

CONTENTS

FOREWORD

From 1996 until 2005 I served as founder and president of the World War II Veterans Committee and from 2005 until the present I have been president of its successor organization, the American Veterans Center.

Our mission throughout all these years has been to recognize and honor our veterans' legacy of service and sacrifice and to preserve their stories for future generations. In the course of my work I have been privileged to meet and get to know hundreds of veterans, from Frank Buckles, the last American veteran of World War I, to newly returned servicemen and women from Afghanistan.

Among all these individuals, Colonel Ed Shames occupies a special place. He is, to use an overwrought phrase, a true American hero. A member of the legendary E Company, 506th Regiment of the 101st Airborne Division – now known globally as the Band of Brothers – in World War II, Colonel Shames was the first member of this storied division to receive a battlefield commission after D-Day.

The arc of his amazing life is traced in this book, which follows Shames from the quiet streets of Virginia Beach, Virginia to the new airborne training camp at Toccoa, Georgia; from rigorous training at bases in England to the historic D-Day landings of June 1944; from nearly continuous battles, including Operation *Market Garden* in Holland, to the heroic defense of Bastogne in Belgium; from heavy fighting through Germany to a visit to Hitler's Eagle's Nest retreat in Bavaria where Shames helped himself to a monogrammed bottle of the Führer's cognac. (A bottle that was opened on a deliciously ironic, wildly improbable and triumphantly fitting occasion: the celebration of his son's Bar Mitzvah 17 years later.)

Along the way we read of Colonel Shames' encounter with "Martin Bormann," detention of Feldmarschall Albert Kesselring, and a gut-wrenching tour of Dachau – he was one of the first American officers to visit that horrific hellhole and the visit still haunts him seven decades later.

We also meet many memorable characters along the way, including Colonel Robert Sink, portrayed memorably in *Band of Brothers* by actor Dale Dye, and Ida, Colonel Shames' wife of 70 years, a lovely, vivacious and spunky lady who is a fully worthy match for her tart-tongued husband every step of the way. "When Eddie returned home in '45," Ida told me, "the real war began."

Ed Shames remains amazingly strong and vibrant at the age of 92 and his memories of the war are remarkably vivid and detailed, and all ably related in this book by author Ian Gardner, who supplies rich context and historical detail.

I have spent many, many enjoyable hours chatting with Colonel Shames and listening with rapt attention to his personal accounts of World War II. He is a master storyteller and I have lamented to him many times what a shame it was that a larger audience could not hear his story.

I rejoice to say that with the publication of *Airborne* his story has been told at long last. It is a valuable addition to the historical record as we mark the 70th anniversary of the end of World War II.

James C. Roberts
President, American Veterans Center
Great Falls, Virginia

INTRODUCTION

As a former British Airborne Reservist, I have always been interested in the history of the sky soldiers from World War II, especially the American 101st Airborne Division. My first book about 3rd Battalion, 506th Parachute Infantry Regiment, in Normandy – *Tonight We Die As Men* – was co-written with Roger Day and published by Osprey in April 2009.

I am in no doubt that my "limited" military background was one of the reasons why over fifty 3rd Battalion veterans put their trust in me. "Trust" is an easy word to use but despite my obvious connection, I feel it still had to be earned, which is why *Tonight We Die As Men* took almost six years to research and piece together. Roger was already well established as a semi-professional historical writer and it was his skill and patience that helped shape the book into what I believe is a first-class piece of non-fiction literature.

Unlike many of our peers, we were not professors of history or university lecturers. Although in theory this should have held us back – and maybe in some ways it did – it quickly became apparent, at least to me, that having no official academic qualifications was sometimes of benefit when it came to dealing with the old boys. Most felt that my casual open approach and sense of humor helped them relax without feeling intimidated or self-conscious.

As my contributor list grew by word of mouth, I spent hundreds of hours on the telephone getting to know "my guys" and their families, all the while learning more and more about their individual experiences on D-Day and beyond. Almost like method acting, it became easier for me to contextualize the huge amount of information being passed to me. Luckily, I found a family in St-Côme-du-Mont – a close-knit village in Normandy near to where much of the 506th action took place – who were willing to take me under their wing. Subsequently, I spent a lot of time "in country" with Michel Léonard, occasionally even accompanied by some of the veterans, talking with locals – who, we must not forget, were also caught up in the fighting – following up leads, finding new ones, but always reporting back after each trip to discuss any details with each relevant contributor.

Since *Tonight We Die As Men* was published, I have followed the exact same research process to produce two further highly detailed volumes – *Deliver Us From Darkness* and *No Victory in Valhalla* – charting the story of 3/506 through Holland and Bastogne to the very end of World War II. Roger armed me with the tools to approach both of these projects without any further editorial assistance and I am now pleased to be taken more seriously as a historian and writer on my own merits.

This combat biography, *Airborne*, was specifically written about Ed Shames, because of his undeniable contribution to 2nd and 3rd Battalions. Ed featured throughout my previous works but this book goes a long way toward filling in the gaps, providing the reader with a better understanding of what he, as a volunteer, put himself through over 70 years ago.

I first met Ed in 2002. We had spent months speaking on the phone but this was the first time we had met in person. We spent three days pondering over maps, working on the battle of Bloody Gully – which took place near Carentan. At that point, I had not figured out the exact location but with a little help from Ed, moved closer to understanding what had happened on June 13, 1944. It wasn't all business and every day we made time for a decent lunch washed down with a couple of beers at my local pub, The Prince of Wales. A few years later as we became more familiar he told me, "Aw, come on Ian, who's gonna believe all this crap!" Maybe he was right, but Ed's service in World War II has many twists and

I always knew that if set into a well-researched narrative Shames' story could be appreciated by many, not just those interested in E Company or *Band of Brothers*.

Due to the success of Stephen E. Ambrose's book, *Band of Brothers*, and the subsequent HBO mini-series, it is sometimes easy to forget that Ed spent almost two years in 3rd Battalion, mostly as Lieutenant Colonel Robert Wolverton's operations sergeant (S3). This book not only puts a little more flesh on Ed's previous service but also explores the rollercoaster ride he experienced after he was reassigned to E Company. Ed's character, as portrayed by Joseph May in the HBO mini-series, was a mouthy individual with a mean attitude, which is not the person that I have come to know. Ed would be the first to admit that back in the day he could be a real "SOB," but always insists that he was fair with it.

That there are inaccuracies in *Band of Brothers* is widely accepted, but perhaps in my opinion the most important inaccuracy is the way Stephen Ambrose described the attack to recapture Foy on January 13, 1945. What really took place and the reasons why, were, in my opinion, completely misrepresented, regarding the participation of the other units involved. The composite version of E Co created by the mini-series troubled some of the veterans, including Earl McClung, Darrell "Shifty" Powers, Robert "Popeye" Wynn, James "Moe" Alley, and Rod Strohl, who were all fiercely proud of 3rd Platoon, which Ed took command of in mid-October 1944. In addition, several other integral members such as Amos "Buck" Taylor, Paul Rogers, and Forrest Guth were never really included by Ambrose or HBO.

In May 2013 Ed came over from Virginia, probably for the last time, on a final tour across Europe with me where we revisited many of the sites identified in my previous research and a few new ones. As a result of hours of conversation and work with Ed, and over a decade of research into the 506th during World War II, Ed's personal recollections have now been set against a factually accurate backdrop that we hope will engage any reader interested in this period both emotionally and educationally.

Despite the close relationship that I now have with Ed, I have done my best to avoid bias and use all the information at my disposal to make this project as accurate as possible; ultimately this is his story – warts and all.

My hope is that *Airborne* provides a glimpse into one man's incredible life experience, a life which has not been without controversial moments. This is the unvarnished truth of a very young man fighting and surviving a war and his actions should be set into context rather than be criticized from our own more comfortable position in the 21st century. *Airborne* deals with the loss of friends and reveals in no uncertain terms that freedom is most definitely not free. Hopefully Ed's war story has something for everyone … sit back and enjoy the ride.

Ian Gardner
August 2014

ACKNOWLEDGMENTS

As usual this section has been one of the hardest parts of the book to complete, as so many people have contributed to *Tonight We Die As Men*, *Deliver Us From Darkness* and *No Victory in Valhalla*. Without this long list of amazing individuals, many of whom have since passed away, *Airborne* could never have been written. If anyone's name has been overlooked – and it has been a long time – I hope you will accept my sincere apologies. Individual thanks are extended, arranged by country, to the following.

United Kingdom

Rosemary Connor, Marcus Cowper, Roger Day, Elsie Douglas, Robert Dudley (my literary agent), Bob Hilton, Emily Holmes, Patricia Howard, Monique Jones, Peter Mills, Kate Moore, John Mundy, Doreen Ramsden, Rosemary and Sarah Pinches, Monica Tovey and Graeme Trim, Francis Wyndham.

United States of America and Canada

Miles Allen, Jannie Anderson, Kathleen "Tachie" Anderson, Fred and Rick Bahlau, Mike Baldinger, Mark Bando, Doug Barber, Manny Barrios, Ralph Bennett, Dave Berry, Lurie Berteau, Joe Beyrle, Joe Beyrle II, Jim Bigley, Marcus Brotherton, Tom Bucher, Sharon Bunker, Roy Burger, Don Burgett, Ray Calandrella, Derwood Cann, Joan Chincarini, Merrick O'Connell, Denis and Donna Cortese, Dan Cutting, Louis DeNegre,

Mario "Hank" DiCarlo, Carole and Harley Dingman, Joe Doughty, Bob Dunning, Mark Durivage, George Dwyer, Teddy and Bette Dziepak, Bud Estes, Bill Galbraith, Judy Gamble, John Gibson, Len Goodgal, Brian Gottlieb, George Grant Jr, Clark Heggeness, Randy Hils, Ben Hiner, Bob Izumi, Ken Johnson, Tom Kennedy, Brenda Kightlinger, John Klein, Laurie Kotsch, George Koskimaki, John Kutz, Gerry and Bobbie Lord, Alfred Lowe, Piet "Pete" Luiten, Walter Lukasavage, Pete and Mary Madden, Clair Mathiason, James "Pee Wee" Martin, Sid McCallum, Jim and Pat McCann, Earl McClung, Karen McGee, George McMillan, Jim Melhus, John Merkt, Tim Moore, Eugene and Vada Montgomery, Dave and Neil Morgan, Gil Morton, Ray and Helen Nagell, Mary Lou Neally, Don Orcutt, Carolyn Packert, Bonnie Pond, Jake Powers, John Reeder, Doyle Rigden, Rich Riley, Bobbie Rommel, George Rosie, Ken Ross, Barney Ryan, Bob Saxvik, John Shank, Ray Skully, Bob Smoldt, Jay Stone, Elsie and Nathan Spurr, Harold Stedman, Tom Stedman, John Sushams, Ann Tanzy, Kathy Tozzi, John Vecchi, Lou Vecchi, Geoff Walden, Aaron Walser, Bob Webb Jr, Bill Wedeking, Chad Weisensel, Harold Winer, Don Zahn.

France and Switzerland

Denis van den Brink, Msr and Mme Brohier, Charles Carel, André Descamps, Charles Destrés, Michel DeTrez, Thérése Dieudonné, Msr and Mme Droin, Msr Dumoncel, Eugéne Enot, Thierry Ferey, Maurice de Folleville, Philippe Frigot, William Hébert, Nicole Laurence, Amand Laurent, Léon Lehay, Jean Pierre Lemesnil, Michel and Martine Léonard, Louis Letourneur, Paulette Menilgrente, Jean Mignon, Msr and Mme Poisson, Susan Rochat, Msr La Rue, Jean Savary and Henry Villand.

The Netherlands

Dick Bakker, Henk Beens, Frits Berens, Donald van den Bogert, Hans den Brok, Jo van Dongen, Bernard Florissen, Gerda den Hartog, Johannes van den Hatert, Peter Hendrikx, Piet van den Heuvel, Gido Hordijk, Jenny and Jan van Hout, Erwin Janssen, Marco and Marion Kilian, Wim and Jos Klerkx, Steph Leenhouwers, Vic van Lijf, Peter van der Linden, Frans Mientjes, Ronald Ooms, Wan van Overweld, Johannes Peerbolte, Tom Peeters, Gert and Clazien van Rinsum, Albert Roxs, Frits van Schaik, Jaap van Schaik, Frank and Chantal Slegers, Ronald Stassen, Willemien van Steenbergen, Noud Stultiens, Jurgen Swinkels, Tom Timmermans, Dirk van Tintelen, Frenk Derks van de Ven, Peter van de Wal.

Belgium

Ivonne Dumont, Jean-François d'Hoffschmidt, Philippe d'Hoffschmidt, Reg Jans, Jean-Marie Koeune, Adjutant Eric "Rony" Lemoine, Maguy Marenne, André Meurisse, Robert Remacle, Joël Robert, Jules and Denise Robert, Philipe Wilkin.

Germany

Florian Beierl, Gerhard Roletscheck.

1

"TAKE THE A TRAIN"

December 7, 1941: The rich vibe of Duke Ellington and his orchestra was suddenly interrupted as a sketchy news flash filtered across the early afternoon airwaves. Shocked by the unfolding bulletin, Ed Shames and his friends Elmer Trant and Melvin Dawley moved closer to the radio. "On Sunday when the Japanese attacked Pearl Harbor, Elmer, Melvin and I were sharing a room at the Laurentian Hotel in Hamilton, Ontario." The preemptive assault conducted by Admiral Isoroku Yamamoto was intended to keep the US Pacific Fleet from impacting on forthcoming Japanese combat operations in Southeast Asia against British, Dutch and US forces on the Philippines. The Japanese air strike sank several important ships and caused nearly 3,700 casualties. The following day, President Franklin D. Roosevelt proclaimed December 7, 1941, as "a date, which will live in infamy," and the US National Congress proceeded to declare war against Japan.

A few months before the attack, we were "happy-go-lucky" 19-year-olds studying to become naval engineers at the Steam Engineering School in Norfolk, Virginia. Politically aware and determined to do our bit in the war, we were still too young for the peacetime American military.

However, the minimum age for the Royal Canadian Air Force was 18, and as they were recruiting potential officer cadets to train as fighter pilots, we decided to give it a go.

Melvin's father was a very successful businessman and we borrowed his car to drive up to Hamilton for our assessments. Before leaving Norfolk, we made a pledge to each other that it would be all or none. Over the next five days the Canadians put us through a series of aptitude tests and stringent medicals. At the end of the week, we were shocked when Elmer was rejected after being diagnosed with a heart murmur. However, Melvin and I were accepted and given 10 days to sign the enlistment papers. Elmer wanted us to go ahead, but we had a deal and that was all there was to it. We went back to the Laurentian Hotel and decided to spend the weekend out on the town. Of course, December 7th was the day that everything changed, and after the Japanese strike we packed our things and returned to Virginia.

Ed Shames' war was about to begin.

———————————

Edward David Shames was born on June 13, 1922 in Virginia Beach, Virginia:

I was the youngest and preceded by sisters Anna and Simmie, and brother George [aged two, six, and eight respectively at the time of Ed's birth]. My father David had studied engineering and fought as an infantryman in World War I. Dad was smart and in the early years worked hard to build up a small portfolio of properties and with my mother Sadie, established "Shames Provisions," a rural country store situated along Virginia Beach Boulevard. In 1927, Dad died suddenly from pneumonia – he was only 42. Assisted by her youngest brother Ben, Mom took over and successfully kept the store going. During the Great Depression, things went from bad to worse, forcing Mom to sell off Dad's properties at a ridiculously reduced price. Thankfully, we lived in the flat above the store. I attended the Henry Clay Elementary School and much of my spare time was spent helping out in the store. One of the pupils, Clifford Irby, was two years older and not only bullied me, but many other younger kids. One morning while walking to school, I picked up a length of lead pipe. During break, Irby cornered me in the toilets and I hit him with the metal "cosh" and split his head wide open. Afterwards we became great friends but I think the incident showed me that aggression could be channeled and controlled if and when necessary.

By the time I turned 11, I had a job selling magazines and saved enough to purchase a small rowing boat to go fishing in Chesapeake Bay. My dad left a pair of Smith & Wesson pistols that I'd use regularly to shoot targets in the local woods. Of course my mother knew nothing about it. When, as a teenager, I began to get interested in hiking my mom gave me a set of local maps and a compass for my birthday, which kick-started my lifelong fascination for topography. Mother always made sure that we had food and even sometimes wine on the table and decent clothes to wear. When my brother George asked if he could attend the Virginia Polytechnic Institute Military School, despite the costs involved, Mom agreed without hesitation. The price of uniform, trunk and school fees was well over $100 and I remember she paid with gold coins that my dad had left. It was then she told me about the golden rule – "He who has the gold, rules!" I've never forgotten it. George graduated in the 1930s and decided to pursue a career as an engineering officer in the Navy. Eventually he was posted to run the main refrigeration plant at Norfolk Naval Base and never went overseas.

Following the attack on Pearl Harbor it was only a matter of time before Ed would join his brother in uniform and he was determined to be at the sharp end of the war.

Four or five months after returning from Canada, Ed read in a national magazine that the Army Operations Center (AOC) at Fort Monroe had announced the creation of a specialist volunteer parachute unit. After Pearl Harbor, the Japanese had successfully invaded the Philippines and American fortitude appeared to be rapidly declining. Senior members of the War Department's civil service had the unprecedented idea of creating a "super unit" recruited directly from the civilian population. The civil servants realized the public relations value of such a regiment, especially one drawn from the general public rather than the regular army. It was correctly assumed that the principle of civilian volunteers would raise the country's morale.

As Monroe was only a few miles away, I went over to their recruiting office seeking further information. The 506th Parachute Infantry Regiment was looking for volunteers, and only the best and brightest people need apply. Plus a qualified parachutist would earn an extra $50 a month! After reading through the glossy brochures, I decided to put my name down as a potential recruit. The minimum age was 21, but as I still had eleven months to go, written permission was needed from my mother, who initially wasn't keen to sign – although eventually after much cajoling from me she agreed.

By late August 1942, Shames received his joining instructions and was ordered to attend the US Army Reception Center at Camp Lee, Petersburg, Virginia.

Camp Lee was about 75 miles from Norfolk and there were hundreds of kids from Virginia, Maryland and North Carolina. After being processed I was put on a troop train with Charles Cartwright, an ex-fireman, who lived in Norfolk on Marshall Avenue. The regular service ran from New York to New Orleans and was packed with young men, all scheduled for different stops along the way. Our destination was a small town in northeast Georgia named Toccoa and when Cartwright noted it was 6am we knew we didn't have much further to go. No more than a "whistle stop," the station had seen more activity in the last four weeks than the previous ten years.

Toccoa would be home for Shames, Cartwright and other 506th hopefuls for the forthcoming months.

Getting off the train, I heard a door slam behind me and this dark-haired guy with large ears walked over and introduced himself: "I'm George Retan. How are you doing?" Up until that moment we hadn't realized that there was anyone else on our train bound for Toccoa. Four years older than me, George, who was from Syracuse, seemed very self-confident and sharp. We shook hands and were still laughing as a sergeant strutted over and instructed us to follow him to a waiting truck.

Camp Toccoa was 5 miles outside town, nestling beneath the powerful shadow of Currahee Mountain. After passing through the front gate and turning right, the vehicle followed the road to an enormous grass parade ground. In the corner closest to the camp was a collection of tents known as "W" Company. Due to recent heavy rainfall the ground was a sea of thick, red mud. Retan, Cartwright and Shames were allocated temporary bed spaces. After a cold damp night, Reveille was something to behold as dozens of shivering figures, some still wrapped in blankets, tried to carefully negotiate their way through the ankle-deep slush for roll call.

Because of the mud, we soon learned that "W" Company also had another title – "Cow" Company. After our names had been checked we underwent a thorough medical examination. A history of broken bones was enough to cause exclusion, as was color blindness or poor eyesight. Mental ability was also considered important, and to pass we had to have a qualifying score equal to, or surpassing, that for Officer Candidate School (OCS).

I was passed A1 fit and given service number 13117836, and the lowly rank of private. As for Retan, when they found out he'd attended one of the best private preparatory schools in the States, Fork Union Military Academy, he was immediately promoted to acting sergeant! One of the guys in my tent, Joe Madona, had come in the day before. Maybe because of the intense overcrowding, Madona managed to rub me up the wrong way. Joe was a short, stocky, Italian American from Winthrop, Massachusetts, so not only a damn Yankee but also an "I-ty" and there's me, a Jew southerner!

During the thankfully short stay in "Cow" Company, Shames and the others were issued their basic equipment and clothing. The following morning one of the regular army cadre NCOs introduced Ed and his new friends to the mountain. The feature marked the western edge of the Blue Ridge Range and over the next 13 weeks would come to symbolize the 506th PIR.

The cadre were, for the most part, from the 82nd Airborne, and temporarily attached as platoon sergeants or squad leaders. It was their job to teach us "civilians" every aspect of military life including physical training [PT].

Ed's group stood in formation on the parade ground as it was addressed by one of the instructors, "Gentlemen, today we are going to put your fitness to the test… You see that lump of rock? It's called 'Currahee,' Native American for 'Stands Alone.' The beast is 1,753 feet high and the summit trail approximately 3 miles long. Any of you who do not make the 6-mile round trip within 1 hour and 10 minutes will fail and be immediately reassigned to a non-airborne outfit. Do you understand me?" Shames looked across at Retan as the squad replied as one: "Yes, Staff Sergeant!" Wearing coveralls and brand-new ankle boots the men doubled past a long row of buildings belonging to Regimental Headquarters toward the start line. Initially it did not seem that difficult, but as the 20ft-wide dirt road began to snake its way upwards the pace increased, and Ed's legs started to burn. At that point some people were already dropping back. About 10 minutes later, as the track approached a rocky outcrop close to the peak it became much steeper and turned sharply before "zigzagging" to a wooden lookout tower on the summit. Without taking a moment to catch his breath, Shames touched the triangulation point and was on his way back down. Legs and feet pulsing in pain, he was now struggling to keep up, and much to Ed's surprise, Madona started shouting encouragement. Passing several stragglers, Retan dropped back, came alongside and delivered a short pep talk as well.

> We all made it back within the required time but it was a daunting glimpse of what might lay ahead. I thanked Joe for his help and inquired how he made the run look so easy. It turned out that he'd been active in baseball and athletics at high school and was still a very keen sportsman.
>
> A day or so later, Cartwright was sent to the Machine Gun Platoon, while Retan, "Shorty" Madona and myself were assigned to 1st Squad, 3rd Platoon, Item Company, the very last platoon from 3rd Battalion to be formed.

Toccoa would be where Ed learned how to take orders, and in the process discover he could go much further and do much more than he ever imagined possible. The 506th had originally expected around 2,800 people but by the time the course began there were almost 7,000 recruits. The vastly overmanned regiment was divided into three battalions. Each had four companies, and 3rd Battalion's were designated HQ, George, How and Item, under overall command of 27-year-old Major Robert Lee Wolverton.

At the time First Lieutenant Charles Shettle was in charge of Item or I Company with the superb Second Lieutenant John Kiley as his executive officer (XO) and cadre man Paul Garrison, as first sergeant. Interestingly, Garrison was a local from Toccoa. Their platoon leader was Second Lieutenant Fred Anderson from Charlotte, North Carolina. Stocky, round faced, and just under 6ft tall, Anderson liked a drink, and loved to tease between telling jokes and delivering endless wise cracks. Although he did not suffer fools, "Andy" was approachable and always on hand to help with any personal issues. He would prove to be an invaluable comrade-in-arms once the 506th landed in Europe.

Forged from Steel

Officially activated on July 20, 1942, the 506th Parachute Infantry Regiment was the brainchild of 37-year-old Colonel Robert Frederick Sink. A southern boy from Lexington, North Carolina, Sink was a graduate of the prestigious West Point Military Academy and had been an early pioneer of parachute tactics and organization. With great energy and determination, Sink, known as "the Fox," was about to put into effect one of the most grueling training regimes ever experienced by any World War II American military unit. But along with rigor came fairness and concern. No problem was too small for his attention. He believed in discipline and order but was not strictly spit and polish. The Fox was also a family man and lived locally with his pregnant wife Margaret and their daughters Margaret (7) and Mary (10), playfully known as "Flip" and "Petey." Back in North Carolina, Bob Sink's father Fred was active in state politics and ran a local daily newspaper, *The Dispatch*, which over the next three years would report every move made by the colonel and the 506th PIR.

The basic recruit accommodation at Toccoa, formerly known as Camp Toombs, was constructed around a grid system and comprised 12 neat rows of single-story wooden huts, each row serviced by its own mess hall. Subdivided into four distinct blocks, the 3rd Battalion area consisted of approximately 36 tarpaper barracks with dedicated latrine and ablutions facilities. Ed, Joe Madona and George Retan were assigned to one of the busy barrack rooms along with Privates Joe Gorenc, Jim Japhet and Don Ross. After Reveille the following morning the men formed up outside on the company street for roll call.

Everything we did from now on was done at the double, even going to our mess, which incidentally had a slogan pinned to the wall stating: "TAKE WHAT YOU WANT – EAT WHAT YOU TAKE."

During the first week, following breakfast, the cadre instructor for Ed's squad, Sergeant Wojtowicz, took the men for calisthenics, drill and PT over on the nearby athletics field situated beyond the parade ground in a shallow valley. The vast sandy oblong-shaped training area was dotted with a variety of apparatus including pull-up bars, 40ft-high scramble net tower and mock-up aircraft fuselages. Closer to the parade ground, the 506th had built a parachute school complete with an outdoor exit trainer, flight swings and a series of 10ft wooden ramps from which to practice parachute landing falls (PLFs).

A wide drainage channel ran along one side of the athletics field. Built into the steep hill adjacent to the creek was a bone-shattering obstacle course with both the start and finish points straddling the brackish water. Fenced on both sides like a racetrack, Colonel Sink's terrifying folly ran through pine woods up and down the hillside and featured amongst its many sadistic creations a 12ft-high log wall and 20ft-high jump platform.

Like the mountain, we were expected to run the torturous course at least three or four times a week. In between, we embarked on a series of 20-mile route marches coupled with fieldcraft lessons and combat training. Hundreds of people washed out during the first few weeks. The cadre closely monitored our performance and any man who couldn't match up to the stiffening criteria was sent packing. Sink made a bet with one of his old classmates from West Point, who then arrived with a platoon of Marines intent on showing us "civilians" how quickly the professionals could lick the assault course. But despite the obvious bravado, they failed to complete, saying certain aspects were just too risky for them to attempt before sheepishly returning to Paris Island to rebuild their wounded pride.

I did my best to avoid the more mundane things like "kitchen duty" or KP but occasionally got caught for general company duties that the army called "Charge of Quarters" (CQ). During one particular CQ, Lieutenant Shettle instructed me to collect a letter from Regimental Headquarters which overlooked the parade ground.

As Ed entered the building, he snapped a quick salute at Sink's executive officer, Lieutenant Colonel Charles Chase, who simply nodded and smiled as he passed by. Also "Point" trained, Charlie was Sink's polar opposite. Steady and cool, Chase was a teetotaler and came from an old established family in New Hampshire. Softly spoken, his speech was measured, unemotional but impeccable, the sign of a true "Connecticut Yankee."

The envelope had already been opened by Sink, who had written in large letters across the front, "Requires your immediate attention!" Being curious, I looked inside and was surprised to read that it was a final demand for payment from a debt collection agency in Baltimore. Upon seeing the open envelope Shettle, who had a mean streak, became angry: "Did you open this – did you read this, Shames?" Standing at attention, I denied everything. Nothing more was said but from that moment, Shettle started to single me out for any trivial misdemeanor or infraction.

As the weather began to improve, the large ventilation grille above the front door of Ed's hut proved woefully inadequate against the heat of a late Georgian summer. One particular evening after a few cups of "White Lightning," Don Ross picked up a trumpet that belonged to another soldier. Originating from San Francisco, 20-year-old Ross had a talent for the trombone but more importantly, the bugle, having played both instruments throughout his teenage years. Ed was spellbound by Don's skill and after several bugle-style renditions mischievously encouraged his friend to step outside and blow Reveille with all the power and finesse he could muster. Although it was well after dark the entire camp sprang into life as people started forming up on their respective company streets!

In fits of laughter, we dashed inside as Sink's voice angrily crackled across the loudspeaker system. "Whoever blew that bugle, I want him found and brought to my office immediately."

Of course Sink never discovered who it was and the event was soon forgotten as summer quickly passed into fall.

Running in formation, I Company was now completing Currahee in less than 50 minutes. The entire regiment was blossoming into Sink's vision with every soldier now willing to take on any challenge firm in the belief that he would overcome it. To show off the regiment's physical prowess, during a Saturday morning visit by the Agricultural Adjustment Administration (AAA Program) the Fox ordered his men to wear swimming trunks and jump boots before running the mountain in platoon order.

But it was not all toil and sweat. Some, like First Sergeant Garrison, got married with full military tradition. Others went on pass to Toccoa and Gainesville or spent off-duty hours in the roadside diners that dotted the area around the camp.

We were getting about three weekend passes a month to Atlanta. Jim Japhet, whose family were wealthy cattle people from Texas, was used to nice things, and always insisted that we stay at the Piedmont Hotel. Of course this four-star palace was way above what Madona and I could afford but Jim always generously picked up the tab. I mean we were used to paying just over a dollar for an evening meal from the Wagon Wheel Bar outside of camp and at that time a steak dinner at the Piedmont cost around $10! As a private, I was earning $50 a month and after deductions such as laundry, PX [postal exchange] and insurance, took home around $20. Shorty [Madona] was a habitual gambler and within 15 minutes of being paid was usually broke, after being fleeced by Barron Dueber, our company communications sergeant from Los Angeles. Not surprisingly, he never approached Jim Japhet for money, but the rest of us were always bailing him out.

Subsequently, Madona and Shames started a shoe-shine business. On an average Friday night the two friends made about $12 each, polishing jump boots for those destined for weekend furlough. Weeks of 12-hour days were spent on dry firing and drills, designed to familiarize the men with their individual weapon, the M1 Garand Rifle. Intercompany rivalry was high and so was the expectation that each platoon would vie to produce the largest number of sharpshooters and marksman. Only the week before, 1st Battalion had set a stratospheric standard during their Skill at Arms contest at the nearby Camp Croft range and 3rd Battalion were not going to be outdone.

Major Wolverton promised three-day passes for every man who scored "expert" and then decided that his soldiers would march at least 30 miles with full combat load across the state line into South Carolina to the Reserve Officer Training Corps (ROTC) ranges at Clemson University. Third Battalion, less the MG Platoon, spent one week at Clemson where some of the previously parachute-qualified officers and NCOs made a display jump in front of the cadets.

The week at Clemson was a huge deal for us and despite achieving "expert" on the M1, because our overall score was slightly less than 100 percent, Don, Shorty and myself were reassigned to crew a .30 cal machine gun in 3rd Squad. While acting as a spotter for some of the other recruits, Andy Anderson noticed that I was able to pinpoint a strike at 700 yards with the naked eye. As a consequence he appointed me gunner, Shorty my assistant and Don our ammo carrier.

The return march on Sunday October 24, commenced at 1900hrs, took 18 hours to complete and covered a distance of 49 miles. For the first few miles everyone chatted and laughed as they marched, but as it got dark and the hours passed, the battalion knuckled down into silence and hunger as the distance gradually began to unravel.

Bizarrely, around this time, when he heard we'd nicknamed him "The Red Death" (because of his permanently rosy complexion), Shettle interviewed every man in the company to ascertain why he was so unpopular. When it came to my turn he chewed me out for not wearing my stripe after being promoted to first gunner on the MG. To be honest Shettle did a passable job but it was still a very strange thing for an officer to do. Just to spite him, I never did sew on my stripe, which constantly needled good old Charlie every time he saw me!

Throughout October and November, most of the officers and some of the cadre were put through their paces on the mock-up fuselages, 34ft-high outdoor exit trainer, flight swings and 10ft jump platforms. The apparatus had been specifically designed and built to prepare and condition the recruits for the Parachute School at Fort Benning. The exit trainer filled everyone with a deep sense of dread. Each candidate was expected to hook the strap of his harness onto a steel zip wire before leaping through the open door and sliding some 250 yards to the ground. Failing to achieve a good "push out" meant a straight drop of around 20ft whereupon a potential "smooth descent" would be violently interrupted by the harness pulling tightly around the crotch!

By the end of November the last few officers completed parachute-packing and ground-training courses and were driven out to a nearby airport maintained by the LeTourneau Company, who manufactured earthmoving equipment. The first jump onto Dicks Hill drop zone (DZ) went well, although the other four had to be postponed for a few days due to bad weather. Afterwards a "Prop Blast" party was held in the Officers' Mess, where each newly qualified parachutist was required to consume a concoction of alcohol from the nose hub of a C-47 while his colleagues shouted "One thousand, two thousand, three thousand..."

Meanwhile Ed Shames and the rest of his company were going through an enhanced specialist program that included parachute ground training, courses in signals and demolition, basic hand-to-hand combat and endless lectures, as well as the usual fitness regime of mountain and obstacle course.

During this phase our barracks were emptying at an alarming rate as hundreds more dropped out either through injury or lack of moral fiber. Toward the end of our time at Toccoa those of us who survived uninjured were running certain sections of the obstacle course with full field pack in under 4 minutes! As the first phase drew to a close and the weather started to get colder we anxiously began looking forward to jump school. But that would quite literally be a walk in the park compared to what was about to happen next.

By early December, the regiment received its movement orders for Fort Benning, and in doing so became the first unit ever to go through the jump school as one complete organization. After Major Billy Turner and 1st Battalion had departed by train, Robert Strayer requested permission from Colonel Sink to march 2nd Battalion, accompanied by half of the regiment's Medical Detachment to the railway station in downtown Atlanta. The 2nd Battalion group, numbering 586 men, set off from Toccoa on Tuesday December 1, and arrived three days later clocking a marching time of 33 hours and 30 minutes, covering a distance of 118 miles.

Not to be outdone by the ROTC-trained Strayer, "Point" man Wolverton was given permission to transport 3/506 by train to Atlanta and from there make the journey (estimated to be around 136 miles) to Benning on foot. The idea was to smash the Japanese Army distance-marching record and in doing so generate extra publicity for the 506th PIR, who were still an independent unit looking for a home. Diminutive and bullish, Wolverton was from Elkins, West Virginia and had a subtle sense of humor. At times, he could be a man of few words but when he did talk, whether questioning or responding, it was clear, precise and very much to the point. Captain Harold "Hank" Hannah and Regimental Headquarters Company joined 3rd Battalion, along with the rest of the medics giving a total head count of just over 700 men.

For the majority of the march the weather was misty, cold and wet. The battalion group, wearing coveralls and helmets and carrying weapons, full packs and three days' rations, ploughed through driving rain singing cadence songs and popular tunes.

3rd Squad made a deal to go all the way. Nobody complained, we just got on with it. What we as a battalion were attempting was unprecedented in US military history and the press, both local and national, took a deep interest. The average rifleman carried around 60lbs. But for those like myself, Joe and Don who were hauling heavier crew-served weapons, plus our M1s, we had to rotate the gun and tripod constantly just to keep up. After stopping for the night, we had a whip round and sent one of the boys across the road to a grocery store for a couple of bottles of cheap whiskey. Gathering around our shelter halves we toasted each other and then got quietly oiled before hitting the sack.

Despite regular 10-minute breaks the rest of the journey was grueling, and every morning it took a good couple of miles to get going again.

Dozens fell out along the way suffering from blisters but were quickly patched up by the medics. The battalion spent four days on the road with Bob Wolverton leading and setting the pace. Due to badly swollen feet, the major had been forced to remove his boots and continue wearing three pairs of socks.

It was then that we began to realize just what a truly inspirational leader Wolverton was. I mean he could have easily got into one of the support wagons like Captains Graham (G Company) and Stoffregen (HQ Company) but instead he chose to remain with us.

Finally, on the fourth night, after almost 45 hours of marching, the battalion approached Benning. With the red lights of the three massive jump towers visible in the distance, Wolverton gave the order to double time.

Colonel Sink and the remainder of the regiment, along with Parachute School commanding officer Brigadier General George

Howell, were waiting at the main gate as Wolverton and his troops hiked past, destroying the Japanese record by an impressive margin. Standing in front of a large welcome sign which read "Long Walkin', Loud Talkin', Non Jumpin' Sonsobitches," the band of the 505th PIR knocked out a series of lively tunes for the momentous occasion.

From here we continued for another few miles deeper into the vast camp to our accommodation, designated Outpost No.1, also known as the "Frying Pan" area. After a sumptuous hot meal and gallons of coffee served in our new mess, weary but elated we gingerly limped off to our beds for a very well-earned night's sleep.

The Benning Shuffle

On December 12, 1942, following two days' recuperation, Shames and over 500 soldiers from 3/506 joined 2nd Battalion, RHQ, the Med Det and Service Company and were assigned to course number 49.

I Company was split up into smaller groups giving Ed and his team the opportunity to get to know people from the other platoons such as Privates Lonnie Gavrock from Memphis, Tennessee, Robert Moon, Jack and Jim Brown from Alaska, Bill Galbraith from California and Joe Beyrle. "A smart operator, tall and blond haired, Beyrle was from Michigan and still owed me and Shorty some shoe-shine money. Despite all the physical training we'd just been through, Bob Moon had an enormous backside and because of his surname consequently took a lot of stick from the rest of us in the syndicate." Lieutenant Kiley was also on Ed's course, having failed to complete at Toccoa after the Troop Carrier C-47 being used to jump the officers was written off when it overshot the runway.

The lean, mean parachute jump instructors were completely unprepared for the level of fitness shown by 1st Battalion during their first week on Benning's specialist pre-para program, known as "the Fort Benning Shuffle." Subsequently, Course 49 skipped the usual regular army physical preparation and went straight onto the next phase, which consisted of ground training and landing drills.

However, this didn't stop the directing staff, dressed in their distinctive khaki baseball caps and white T-shirts, trying naïvely to break us down. Eventually they realized that we could cope with pretty much anything they could throw at us, including countless press-ups, which they stupidly thought to be our weak point! Eventually the instructors were forced to back off and use more polite verbal forms of encouragement. However, the regiment kept its own physical training program going with regular PT sessions, and 9-mile morning runs around the perimeter track of nearby Lawson Army airfield.

By Christmas Eve, after passing all the required training blocks, Ed and his syndicate had reached "C" stage and were waiting for one particular test out at the enormous jump towers. Each crane, originally built for the New York 1939 World's Fair, was 250ft high and fitted with four arms, each one designated for a different aspect of parachuting including controlled descents and free fall.

Nobody was looking forward to the "shock harness." When it came to my turn, I was attached to a long beam and hoisted upwards toward the top of the tower. Suspended in a parachute harness underneath the apparatus, parallel to the ground, my hand was physically shaking as I clutched onto the release handle. When the instructor shouted from below, "Arm number one – ready? OK, RELEASE!" I pulled with all my might and dropped like a stone until the risers arrested my fall. It was a scary experience but we only got one attempt: anyone who couldn't do the test was immediately failed.

While Ed and his friends were going through "C" stage most of the previously parachute-qualified officers and senior NCOs were learning to become jump masters. The two-week course covered aircraft inspection (inside and out) prior to emplaning, plus instruction drills, under-slung loads, equipment checks and the specific commands necessary for jumping a "stick" of up to 20 men.

Sink's adjutant at the time, Frank Thorpe III, took it upon himself to organize a written test for those of us who, after completing jump school, wished to be considered for OCS. About 60 people were selected, including Retan, Japhet and myself. Despite being somewhat surprised when Colonel Sink walked into our meeting room, we respectfully stood to attention. Screwing his cap around on his head, the colonel finally shaped it into position before speaking: "Thank you all for the gallant interest you have shown in becoming officers, but contrary to what Captain Thorpe might think, I simply cannot allow this to happen. However, at a later date, if in combat you prove worthy, and I know who you are, then it might be possible to award some of you with battlefield commissions. Dismissed. To your duties, fall out." We were somewhat confused by the ruling but Sink had his reasons and his word was law.

Before Ed and the other students moved onto parachuting, they spent time in the sweltering packing sheds learning how to pack the 'chutes that they were going to use. Lead-filled canvas bags allowed the silk to be held in place while the canopies were laid out on purpose-built benches. The rigging lines of each parachute were all connected at the top of the 28ft-diameter canopy by what is known as the "apex tie." Looped at each end, the 7-inch-long cord is the last physical connection to the aircraft upon exit. "Many, like me, had never been in a plane before and the smell of aviation fuel coupled with the stifling heat was something else," recalled Ed.

During our first jump from Lawson Field on New Year's Day, I got a bad exit and injured several ligaments when the static-line became wrapped around my leg. Despite the pain, I followed the drills that had been drummed into me, "1,000, 2,000, 3,000, check canopy, check oscillation, get your back into the wind, check drift, feet and knees together, knees slightly bent, chin on chest and prepare to land." My landing was heavy and while struggling to unhook my reserve and complete the harness release drills, I realized that this was something that I wasn't going to like! But I'd earned the right and the anxiety was something that I simply had to get accustomed to. The swelling was so bad that the medics strapped and completely immobilized my knee so I could make the next jump a couple of hours later.

The following day we completed our remaining three descents and straight afterwards I checked into the base hospital for emergency treatment. Some of the other companies made five jumps in one day so you can imagine how exhausting that must've been for them. I was lucky. Bob Moon smashed his ankle so badly on one landing that he was forced to quit the outfit.

Uniform pressed, jump boots polished and pants perfectly pressed and bloused, it was a proud day when we were awarded our wings and given a two-week furlough. Before the course broke up, Colonel Sink had the last word: "You must keep in mind that not only are you now a member of the Airborne Elite, but that you belong to one of the finest regiments in the US Army. Good luck, behave yourselves at home and start looking forward to the tactical phase at Camp Mackall." With the exception of First Sergeants Paul Garrison, Jim "JP" Shirley (HQ Company), Gordon Bolles (H Company) and several others like Staff Sergeants "Geetchie" Lindler and John Taormina, 99 percent of the cadre remained behind at Toccoa to train the 501st PIR (who were already part of the recently formed 101st Airborne Division), 511th and 517th respectively. Despite being turned down for OCS, Jim Japhet was promoted to sergeant and assigned to 1st Platoon under Second Lieutenant Gerry Howard. Gerry was a gentleman who really seemed to care about his men. Meanwhile, Andy Anderson asked Retan to take over 3rd Platoon as our platoon sergeant. Seeing Jim and George reassigned was a blow but I figured my chance would surely come. It was just a matter of time.

Walkin' tall

The regiment returned to Fort Benning and spent the next two weeks at their old dilapidated camp in the Frying Pan area close to Lawson Field. During that time they were prepared for the Fighting in Built Up Areas (FIBUA) phase of training, which was to take place across the Chattahoochee River in Alabama. While here in "'Bama," Shames (who had still not fully recovered from his parachuting injury), Ross and Madona did their next jump with full equipment on February 19. After completion, the unit headed by train to the town of Hoffman in North Carolina, 15 miles down the road from Fort Bragg. "Being a southern boy, I loved our new home at Camp Mackall, with its purpose-built barracks and wonderful mess halls complete with jukeboxes." Over the next few months the training intensified with plenty of two- and three-day field problems.

One particular Thursday afternoon, we'd just completed a 25-mile battle march in our newly issued jump jackets and pants and had stopped for the night. The following morning, Lieutenant Anderson asked me and the other gun commanders to deploy in depth and provide a defensive ring around the platoon with our machine guns. Using a borrowed map, I selected a fantastic spot that not only had great cover but also provided superb arcs of fire. As Don and Joe were digging in to set up the gun, I began creating a detailed overlay complete with military abbreviations and icons showing our company and platoon Command Posts (CPs), plus prerecorded targets and their ranges.

A few hours later, Anderson and Wolverton arrived to inspect our site. Standing to attention, I saluted and gave Wolverton [who had recently been promoted to lieutenant colonel] my name and rank and then explained my arcs and why I chose this particular spot.

After looking around for a few minutes the colonel asked, "Who laid this position out?" "I did, sir." "You did. You mean by yourself?" "Yes, sir." Then, completely against protocol, I seized the opportunity and told him that I could read a map just as well as any officer he had in his battalion. That got his attention. Slightly taken aback, Wolverton responded, "Go on then, explain to me how you planned it." "Er, using these map overlays, sir." "Overlays? What overlays?" After handing over my map case to Wolverton, he inquired how a kid like me knew so much about topography. "Maps are my hobby, sir, and have been since I was a kid."

At that moment, Wolverton turned toward a rather bemused-looking Anderson, "Please wait here, lieutenant, while I go find Charlie Shettle." Only recently Wolverton had been captured on a training exercise and tied to a tree by the "enemy" who then commandeered his jeep. The colonel had found the blunder in intelligence deeply embarrassing and unbeknown to Shames was now on the lookout for new blood for his Planning & Operations Department, or S3 for short.

A few minutes later, Wolverton returned with not only the Red Death but also the two other platoon leaders, Gerry Howard and Jim Nye. At that point, Madona, Ross and myself were pushed to one side while Wolverton, still holding my map case, discussed the gun position with Shettle and the others.

We couldn't believe what happened next. After dismissing all the officers, Wolverton took me aside and inquired, "Shames, how would you like to be my operations sergeant?" "Sir, doesn't that require the rank of staff sergeant?" "Yes, but don't get ahead of yourself here! I'll promote you to buck sergeant, and see how you pan out over the next week or so, eh? Can you come to my office at 0800hrs on Monday so we can sort out the paperwork?"

Shortly after breakfast on the Monday morning, I asked First Sergeant Garrison if I could leave for Battalion HQ. Garrison demanded, incredulously, "What in the hell are you talking about?" and then ordered me to accompany him to see Shettle, who unsurprisingly gave me a hard time before finally letting me go.

After saying goodbye to Shorty and Don, I moved my gear across and reported to Captain Carmen. Charles Carmen was also Jewish and had recently been posted in as the new planning and operations officer (S3). True to his word, after the first couple of weeks, Colonel Wolverton made me up to staff sergeant, and I soon settled in and started to get to know the other members of his staff.

Ed was somewhat disappointed to learn that Wolverton's adjutant and personnel officer, First Lieutenant Alex Bobuck, and the executive officer for HQ Company, Second Lieutenant James Holstun were both hardened anti-Semites. Nicknamed "Jeb," 28-year-old Holstun was from New Orleans.

I believe Holstun's family were influential financiers and even owned their own bank in Louisiana. Both men made their position quite clear from the moment they discovered I was a Jew. However, it didn't matter because Bobuck's assistant, Sergeant Major Paul Simrell, was a lovely man and, although my senior by several years, quickly took me under his wing. Simrell had been an administrator before the war on the famous Panama Ship Canal. Paul was brilliant at his job and pretty much ran the S1 along with his clerk, Tech Corporal Ray Calandrella.

I soon discovered that if Colonel Wolverton wanted anything doing by personnel, instead of asking Lieutenant Bobuck, he went straight to Simrell and Calandrella! Private First Class Elwood Kendall was our runner and it was one of his jobs to play prerecorded bugle calls on a phonogram connected to the camp loudspeaker system. The old records were all worn out and one morning Wolverton happened to mention, "Wouldn't it be great if we had a real bugler?" Without thinking I replied, "Well we do, sir!" "What do you mean? Who?" "Private Ross, sir, do you remember he used to be on my machine-gun team?" "Ah yes, yes, I recall. Send Kendall over to fetch him will you please."

Dressed in summer uniform and best parade boots, Ross knocked and sheepishly entered Wolverton's office. The colonel was sitting at his desk surrounded by the staff including Shames. Pointing to a bugle on the table, Wolverton politely ordered, "Let's hear you blow it then." "What would you like to hear, sir?" "How about Reveille, Assembly and Officer's Call for starters?"

Pursing his lips, Don blasted out the requests one after another. It wasn't long before Colonel Sink heard and came striding across to the 3rd Battalion HQ. Realizing that if Sink got his hands on Don, that would be the last they would see of him, Wolverton and Shames bundled Ross and the instrument into a nearby locker. Entering the office Sink looked around and inquired what was going on. Pointing to the gramophone Wolverton responded, "Nothing to worry about, Bob, we were just trying to fix that old record player of ours." Looking somewhat puzzled, the Fox turned, but as he was about to leave he commented, "Better make sure you get it fixed by this evening or there'll be hell to pay!"

Apologetically we pulled Don back out of the locker and I took him over to I Company to give Shettle the good news. To protect our new asset, Wolverton assigned Don to be a member of his "personal security" – a team he'd recently formed from the junior members of staff to guard the battalion CP during future field problems and deployments.

When off duty, Ed, Don, "Shorty" and Joe Gorenc would often head to nearby towns such as Pinehurst or Rockingham for a few drinks. Joe was from Sheboygan, Wisconsin and like Shames had a fascination for maps. "Gorenc was such a great guy, I knew he would be the perfect addition to my new team."

Conversely, Bob Wolverton hung out at the Country Club in Southern Pines. During a party, Wolverton and regimental communications officer, Captain Bob Moon (no relation to the unfortunate private of the same name), were arguing with Robert Strayer about the overall distance they had marched in December. Determined to prove Strayer wrong, Wolverton decided to drive the exact route and accurately calculate the distance from its original start point at the train station in Atlanta to the barracks at Benning. As it was Easter weekend, Wolverton and his driver Private First Class Vernon Law, with Ed in the back seat of the jeep, set off on the Friday morning from Rockingham.

On the way to Atlanta we stopped off in Columbus, South Carolina, at Fort Jackson where the colonel visited an old friend from West Point. Later that afternoon, after reaching the train station we reset the trip meter to zero and began clocking the first part of the route to Fort MacPherson. From here we drove up to Warm Springs where we stopped off for the night in a schoolhouse. The following morning, we continued along the remainder of the route to the Frying Pan area of Benning where our old barracks were situated. You can imagine our surprise when we realized that the total distance covered was in fact 149.8 miles! A little different to what had previously been imagined.

Without a doubt, working closely with Colonel Wolverton changed my military career and our relationship grew into an unusual and I think unprecedented form of trust. The colonel's wife, Kathleen, was a beautiful lady, whom everyone respectfully addressed as Mrs Wolverton. The Wolvertons were also very proud of their son Lach (short for Lachlan) who was around nineteen months old at the time.[*]

I started to spend more and more time with the boss, and less time with Carmen who we all came to realize was slightly unhinged. Maybe for that reason, Wolverton began to rely on my professional judgment, advice and opinions rather than Carmen's.

In early May, Colonel Sink, Hank Hannah and regimental supply officer, Major Carl Buechner, visited Fort Bragg for a meeting with Airborne

---

[*] Many years later, for personal reasons, Lach changed his name to Lock.

Command to learn more about the regiment's forthcoming role in the Tennessee maneuvers against the US Second Army. Military training ramped up with further tactical night parachute jumps, each more complex than the last. The final stage, in South Carolina on June 3, was a command post exercise, which took place in pouring rain and began with a full regimental parachute insertion followed by an attack that lasted almost 24 hours.

All the while, Ed Shames gained more experience in intelligence work.

Captain Carmen had graduated top of his class at West Point and despite being screwy was one of the smartest people I'd ever met. He taught me many things, including how to build a proper sand table. Topographically shaped with sand or earth, complete with scale buildings and trees, the large box or table represented a three-dimensional "living" model of any assembly area, target or DZ we cared to create.

By June 6, the regiment had set up camp near Sturgis, Kentucky in readiness for the six-week-long exercise in Tennessee. A day or so later the men jumped into the mountains as reserve for the 101st Airborne Division. The drop was low, under 350ft, and many were injured landing on the high rocky slopes.

One of the guys I knew from I Company, Private Bernie "Red" Swann was badly concussed during the drop. It took several days for all the casualties to be recovered. By the time they found Red he still couldn't remember his own name or anything else.

On June 10, 1943, the 506th Parachute Infantry Regiment was finally recognized by the commander of the 101st Airborne Division, Major General Bill Lee and unofficially attached to the division. For the next few weeks the regiment was temporarily assigned to III Corps and on

July 13 jumped into the Lebanon training area of Tennessee. The purpose of the exercise was to learn how to establish roadblocks, demolish bridges and interrupt lines of communications. At the start, 3rd Battalion was misdropped and Colonel Wolverton, Ed Shames, Don Ross and the rest of Company HQ landed in a "German"-designated bivouac area. This would be the last jump Ed and the boys made on American soil as from here the regiment was returned to Fort Bragg in preparation for overseas deployment. On July 21, 1st and 3rd Battalions headed by train to Bragg, followed the next day by 2nd Battalion.

The time at Bragg was full of meetings and conferences trying to make sure that the regiment was prepared and had everything it needed for Europe.

Don Ross was appointed to the S3 and joined Kendall as our second runner. I also managed to persuade Wolverton and Carmen that Joe Gorenc should be my assistant. So he was promoted to Tech Sergeant and earmarked for transfer. It would have been lovely to have had Shorty on the team, and Lord knows I tried but as he didn't have the necessary skills, Wolverton said no.

During the latter part of August, Colonel Sink went on compassionate leave back to Lexington for the birth of his third daughter Robin. Before he left, Sink asked Wolverton to help Charlie Chase look after the regiment. While Wolverton was over at RHQ, Carl Buechner, who by then was his executive officer, was left to mind the store.

Buechner decided to change many of our working practices and really screwed things up, especially for me and the S3. I guess he was trying to prove a point after being overlooked at regiment but when Wolverton returned there was hell to pay.

A couple of weeks before we were due to embark, we were all given leave. I went home to Virginia Beach to say goodbye to my family and friends. On my last night, I decided on a whim to visit Ida Aframe. I'd known Ida since junior high and her older sister had married my cousin a few years earlier. Ida was absolutely beautiful. I mean everyone loved that girl. Her father was an important businessman in the local community and the family was pretty well to do. Ida was now a volunteer at a nearby hospital, where she worked as a nursing assistant. We sat down together in the staff rest area and talked. When it was time for me to go, she kissed me on the cheek, wished me good luck and promised to write. Ida kept her promise and we started regularly corresponding via V-mail. In fairness to Ida, my letters were a little more intimate than the ones she sent me! The next day, I went back to Bragg and 48 hours later moved out by train to Camp Shanks.

Between September 5 and 6, 1943, the regiment was ferried out to His Majesty's Troop Ship *Samaria* moored in New York Harbor. As the *Samaria* passed the burned-out hulk of cruise liner SS *Normandie*, Ed took a long look at the Statue of Liberty and wondered whether and when he would ever see it again.

2

"BEYOND GOLDEN FIELDS"
Ramsbury, England

The *Samaria* reached Liverpool on September 16, 1943 and the regiment moved out to the nearest operational railhead for transportation south. Early the following morning the paratroopers arrived at a Victorian-era station in the Kennet Valley, 68 miles due east of London. In the darkness, a sergeant from the divisional advance party welcomed everyone to Hungerford – emphasizing the word "Hunger" – before directing each battalion to its designated trucks. From here the 3rd Battalion was driven a short distance to a camp in the picturesque village of Ramsbury. Situated on the northern edge of town, beside Love's Lane, Camp Ramsbury consisted of 17 sparse wooden barracks and a Nissen hut, which became Colonel Wolverton's HQ.

Adjacent to the main entrance of the camp and connected by a tall hedge-lined path was Parliament Piece. The imposing 16th-century manor house had already been requisitioned as a billet, mess and club facility for the junior officers. Colonel Wolverton was allocated accommodation a couple of miles east of the village at Crowood House, which at the time was the home of Robina Clifton Brown and her three teenage children.

The next day Don Ross was up early to blow Reveille, closely followed by Assembly. Don would soon become a celebrity among the local children who developed a fascination for his bugle calls, which could be clearly heard across the village. With the entire battalion now formed up on the grass "parade ground," Colonel Wolverton explained that they were in the county of Wiltshire and that there were strict protocols governing how they behaved toward the local population. Everyone was issued a booklet entitled *A Short Guide to Great Britain* that outlined British customs and rationing and the complicated British currency of pounds, shillings and pence.

The enlisted men's mess hall was situated just down the road from the camp in an old schoolhouse along Back Lane. When Ed and Paul Simrell returned from breakfast on their first morning in Ramsbury, Wolverton advised them that they, along with several other senior NCOs and officers were going to be billeted in private homes around the village.

I guess it was all to do with integration. Paul and I were sent to the Blain family who owned Hills Grocery Store in the High Street. As we were standing in the hallway it quickly became obvious that Tom and Gwen Blain were somewhat wary, and needlessly overprotective of their two daughters Joan (12) and Margaret (14). Mr Blain showed us upstairs to a room that, much to our surprise, had already been furnished with beds by the army.

From their bedroom window, Ed and Paul had an impressive view across the High Street toward the square and the enormous elm tree, whose ancient gnarled branches partially obscured the upmarket Bell Hotel.

Despite being given keys to both the front door and bedroom, we weren't allowed access to the family bathroom, even though it was only across the landing. Instead we were asked to use the ablutions over the road at the Memorial Hall or the showers at the camp. Although Simrell was single, I never saw him go out on a date and despite the constant rhetoric about Panama, he never once mentioned his family, although I often asked. On the other hand he always took an interest in my home life, especially when I was writing to Ida and my sisters or when I had to co-sign the papers allowing my mother to sell off dad's last few remaining assets.

During the last week of September, all the S3 departments gathered together for a divisional meeting hosted by Regimental HQ at its base at Littlecote House in preparation for the regiment's first parachute exercise. Ed was at the meeting with Charles Carmen when Hank Hannah, now the regimental S3, produced several large-scale maps covering Littlecote and its surrounding area. The detailed Ordnance Survey sheets caused quite a stir and Hannah revealed that he had been in London over the weekend visiting Covent Garden when he had stumbled across Stanfords Hiking and Map Shop in Long Acre. After the meeting Ed obtained permission from Wolverton to visit Stanfords whenever necessary to purchase maps of Ramsbury, and Pentico Woods and Marridge Hill, both of which had been recently designated as training areas.

In the event, the exercise turned out to be a washout, when heavy rain canceled the jump. The primary objective for 3rd Battalion was to "destroy" a simulated series of coastal batteries and strong points. During the subsequent 30-mile night march across waterlogged fields, most of the charts purchased and issued by Ed disintegrated in the foul conditions.

Military training intensified with both day and night assemblies, undertaken over and over again. If necessary, especially after a parachute drop, it was Don Ross's job to blow Assembly and bring everyone in on Colonel Wolverton's command group. For many of these two- or three-day maneuvers, Ed and his small team created the sand tables, designed to help the men understand and appreciate the ground they were about to attack. Live firing also took place on the ranges at Pentico farm, where all manner of squad-level battle drills took place, including bazooka and demolition training.

Sometimes on weekends off, when I had access to the colonel's jeep, I used to drive over to Stonehenge. Back then you could sit on the stones and there was nothing more relaxing than lying in the autumn sunshine with a good book. One Saturday morning, it rained so hard that I headed back to Ramsbury, only to find Mr Blain overworked at the store. Putting on a white dustcoat, I jumped straight in and began serving. Up until then Mr Blain had no idea that I'd grown up in a similar environment helping my mother. After we had dealt with the backlog, which took most of the afternoon, Tom asked how much he owed me. "Oh, that's OK, sir. Uncle Sam pays my wages and I'm only too pleased to be of assistance." That night, the Blains dropped their guard and allowed Paul and I to use their private bathroom. On Sunday morning, there was a knock on our door and Gwen came in with a couple of freshly boiled eggs, a rare luxury in those days.

I continued to help out whenever time permitted and it didn't take long for their home to become our home. Tom, who was in his late forties, had served in World War I and I think felt a connection that grew deeper as time went on. However, Paul never really got to know Tom and Gwen quite like I did as he spent so much time over at the office. Strangely if ever we were relaxing in the living room, the girls would always be somewhere else, except if they needed to speak to their parents. That being said Joan and Margaret were always keen to hear about Virginia Beach and what Ida had said in her latest letter.

Behind the house a lovely garden sloped down to a crystal-clear millstream flowing from the river Kennet. Over on the right, just beyond the barn, was a makeshift garage, where Tom kept his car, an old Austin, raised up on bricks and minus its wheels. I don't think our new family would've minded if I'd have brought friends into the house but we didn't want to take advantage of their kindness and besides Shorty Madona was now only a stone's throw away at The Bell [the village pub].

Before leaving the States, Shorty had been transferred to 2nd Platoon, most of which was now billeted in a row of stables opposite the pub which was then owned by Simonds Brewery.

As we were under Double British Summer Time, and it was still light at 9pm, I'd often go over to see Joe and Sergeant Ernie Mann to shoot the breeze with 1st Squad, drinking hooch whiskey made in their own still – while up on the hill, planes from the nearby airfield droned away in the background.

Most evenings I'd find Bill Galbraith and the Brown twins from 2nd Squad out in the courtyard practicing football moves with Shorty who had just been selected for the newly formed regimental football team called "Sky Train." Madona's new boss was Jim Nye. Lieutenant Nye was an intolerant bastard with a nasty "GI" attitude and I never met anyone who ever really got on with him, especially after he punished Shorty and the boys when H Company stole their "honey bucket" [portable latrine] one night and emptied it all over the front entrance of the pub.

Old man Smith used to run The Bell, which was where Shorty and I had our first taste of high-strength Lemon Hart 151. The Demerara rum was sweet and deadly and most definitely not for the casual drinker! Ramsbury had a number of great pubs; but personally my favorite was the Crown & Anchor at the top of the village. Quite often on our way to the C&A for a few pints of "Arf 'n 'Arf" [mild and bitter], Shorty and I would stop at the battalion laundry run by Barron Dueber in Oxford Street, to pay off Joe's most recent gambling debts. Much to my dismay, Shorty still couldn't grasp the fact that Dueber was a dishonest snake who played him like a cheap banjo. Knowing full well that Paul and I were close to the boss, Dueber always made sure that our laundry and alterations were given priority over everyone else. I mean we weren't complaining, but if he had thought for one minute that we were of no potential use to him – he'd have sent us straight to the back of the line.

In case of "map emergencies," Captain Carmen always made sure we had an ample supply of weekend passes to London. These "red cards" were a rare commodity and it used to drive Corporal Ben Hiner, the battalion mail clerk, nuts when he occasionally saw me taking advantage of the privilege. Joe Madona and I would often thumb a ride to Hungerford railway station and 90 minutes later we'd be in London signing into the American Red Cross Center at Russell Square.

Sometimes I'd target the nicer hotels such as the Regent Palace in Piccadilly on behalf of Colonel Wolverton, specifically to scope out possible places for him to stay. During one of these "research" trips I noticed a billboard in Covent Garden publicizing a concert to honor Chinese President Chiang Kai-Shek by the London Philharmonic Orchestra. I loved symphony music and especially Sir Thomas Beecham, who was conducting the show at the Royal Albert Hall. Although the cheapest ticket I could buy was £10 ($40), it was well worth it.

George Retan had become a bit of a loner but occasionally I'd see him at Crowood House where he was now based with his platoon. Once or twice we visited London together, where of course we stayed at the Regent Palace. Piccadilly was like Broadway to us and had prices to match but we loved the party atmosphere. The ornate hotel was located on Glasshouse Street close to Piccadilly Circus and Shaftesbury Avenue. From the underground station opposite, you could look right down Regent Street toward Buckingham Palace and beyond to Big Ben. At the time there was only one bathtub for every two rooms, but the Regent was still one of the best hotels in Europe. Several high-class restaurants and bars were on the ground floor but these were too expensive even for Retan, so we would eat across the street in the American Red Cross Club at Rainbow Corner [now the Criterion Theatre] where you could purchase a decent hamburger for 5 cents!

Nothin' stops at this station

By now the HQ building at the camp was subdivided into a number of separate rooms mostly belonging to the various "S" departments. Wolverton and Buechner had their own offices, while Alex Bobuck and mess officer Second Lieutenant Jack Esco were sharing our already cramped space. Bobuck really was an officious SOB and tried his best to make things difficult for me at every opportunity.

Generally speaking Ed's department was exempt from CQ until First Sergeant Jim "JP" Shirley decided to put Kendall on the HQ Company guard roster.

After I removed Elwood's name, JP threatened me with immediate disciplinary action. When Wolverton learned what was happening, he reprimanded JP and then Captain McKnight, giving them both a warning not to bother us again.

One morning Captain Carmen called me over. "Shames, I've been thinking about developing our own form of secure code that we could use in the field." Believing Carmen was joking I replied, "Excuse me, sir … maybe we can base it on Hebrew?" But he was deadly serious.

This was the latest in a series of bizarre initiatives, and fearing more, Colonel Wolverton ordered Carmen to take temporary command of HQ Company after John McKnight was posted to I Company, while he placed him on the transfer list. Several weeks later, somewhat reluctantly, Charles Carmen packed his bags and headed for the CBI (China, Burma & India Theatre of Operations).

Before leaving, Carmen asked if I wanted to go with him. Of course my answer was "no," but if I'd have known then that his replacement was going to be Charlie Shettle, I would've probably reconsidered his offer! Biting the bullet, I struck up an uneasy partnership with Shettle, but it quickly became clear that as a department we were probably going to have to carry good ol' Charlie every step of the way.

Battalion HQ underwent another unexpected change. George Grant, who had previously been regimental supply officer, replaced the belligerent and unpopular Carl Buechner as executive officer. Related to President Ulysses S. Grant, Major Grant was also a misfit.

Wolverton told me that Colonel Sink had deliberately pushed him over to us and there was nothing we could do about it.

Sideswiping Ray Calandrella, the major insisted on bringing along his "prodigy," Bill Atlee, who clearly had very little office experience, to work alongside Paul. Grant demoted Ray who, like everyone else, was totally bewildered by the decision, and sent him to the assault/reconnaissance section under Jeb Holstun, who ironically was now our intelligence officer. However, when Bill Atlee's British uncle "Kermit" turned out to be Deputy Prime Minister Clement Attlee, everything fell into place. I think ultimately Sink was playing a game with Wolverton by trading off individuals like Grant and Buechner, which rightly or wrongly only served to destabilize the team. Despite being a family man, Major Grant was definitely a loose cannon and, from what I saw, thought himself as being a cut above everyone else, including Colonel Wolverton.

Perhaps due to these circumstances, Bob Wolverton began to confide more than ever before in Ed.

The colonel had a premonition that he wasn't going to make it and despite me telling him not to be so ridiculous, proceeded to write a series of letters to his son. Each note was intended to be opened by Lach "in the event of his father's death" on subsequent birthdays up to the age of 21. The boss pondered over these retrospective paternal messages for weeks and openly discussed every painstaking line with me, and occasionally, Hiner. Colonel Wolverton rewrote the content countless times until he was finally satisfied with the result. Then a naïve 21-year-old, I felt out of my depth and somewhat put upon. But now, as a great grandfather looking back on those intimate discussions – it was a rare, once in a lifetime privilege that underscored a growing change in my awareness.

By now, as we had such an abundance of maps, Joe Gorenc and I decided to hold map reading and navigation classes over at the Memorial Hall several evenings a week.

The extra-curricular lessons proved invaluable for those who bothered to turn up, and no doubt saved many lives after the battalion entered combat on D-Day. Regular dances were also held in the hall and were always well attended by the WAAFs from Ramsbury Airfield. After a succession of brawls between the paratroopers and members of the 28th Infantry Division (ID), Wolverton, thinking that a bit of culture was needed, asked Shames to organize a special classical concert.

I booked a four-piece chamber orchestra, who were doing the rounds at the time, playing well-established venues and the occasional officers' mess. Unlike me, the audience didn't appreciate the show and started a riot. I followed the musicians out through the back door and made a hasty getaway, leaving the Military Police desperately trying to calm things down.

Training ramped up with jumps on November 11 and December 13.

Shortly after Christmas, some of us, including myself, were invited by the British to carry out parachute descents from a barrage balloon at Bulford. Before we departed I heard that First Lieutenant Jim "Skunk" Walker from H Company had managed somehow to steal a British staff car from the vehicle park which he subsequently presented to Colonel Sink, who I understand graciously accepted the gift.

In February, the commander of the division, Bill Lee, became ill and was replaced by Major General Maxwell D. Taylor. Taylor was an experienced and charismatic leader who had seen active service in Italy with the 82nd Airborne. Shortly after Taylor's arrival, Wolverton asked Ed to action a letter from the local Jewish community.

A synagogue in Swindon was inviting any Hebrews from the battalion to attend their upcoming Seder – the first night of Passover. I typed and pinned a notice on the bulletin board outside HQ and around 18 people put their names down. Because of the response, I asked Wolverton if he could organize a truck for us. "Why don't you go ahead and sort that out, Shames. Take this note and requisition whatever you need from the motor pool." I drove over to Service Company at Froxfield in the jeep. When I handed them the note and explained my reasons, the officer in charge quipped, "That's the trouble with this outfit, there are too many damn Jews!" Slightly taken aback, I called the lieutenant a "son of a bitch" before he pulled rank and threatened to charge me with insubordination. Trying my best to stay calm, I politely requested that he call Colonel Wolverton, who immediately put the guy in his place. Sometimes, I had to ask myself just whose side some of these jokers thought they were on?

Around this time the division was alerted for the invasion of Europe, which kick-started several dress rehearsals beginning with a demonstration jump by 2nd and 3rd Battalions. The DZ was located on farmland east of Welford Airfield (6 miles north of Hungerford) and the drop was witnessed by General Eisenhower and British Prime Minister Winston Churchill.

A number of training areas were established along England's southern coast so that the Allies could test their plans for assaulting Hitler's "Fortress Europe" in realistic settings. Slapton Sands, in a part of Devon known as the South Hams, was chosen to represent "Utah" Beach. "Utah" was the codename given to the area at the base of the Cotentin Peninsula where "U" Force was to land on D-Day.

In total there were seven major exercises conducted within the Slapton Battle Training Area and the 101st Airborne participated in two of these: Exercise *Beaver* at the end of March and Exercise *Tiger* in late April. The latter was to closely follow the plans that had been laid down for the forthcoming assault on Utah Beach. After a naval bombardment by two cruisers and seven destroyers, the 4th ID would secure a bridgehead and then move inland. The 101st was scheduled to deploy from trucks northwest of Slapton Sands before dawn on "D-Day" moving out to meet up with the 4th ID, while the 82nd Airborne were given the task of securing the area to the east of the bridgehead.

Security was taken very seriously and strictly enforced. While en route to the exercise area, all personnel from the 101st were ordered to change into fatigues for the exercise rather than wearing their by now all too familiar jumpsuits, as it was vitally important that the Germans were kept in the dark regarding the purpose of *Tiger*. To further confuse the enemy the 101st was renamed the "1st Tank Destroyer Group," and the titles of all sub-units within the division were altered in a similar way. The 506th was redesignated the 801st Tank Destroyer Battalion (Towed) and 3rd Battalion became Company C. Bob Wolverton, together with his small advance party, left Ramsbury for the exercise area by jeep.

The weather was beautiful, and we felt like tourists, even stopping at Paignton Zoo to take a look at the animals. There was this big old tiger pacing up and down in its cage, and in a moment of dumb stupidity I called out to the animal. I had my hand on one of the bars as the tiger suddenly turned and lashed out. I jumped back in surprise and found the cat had ripped the top of my thumb with its claw.

Of course everyone thought it was highly amusing and somewhat ironic that Operation *Tiger* had already got the better of Shames!

Exercises *Beaver* and *Tiger* were rehearsals for the role the 101st would undertake once it actually landed in France. However, General Taylor insisted upon a full-scale rehearsal of the entire division's movement, both parachute and glider, from its camps in the Kennet valley to its planned D-Day departure airfields. This vital exercise was codenamed *Eagle*. On May 9, the battalion left Ramsbury for Exeter, while elements of the 1st and 2nd Battalions made for Upottery. Several nights later the regiment clambered aboard their designated aircraft and was flown back to the Kennet Valley to be dropped near Welford, along with the rest of the division, under a full moon.

Toward the end of May, unbeknown to all but the most senior officers, the 506th began final preparations for the invasion.

Even I figured that this was probably just another dress rehearsal until Wolverton, Shettle and myself, along with our supply officer First Lieutenant John King, were ordered to attend a SHAEF [Supreme Headquarters Allied Expeditionary Force] briefing at Southwick House near Portsmouth. We traveled down to the south coast in a SHAEF-operated weapons carrier with me, King and Shettle in the back. Shortly after arriving we were shown to a room, filled with airborne commanders and their respective S3 and S4 departments. I recognized the American captain who briefed us, as he'd previously visited Colonel Wolverton and our department at Ramsbury. Although the meeting at Portsmouth was secret, the SHAEF officer wouldn't allude to any exact mission details but instead gave us a broad outline of what to expect and where before personally issuing a set of large sealed packets to each battalion commander including Wolverton who seemed very excited.

Upon my return to Ramsbury, I walked back to the Blains and found Joe Gorenc waiting by the front door. Unbelievably, although he never really gambled, my buddy had just won nearly $2,000 and didn't have a clue what to do with the cash, which was bulging from an old envelope. "Oh my God, how in the heck did Dueber allow you get away with that?" Joe could hardly contain himself, "Aha, Dueber wasn't playing, this was a big crap game up at the camp and I got lucky." Of course I couldn't tell Joe where I'd been or what was most probably about to happen. Because all the outgoing mail had just been stopped, I suggested for the time being we hide the dough behind a cabinet in my room which would remain locked until we got back from the upcoming marshaling exercise at Exeter.

3

"THE OTHER SIDE OF TOMORROW"

The marshaling area, Exeter

Early on May 26, 24 hours before the bulk of the battalion departed for Exeter, the advance party consisting of Wolverton, John King, Ed Shames and driver Vernon Law left Ramsbury. It was difficult to imagine that there was a war going on as the jeep headed west to Devon. Approaching the airfield they could see camouflaged huts dotted around the perimeter and a large control tower. On the southern side of the road, just opposite the main gate, was the tented camp still in place from Exercise *Eagle*.

After signing in with security, the four men were reintroduced to the ring-fenced battalion area. The space was made up of a number of pyramid tents, laid out around the larger S3 briefing tent, which was only just big enough to hold a company of 140 men.

After we'd been sealed in, Colonel Wolverton handed me a number of maps and aerial photographs and said, "Shames, these are your instructions.

As you've probably guessed by now – this is it. Tomorrow, when the trucks arrive, take as many extra people as you need. Is that clear?" It was only then I realized that this was the moment we'd all been working toward and we were really going to war.

Outside my tent was a pile of fresh soil that the engineers had dumped specifically for use by the S3. My instructions revealed that we were to be dropped about 3 miles due north of Carentan onto DZ D, to capture and hold two wooden bridges and a passenger ferry crossing the Canal de Carentan, which we were calling the river Douve, near the village of Brévands. The bridges were about 6 miles inland from le Grande Dune [Utah Beach] and nearly 2 miles east of St-Côme-du-Mont, providing an important link between Utah and Omaha, the two American invasion beaches. The bridge nearest Carentan was wide enough for vehicles whereas the bridge further downstream was only suitable for pedestrian traffic.

The next morning we all gathered in the HQ tent to await the battalion. Following their arrival Wolverton called a meeting of company commanders, executive officers, and platoon leaders to reveal and explain the basic points of our D-Day mission. HQ Company, along with my department, supported by H Company, was to secure the road bridge, while G and I were to hold the footbridge. The battalion was to protect these vital structures until relieved by the 4th ID arriving from Utah Beach. Two platoons from C Company, 326th Airborne Engineer Battalion (AEB), were to assist us in holding the bridges and, if the need arose, prepare them for demolition. All those present were given aerial photographs, maps, and additional briefing notes. As the officers were leaving, Colonel Wolverton asked them to assemble the entire battalion, because he wanted to personally inform the men of their mission.

Afterwards Shames and his temporarily enhanced team returned to the S3 tent to begin assembling the sand table, formed from four large sheets of plywood. Joe Gorenc was anxious – but about his money rather than the invasion. Ed reassured him, telling him not to worry as Paul now knew about the cash so if anything should happen to Joe, his winnings would be safe. With everything now topographically complete, the colonel came in with Shettle to inspect.

"Who put the 'AVOID AT ALL COSTS' sign on the church steeple at Carentan?" asked Wolverton. I admitted "Er ... me, sir, the SHAEF notes say it's a suspected German Corps HQ and I thought it might be a good idea to flag it up!" After studying our near-perfect 20ft-square scale model, Wolverton turned to Shettle and said, "Charlie, what do you think about Shames briefing the battalion?" Although I didn't foresee that one coming, of course Shettle had no problem with me taking over, as I suppose it probably freed him up elsewhere. Wolverton then requested that firstly, I was to advise all the company commanders, then rifle companies, support weapons and lastly individual platoons including the demolition engineers from C/326. As the colonel was leaving he handed me a white mattress cover. "What do you expect me to do with that, sir?" "They want us to carry and use 'em as body bags to store our own remains should we be killed." "You gotta be joking, colonel. Who thought of that?" "The Medical Detachment – now don't forget, to make it easier for them to identify, you'll need to write your name, rank and serial number somewhere on the outside."

Ed dutifully did what the boss had asked and afterwards stored the mattress cover in his musette bag.

Shames' tent was one of several that the soldiers had to visit as part of their preparations:

From my stand, each group would then head to the gas tent to check their respirators before moving onto first aid, which subsequently became part of a daily circuit. The colonel ordered me to make sure our facility was manned around the clock and to task my team, which now included Corporal Hiner, in any way I saw fit.

When all the maps and aerial photographs were pinned in place around the tent, I sent Ross, Kendall and Hiner to fetch the company commanders along with their respective executive officers for the first session, which had been scheduled to last around 30 minutes.

The sand table was orientated north so that any remote compass bearing would match the actual locations on the map. Six farms ran along the road that led to the vehicle bridge, each lovingly recreated in miniature. The farmhouse nearest the junction leading to the bridge was earmarked as the battalion aid station and supply store. Unfortunately, intelligence could not tell how many of these properties were occupied by the Germans, so all had to be viewed as potentially hostile. Where known, the identity of enemy units and their respective strengths were marked, although the actual bridges were rather a gray area.

As we were discussing the various flooded spots around the DZ, Jeb Holstun callously blurted out that he'd rather be fighting Jews and Brits. I don't know if he was trying to be funny but I didn't find his comment the least bit amusing. After the way he and his buddy Bobuck had treated me over the last few months, I just exploded, "You damned SOB! If you ever come between me and a Kraut, I swear I'll blow your damn brains out!" Following a short but heated argument he backed down, but you can imagine the atmosphere immediately afterwards.

I made it clear to everyone, whether officer or private, that they were free to return at any time and talk to either myself or Gorenc. One of the guys, Sergeant Frank Padisak, from 1st Platoon, H Company, took the offer literally and kept coming back. Late one night he woke me and asked for another run through across the sand table. Afterwards, Joe passed a flippant comment about Padisak, who was going over the same information time and time again. Joe was smirking as he said, "What's wrong with this guy, is he just plain stupid or something?" Joe was embarrassed as I began to put him straight: "Can't you see what's driving this man? Padisak's holding himself totally responsible for the lives of his squad, and the extra work he's putting in here is providing a confidence and level of understanding that I wished some of the other squad leaders were capable of showing – now shut the heck up and go back to bed."

One afternoon, when I Company was rotating through the tent, Ed asked many of his old friends to sign his 100 Franc invasion note including, of course, Joe Madona, George Retan, Jim Brown, Red Swann, Bill Galbraith and Lonnie Gavrock.

Even when we had the cancellation on June 4, over at the airfield, I was told to stay put by Wolverton, who promised to arrange a seat and 'chute for me as per usual on his aircraft – which was also designated as the number one, lead plane, spearheading our assault. Likewise, I couldn't be there the following evening when the colonel recited a prayer he'd written after proposing his "one year from today" reunion idea to the battalion.

Afterwards the colonel asked the troops to kneel, lift their heads to the heavens and delivered the most powerful prayer that any soldier, army or nation could imagine. Afterwards the men stood and for a full minute there was total silence as everyone gathered their thoughts.

Although I couldn't be at the gathering, I'll remember the colonel's poignant and emotive words to the end of my days: "God Almighty! In a few short hours we will be in battle with the enemy. We do not join battle afraid. We do not ask favors or indulgence but ask that, if you will, use us as your instrument for the right and an aid in returning peace to the world. We do not know or seek what our fate will be. We only ask this, that if die we must, that we die as men would die, without complaining, without pleading and safe in the feeling that we have done our best for what we thought was right. Oh Lord! Protect our loved ones and be near us in the fire ahead, and with us now as we each pray to you." Ironically, the prayer turned out to be for him.

During the evening of June 5, Kendall arrived with orders to escort me to the airfield. On our way through the various checkpoints, I learned that Ross, Gorenc, Calandrella and Atlee were already loaded and waiting on the number one plane while Shettle and Hiner were aboard another. Out at the aircraft, fitting our 'chutes and equipment, I acknowledged Don, who happened to be sitting nearest to the cargo door, chain smoking.

Moments later, Colonel Wolverton appeared in the opening, saying "Shames, I'm so sorry but a British journalist, Ward Smith, from the *News of the World* is now occupying your seat. It was a last-minute thing so I've had to remanifest you and Kendall onto alternative aircraft."

After the boss pointed out our respective chalk numbers, I saluted, turned, and we trotted away across the airfield.

It was getting dark as Shames reached his surrogate plane, he had no idea who was onboard, but after a brief safety inspection, the jumpmaster, a lieutenant, designated Ed as "push out man" before directing him to the number 19 position. Struggling uphill toward the cockpit, he fumbled apologetically through the red low-lit interior.

Boot camp for the brave

Shortly after 2350hrs on June 5, 1944, 45 C-47s from the 440th Troop Carrier Group took off for France via Portland Bill. The moon reflected silver and shimmered on the English Channel, 1500 feet below. Talking over the roar of the twin 1200hp radials was almost impossible as Ed sat, deep in thought, frustrated when he realized he had forgotten to blacken his face and there was now no way of rectifying the problem. Continually buffeted by the weather and the other aircraft in the formation, Ed's plane rocked and fell a few feet, only to quickly return to its position in the armada. Shames felt completely alone in a plane full of strangers and under his breath, cursed the colonel for his actions.

Perplexed by the sudden change of plan, I could never have imagined the final consequences of Wolverton's decision.

Approaching the Cotentin Peninsula a layer of clouds became visible to the pilots. Rising to a height of 3,000 feet, the formation decreased altitude and flew under the overcast in an attempt to keep visual contact. During the straight run into the DZ heavy antiaircraft fire destroyed one plane and forced a number of other aircraft off course including the one Ed was on.

Four minutes out from the DZ, the plane slowed to 120mph and the red light by the exit door flicked on, signaling the jumpmaster to call "Hook up" and begin his safety checks. After successfully checking each other's equipment, parachutes and fastenings, every man in the stick responded to "Sound off for equipment check" by shouting in sequence, starting with Ed, "Nineteen OK! Eighteen OK! Seventeen OK! ..." Satisfied that all was correct, the lieutenant beckoned everyone forward before returning to his designated position in the aircraft. It would be Ed's job as "push out man" to drive toward the door, ensuring momentum and a timely exit procedure.

At 1:40am the green light came on and as I began to push, the guy in front stumbled and fell. The delay trying to pick him up was only a few seconds but it was critical.

Running headlong down the fuselage, Shames grimaced as the crew chief snatched his static line, and he leapt into the black, tracer-tipped void.

The minute-long descent gave me plenty of time to look around at the incredible "firework" display across the peninsula. I was heading for a burning industrial area and began desperately trying to control my drift before landing heavily amongst a herd of cows in a muddy yard. A nearby building was on fire and I could see a tall chimney towering above me. Below it, illuminated in the flames, was a logo depicting a carnation… God, no – it can't be? Christ Almighty, I couldn't believe that I might be on the edge of Carentan, inside the Gloria Milk Factory! My sand table words "AVOID AT ALL COSTS" began running through my head over and over again. Physically shaking, I cut the risers that connected the main 'chute to my harness, assembled and loaded my M1, shouldered my equipment and moved out toward the Bassin à Flot, the canal that connected Carentan with the Douve.

Clambering over the perimeter fence, I could hear the cows mooing. The noise they were making probably saved my life! I didn't see anybody else from my aircraft. Most of those poor bastards would have landed behind me across the city and wouldn't have stood a chance. Yes, I was damn lucky but I still had to find a way across the Douve and that wasn't going to be easy.

Leaving behind the noise of Carentan, following his mental map, Shames moved on a compass bearing northeast before reaching a small swing bridge.

Occasionally, upon looking up, I saw the red lights from a "marker plane."

Dozens of these aircraft had been designated to fly high and fast at regular intervals across the peninsula on an easterly bearing to aid ground navigation. Crossing the bridge, he passed the entrance to a brick factory and then found himself in an industrial area. The post-drop silence was punctuated every now and again by a burst of tracer fire, arcing into the night sky.

Silhouetted by moonlight, I could just to make out two rows of tall trees lining the Bassin waterway. Knowing from the sand table that there were two lockkeepers' cottages a mile or so ahead, I decided to move away from the road and shadow the canal from some open ground to my right. It was shortly after this that several other paratroopers from the battalion started to join me.

A little later we passed a derelict farm that was set back from the road. I was amazed that we had got this far and not been seen. We soon came to another, which looked as though it might be occupied and decided to ask for help. I reasoned that it was probably safer to approach an isolated building because if challenged, we could easily withdraw and carry on down the road. Deploying the men around the house, I knocked on the door. An elderly man answered, and I told him that I was an American and the invasion had begun. He must've understood because he almost collapsed with shock. From somewhere behind, a woman started to scream hysterically. I forced my way past the old guy, clamped my hands over the woman's mouth and carefully lowered her to the ground. After she calmed down a little, I got on the floor beside her and encouraged the old man to do the same. I wanted to show the Frenchman my map.

Illuminated by torchlight underneath a raincoat, I pointed at Ste-Mère-Église and the old man pointed at Brévands – the settlement opposite our objective. He then showed me the location of a nearby minefield but I nearly had a fit when he gesticulated toward Carentan and a German vehicle park – *"Allemagne camion ici, ici"*– that we'd passed back down the lane! Thankfully the farmer didn't seem to think that there were any more enemy soldiers between his house and the Douve.

Now certain of our exact position, as I doubled the men up the road toward the lockkeepers' cottages we noticed two figures staggering toward us. As a regiment we'd been told not to open fire on anything unless it was totally necessary [so larger enemy forces were not alerted to their presence]. These two men stank of booze, and were probably returning from a night out. I ordered that their throats be cut and during the struggle one of the Germans discharged his pistol and the bullet grazed the bridge of my nose. After the two drunken Krauts had been dispatched, they were searched and I kept one of their pay books, believing it might be useful to Colonel Wolverton.

Shortly afterwards, the group reached a stone bridge that crosses the river La Taute at St-Hilaire-Petitville, where the river drained into the Douve just east of the Bassin á Flot lock gates. Ed reasoned that attempting to cross the old bridge would lead to almost certain death. However, the lock gates were fitted with a metal gantry and Ed thought that this might be a better way to cross over the waterway and then try and find a more convenient place to swim the river.

The men soon found a spot that looked as though it might be suitable to wade across and Ed decided that he should be the one to go first.

I tied a jump rope around my body and two men held the other end as I slipped into the freezing water. I couldn't reach the bottom and, struggling to catch a breath, was forced downstream by the outgoing tide. The two guys hauled me back to shore and we continued along the bank toward the lock at La Barquette, the objective of the 501st PIR who had also dropped onto DZ D.

A little further upstream, Ed's group was joined by Sergeant Stan Stockins from HQ Company.

After successfully crossing the Douve we met five soldiers from the 501st led by a captain. The officer asked who I was, where I was going and if I knew where we were. "Sir, I'm Colonel Wolverton's operations sergeant from 3rd Battalion, 506th and yes, I do know where we're going. Would you take command?" "I don't think that'll be necessary," he replied. "Sergeant Shames, for the time being we'll go where you go, so lead on." We followed an easterly bearing that took us across open salt marshes. Luckily there wasn't much flooding here and the early morning mist was now providing superb cover. As it started to get light, I began to pick up the pace and told the group that I wasn't waiting around. Due to their heavier loads some of the men started to moan but still fell in behind me like ducklings waddling after their mother. But I was no lightweight: on top of my basic load, I was carrying a number of smoke grenades, air recognition panels, dozens of waterproofed maps and a walky-talky radio, which unfortunately wasn't impervious to the saltwater I'd just swum through.

We hadn't gone much further when we ran into Colonel Howard Johnson, the commanding officer of the 501st who belligerently demanded, "Which way's the goddamned lock?" I showed him La Barquette on the map and pointed. He set off taking the 501st people in my group with him. By now it was nearly broad daylight so I stepped up a gear, keeping the river to our right as we approached the road bridge. On arrival Captain Shettle squawked, "Boy are you a sight for sore eyes! Why on earth are you still wearing your parachute pack tray?" Due to the shock and excitement of landing in the milk factory, I'd forgotten to take it off and was wearing it like an extra layer of clothing. This may sound crazy but the harness made me feel safer, so I kept it on like some sort of lucky charm.

When I first saw the bridge it looked much smaller than I'd imagined, I mean compared to the aerial photographs and my scale model.

Charlie Shettle and a small force were sheltering behind a 10ft-high berm topped by a single-track road that led to the bridge, forming part of the river Douve's flood barrier. Due to the obvious inactivity along the coast, Shettle and the others were beginning to wonder whether the invasion had been postponed, leaving them all stranded.

Charlie quickly went on to explain that he was now the most senior officer present and would I consider acting as his executive officer, at least until Colonel Wolverton, Major Grant or Captain Harwick (commanding officer of H Company) turned up. He then dropped another bombshell – we had no way of communicating with Colonel Sink or anyone else, as all our radio kit had been lost on the drop! We quickly tried my waterlogged radio but it wouldn't work. "Sir," I inquired, "have you seen anybody at all from the lead plane?" "No Shames, no one, not even Lieutenant Bobuck." "What about Sergeant Major Simrell, have you seen him, sir?" Lowering his voice

Shettle responded, "I'm afraid not, but Lieutenant Esco, Corporal Hiner and Kendall all made it safely and are about somewhere. We have around 40 people on site at the moment, including two platoon leaders from H Company, Lieutenants Christianson and Madden, plus a German prisoner who they've already got digging trenches, but so far that's about it."

4

"THE RIVER RUNS RED"

D-Day, the wooden bridges at Brévands

By first light, First Lieutenant Ken Christianson and a couple of men from his 2nd Platoon were the first people to arrive at the road bridge. At this point there should have been around 250 men at the position. The area was surprisingly quiet, except for a few random airbursts coming from a German 40mm antiaircraft gun positioned on a hill 2 miles away at L'Amont near St-Côme.

Looking toward the coast from Shettle's objective at the road bridge, the sharp bend in the river meant that it was virtually impossible to see the other crossing point. However, the berm did provide excellent protection from the sporadic German fire now coming from the opposite bank. Christianson had been asking for volunteers to scout across the bridge to test the enemy strength. As Ken was looking around, a Lancaster bomber came out of nowhere and crashed vertically into the ground 1 mile northwest of the footbridge, close to a small farmhouse called Les Rats. Piloted by Wing Commander Edward Carter, the RAF plane had been bombing an abandoned gun site at Pointe du Hoc when it was hit from below by a German night-fighter. The four-engine aircraft screamed into the ground 15ft from the farmhouse's front door and exploded; there were no survivors.

Thirty minutes after Carter's plane came down, as Christianson was giving a final briefing to his five-man assault team, the horizon lit up, followed by a deep rumbling noise. The Allied naval bombardment of Utah Beach had begun, signaling the invasion was underway – everyone breathed a deep sigh of relief.

As the H Company team, led by Staff Sergeant Fred Bahlau, sprinted across the heavily timbered bridge, a cacophony of small arms and mortar fire erupted from the other side of the river. Adjacent to Shames, Corporal Tom Bucher was providing covering fire with his machine gun. Suddenly a burst from a German machine pistol tore up the embankment, forcing Bucher to relocate. Meanwhile, across on the other side of the river, Bahlau's men were struggling to make progress through the soft, exposed mud banks. One of the H Company guys, Hank DiCarlo, was wounded in the upper right chest and had to make his way back under the bridge by spanning the trusses with a discarded builder's plank.

H Company also had a 60mm mortar team on site, able to provide a protective umbrella, while Christianson organized a relief group led by Pete Madden and Harry Clawson. Knowing Bahlau's team could not hold off a larger-scale attack, Shettle ordered the bridge to be rigged for demolition. As Shettle and Christianson were keeping the rest of the enemy force occupied, Shames looked after their defense.

Shettle ordered me to scout around and find out what our ammo state was. Any spare 60mm shells I could find were to be dumped next to a growing pile of C2 plastic explosive. Plus, I was also to make sure that everyone kept their heads down as Corporal Bucher had just been shot in the throat.

Ed's search turned up just one mortar tube, minus its base plate, and several men who had no weapons at all. After returning to Shettle, Shames reported his findings and left the tube beside the C2.

After arriving earlier with Captain Shettle, Sergeant Ralph Bennett from H Company had been ordered by Lieutenant Christianson to support Bahlau's group with his 60mm mortar. As Bennett and his team were firing blind, Ed decided to give him some assistance. Shames ordered Sergeant Stan Stockins – known for his strength – to throw the C2 across the bridge toward the Germans, reminding him to keep below the berm. After tearing the 1lb blocks in half, Stockins had to insert slow-burning waterproof fuses, then pause momentarily before hurling each spherically molded charge as far as he could across the river.

While he was doing this, Stan's head was exposed for a split second – he was killed instantly by a high-velocity bullet that tore through his face. Ed was the first person to reach him.

I think the shot came from a two-story house across the river. After turning Stockins onto his back, I realized there was nothing we could do for him. Then our regimental Anglican Chaplain Tilden "TS" McGee came across, and said a few words over the body.

After Stockins was killed, I got permission to use the 60mm tube I'd found earlier. Shettle thought it was worth a try even though the base plate and bipod were missing. Placing the tube on the ground, with the aid of a colleague, I used my left hand to adjust the angle and we began dropping shells. I had no idea where they were landing but hoped it would keep the enemy away from the bridge.

In the meantime, DiCarlo was beneath the bridge dripping blood into the Douve as he slowly and painfully inched his way along the plank between trusses under the bridge's 130-yard span. As he neared the friendly bank, two colleagues hauled him up and dragged him off behind the berm, leaving him beside Stockins' bloodsoaked corpse to await treatment and evacuation to the newly established aid station at Fortin farm.

Ed was still operating the mortar tube, which with each shot sank a little further into the soft earth until the muzzle settled just below ground level. At that point he sensibly decided to cease his fire mission. A few minutes later, Shettle and Christianson sent Pete Madden and his group across the bridge. Their job was to protect the regimental demolition engineers who were trying to rig the bridge with explosives. As the group reached the far side, they joined up with Bahlau and his battered force. The group was now about a dozen strong and formed a defensive line along the enemy-held dike upstream of the bridge. Because of overwhelming enemy fire, the demolition men had to abort their mission. Madden could see there was no point in staying and during a brief lull withdrew back under the crossing.

Shettle's group was getting low on ammunition when he ordered Jack Esco to retrieve some bundles that had landed in the river. Machine-gun fire was ripping across the top of the berm and any man going over faced a short future – rightly or wrongly Esco refused the order. There was no reasoning with Shettle, who furiously relieved Esco of his duties and sent him back to Fortin farm, where the mess officer made himself useful, tending to the wounded. Once the immediate need for ammunition had passed Shettle decided to leave the bundles where they were and ordered everyone at the bridge to start digging in.

As the day progressed, more people arrived and were allocated positions along the berm. On several different occasions Ken Christianson risked all by dashing across the exposed access road that led to the bridge. Ken was desperately trying to make contact with G and I Company who were tasked with holding the footbridge. Both companies were also in poor shape and missing their commanders, Harold van Antwerp and John McKnight. Shettle ordered regimental demolition man, Private First Class John Agnew, to blow a trench through the road, parallel to the berm, making it much safer for Ken and others to cross.

I dug in behind the northeastern side of the bridge beside Captain Shettle and Chaplain McGee. Rooting around inside my damp musette bag, I pulled out the waterlogged handy talky portable radio, which was still the only communications device we had. After a while we got the thing working but were unable to tune it into any of the battalion or regimental frequencies. Unbelievably the only thing we could pick up was BBC World Service broadcasting to the ships off Utah Beach, so at least we knew the beach landings were underway.

Stragglers were continually drifting into our positions. Once I'd established who they were, Shettle and I questioned them to try and find out what was happening around the area. We were anxious for any news about Wolverton, the 81mm Mortar Platoon [which had vanished into thin air] and our friends. But nobody we interviewed seemed to know anything about anyone.

One man who came in was 32-year-old Second Lieutenant Rudolph "Rudy" Bolte, a recent replacement from 1st Platoon, H Company. Rudy had been severely concussed by an explosion from one of the monstrous 14-inch rounds being fired from the battleship USS *Nevada*. A number of these half-ton shells sporadically flew overhead, sounding like subway trains racing through a tunnel.

As Charlie and I started talking to Bolte, we realized he was not in very good shape. Shettle told him to go find a place to dig in and come back as soon as he started to regain his composure. He didn't return and later that evening I was sent down the line only to discover Rudy at the bottom of his foxhole. Crouching near him I addressed him, "Excuse me, sir, but Captain Shettle wants to know why you haven't rep…" I stopped in mid-sentence as Bolte looked right through me with piercing green eyes. He was clearly still very screwed up, so I went back to Shettle to report what I'd seen. Nothing more was said, Charlie just left Rudy alone, in the hope that he would eventually pull himself together.

Rudy was later evacuated with concussion to a hospital at Cherbourg a day or so after the port was liberated.

Half a mile or so behind the bridges, mortar and small-arms fire seemed to be growing louder. The German I.Bataillon/Fallschirmjäger-Regiment 6 had been trapped by elements of the glider-borne troops, who had recently arrived in the second wave, and were desperately trying to withdraw to their regimental HQ at St-Côme-du-Mont. Amid all this action, Ben Hiner and a couple of others were sent out by supply sergeant Bob Webb, of HQ Company, to look around the DZ for lost radio equipment. Shettle also had men scout around for supply bundles. One of these patrols, led by H Company executive officer Dick Meason, brought back about a dozen prisoners from Ost-Bataillon 439. Initially after interrogation, Shettle suggested that the sorry-looking bunch of Ukrainian volunteers should be shot but he was talked down and eventually agreed to lock them all in a barn behind the aid station down at Fortin farm.

As darkness fell, Shettle ordered five men from C Company, 326th Airborne Engineers, to rig two of the vehicle bridge trusses with explosives. It was after dark before the engineers eventually completed the task. During the night, enemy activity increased and there was an exchange of rifle and machine-gun fire. Shames started throwing fused C2 over the berm and, together with support from Ralph Bennett's 60mm mortar team, managed to simulate a short artillery barrage. The Germans pulled back and things went quiet.

It was then that Shettle surprised me by saying that I ought to be an officer! At first I thought the Red Death was just being sarcastic but he was in fact quite serious. Although Charlie was clearly impressed by the way I'd handled the briefings back at Exeter he was now beginning to see a different side to me, perhaps even one that I never knew existed before now. Acknowledging his comment, I moved off down the berm encouraging our boys to stay alert and remain focused – as our part in this battle was by no means over.

Jericho Rain

Shortly after dawn on June 7, dozens of C-47s appeared in the distance dropping food, ammunition and medical supplies for the 101st. Several of the transport planes strayed over DZ D, drawing flak before delivering supply bundles onto an open area north of Fortin farm.

On the small hill overlooking the footbridge, a camouflaged German 88mm antiaircraft gun was firing on anything that moved within its arcs, including the C-47s. At the time, First Lieutenant Joe Doughty was in charge of defense, assisted by Jim Nye and several other junior officers including Second Lieutenant Charles "Sandy" Santarsiero and George Retan from 3rd Platoon, I Company. Incredibly, that morning a small force led by Sandy and George had ambushed and captured two companies of retreating German coastal artillerymen who had been manning gun positions behind Utah Beach.

I'd heard small-arms fire in the distance and a little while later Second Lieutenant "Sandy" Santarsiero arrived. He had been responsible for some of the noise and was clearly very excited by all the action. The lieutenant brought along some prisoners and wanted to know what to do with them?

Around lunchtime, as Sandy was herding the prisoners back toward the bridge, it came under attack by a flight of P-51B Mustangs from the US 353rd Fighter Bomber Squadron. The air strike – over in under a minute – rendered the bridge unserviceable. One of the aircraft, flown by First Lieutenant Charles Huffman, lost altitude coming out of the target, rolled to the right, jettisoned two bombs and clipped the ground with his right wing tip. The Mustang tumbled several times before disintegrating in flames across an area known as "white tree field" several hundred yards behind the bridge – the area where Sandy had ambushed the Germans a few hours earlier. Joe Doughty sent out a small patrol to the site to see if any of the .50 caliber machine guns could be recovered but all four were too badly twisted to be of any use. Huffman's dog tags were recovered from his grisly remains, which were discovered hanging from an old poplar tree at the end of the debris field.

After watching the plane crash from Fortin farm, Ben Hiner and Bob Webb were alerted by Elwood Kendall, who arrived with some alarming news from Shettle: I.Bataillon/Fallschirmjäger-Regiment 6 had been spotted no more than 600 yards away, moving past a gap in the trees north of the farm, heading west in the direction of St-Côme-du-Mont. Since mid-morning the 501st at La Barquette had been in combat with the German paratroopers, who had suffered heavy casualties. It was not long before Ken Christianson and three other soldiers quickly developed a plan to deal with the looming threat. Taking four of Webb's men, the lieutenant crossed the Pénême road and ran toward the German paratroopers, yelling and firing wildly into the air. It was a crazy move that took the enemy completely by surprise. For the next three hours, Webb, Hiner and ten other troopers formed a defensive line along the road, successfully keeping the enemy away from Fortin farm and the bridge.

It seemed to me that by now the Germans were in the process of withdrawing. Most of us stayed near the bridge as per orders. However, one or two patrols were sent out to try and make contact with other units. Although we were unable to see the footbridge from our position, we could hear the 88mm gun and were acutely aware of the recent air attack.

But when Sandy arrived with a second group of POWs, "the crap really hit the fan!"

Santarsiero's second group of prisoners was standing in full view behind the bridge when four P-47 Thunderbolts roared in low overhead. Perhaps concluding that the bridge was in enemy hands, the pilots acquired their next ground target. Shames was helping to process the second group of POWs when the planes began their initial attack run from the direction of Fortin farm. Remembering the earlier attack, everyone panicked and ran for cover. The first 500lb bombs shook the ground like an earthquake and sent plumes of earth, water and wood cascading skywards. During the ensuing attack, both ends and the center of the bridge were taken out, leaving the crossing completely unserviceable. As Ed later recalled, "I was out of my foxhole and ran toward the nearest trench, jumped in feet first and landed on Chaplain McGee's back!"

Then two of the Thunderbolts returned and started strafing the bridge with cannon fire:

One aircraft began firing its eight .50 cal guns and the cannon shells tore into the ground around our position. The second plane was circling and preparing for its attack. I shouted to McGee, "Smoke, we gotta let 'em know!" I still had the orange canisters and air recognition panels in my musette bag. Scrambling out of McGee's foxhole my helmet fell off. I then started to "pop" the grenades and jumped frantically up and down waving the smoke all around before throwing them on the ground when my hands began to burn.

The second aircraft was now well into its dive and firing. By this time we were both out in the open, I "popped" more smoke as McGee frantically waved the air panels. The cannon shells went wide and we realized there was no point in carrying on and tumbled back into the foxhole. Fortunately for us the pilots must've realized they'd made a terrible mistake because they aborted and flew away waggling their wings.

Incredibly only one person was killed during the air attack. The sandy soil around the bridge area had allowed the men to dig deep foxholes and these undoubtedly saved many lives. If the air attack wasn't enough, the embankment then came under German mortar attack and Pete Madden was blown out of his hole, receiving extensive shrapnel wounds to his back and right leg. Shortly after the bombing, Shettle gave permission for Sandy, along with a small patrol, to try and make contact with Colonel Sink.

At around the same time, down at Fortin farm, elements of I.Bataillon/ Fallschirmjäger-Regiment 6 surrendered to Ken Christianson, Bob Webb and Ben Hiner. After they had been disarmed and searched, the German parachutists were added to the "white tree field" prisoners and marched down the road to a larger barn. About 30 minutes later the building came under fire from the German 88mm gun on the hill opposite the footbridge. Dozens of German POWs were torn to shreds during the barrage. One of the shells fell short and exploded in the backyard of Fortin farm, instantly killing the farmer's wife, Odette Fortin, and Georgette Revet, an eight-year-old girl who had been sheltering at the house.

That evening a runner from the 501st brought Captain Shettle word that 260 Germans, all Fallschirmjäger and many of them seriously wounded, were being sent to Fortin farm. The Allied net was closing around St-Côme-du-Mont and the enemy forces began to withdraw in disarray along the railway lines into Carentan.

Give blood

By midday on June 8, thanks to Santarsiero, communications had been established with Colonel Sink's CP at Angoville, resulting in a successful bombing mission against the "88" at Brévands, the same gun that had earlier targeted the barn. The remaining wounded at Fortin farm were evacuated by jeeps belonging to the 326th Airborne Medical Company. By this time the supply officer, John King, was driving around on a captured German *Kettenkrad* (tracked motorcycle) looking for missing equipment and stragglers. Later in the afternoon Colonel Sink entered St-Côme-du-Mont and "liberated" 3rd Battalion surgeon Stanley Morgan, several members of the Medical Detachment and a number of wounded who had all been captured on or after D-Day. Much to Ed's disbelief, among the soldiers was Alex Bobuck, who had fooled the Germans into believing he was some sort of administrative medical pen pusher.

To me Bobuck did his best to steer clear of any fighting. I told him so and he didn't like it one little bit.

Back at the bridges the 327th Glider Infantry Regiment (GIR), who had landed on Utah Beach with 4th ID, was preparing to take over. By evening almost 150 men from 3/506 were placed in reserve and divided into three groups. After dusk H Company, with Christianson in command, was sent to an orchard in St-Côme, while Santarsiero took G and I Companies to a temporary bivouac field at Beaumont farm directly behind Sink's CP. Meanwhile, Shettle and Shames led HQ Company and marched them to Folleville farm, situated on the far northern edge of St-Côme, where they established 3rd Battalion's CP. The command post was to act as a hub, while the three rifle companies became the spokes allowing the decimated battalion to take control of a much larger area.

Most of the troops from HQ Company had occupied the two stone barns attached to the house. Shettle found a nice room upstairs in the main house and soon settled in. As for Hiner, Kendall and myself, we made ourselves comfortable in the kitchen which had a lovely Aga stove in the center. After we got the Aga going, I asked Hiner to take care of things while I took a quick nap and curled up next to the warm oven. I was so exhausted that the moment my head hit the "back pack" pillow, I lapsed into a deep comatose sleep almost like I'd been anesthetized.

The following day I learned the fate of Colonel Wolverton. Just up the road, H Company had discovered his mutilated and bloated remains, still harnessed, hanging from an apple tree in their bivouac area. Those German bastards had used the colonel's body as target practice and we figured that he must've died less than a minute after leaving the plane and never set foot on the French soil he came so eagerly to liberate. Uncannily, just like the last jump back in the States, the colonel had landed right in the middle of an enemy bivouac area… it was murder, no other word for it.

After talking to some of the medics, Ed was even more saddened to hear that virtually everyone from Wolverton's aircraft was now listed as missing, including Gorenc, Ross, and Calandrella.

The bad news kept coming, as Ed learned Paul Simrell had been killed. Paul's body was found in close proximity to that of Bill Atlee and Jim Shirley although they had jumped from different planes. Major Grant's remains were discovered later in a marshy area at the far end of St-Côme overlooking the railway.

I was completely overwhelmed by the loss of Colonel Wolverton and Paul Simrell. We were all so damn close-knit and at the time I thought I'd never get over the feeling of anger and frustration. There still had been no news of Shorty Madona, George Retan or Jimmy Japhet and I prayed that wherever they were, they were OK. Not surprisingly, I didn't feel the same toward Lieutenant Holstun who had been killed by his "friends" the Krauts. Bizarrely a rumor quickly began to circulate that it was me who'd shot him! This was completely untrue, although I'm not ashamed to say that I played along for a while until the bubble burst.

In fact, shortly after the drop, Holstun was cut down by enemy machine-gun fire north of the DZ, while leading a patrol that included a couple of men from I Company who survived to set the record straight.

As Ed and Ben, who was now the acting chief clerk, were doing their best to try and get some sleep at Folleville on June 10, Second Lieutenant John Williams from H Company came into the kitchen with one of his soldiers. Williams asked if he could leave "Chick" Dworsky in the house to clean a 9mm German Luger pistol. Not long afterwards, Williams, who had been a late replacement for "Skunk" Walker's platoon, arrived to collect his prize.

When Williams came in, I was dozing on the floor underneath the window. To begin with I wasn't really paying that much attention, until

Lieutenant Williams pulled a fully charged clip from his pocket and started fumbling around trying to load it into the magazine housing. He quickly became abusive when Ben asked him what the hell he thought he was doing. As I stood up and told him to put the gun down, he ordered me to mind my own business, and then it went off. Ben screamed and fell onto the stone floor in front of the stove, clutching his stomach. In a split second, everything rolled into a blur. The bullet had gone right through Ben's abdomen and out the other side. Williams did nothing, just stood in a daze. Kendall arrived and immediately gave me a hand to bandage the wounds and arrest the bleeding. It was then I looked up and shouted at Williams, "You stupid son of a bitch, get the hell out of here and find a doctor ... NOW!" While we were waiting, I held Ben's head and stroked his hair trying to calm him down. What seemed like an hour was probably only ten minutes until Williams came back with Doc Ryan. By now, despite our covering him with a blanket, Ben was pale, clammy and in deep shock. Placing Ben on a stretcher, we carried him semi-conscious out into the courtyard to a waiting jeep, praying that he was gonna be OK. Ben's life now hung in the balance and as they left, I wondered just what Shettle would say to Hiner's wife, Ruth Anna, if he died in this terrible way?

Restructuring

After being on the run from the Germans and isolated since D-Day, Captain Robert Harwick was given charge of 3/506 on June 9, and immediately began the job of replacing many of the missing company commanders. In the shake-up that followed, Shettle took over command of HQ Company until a permanent replacement could be found.

Far from beaten, on Sunday June 11, the German Fallschirmjäger-Regiment 6 withdrew from Carentan and took up positions southwest of the town. The Germans had been joined by the newly arrived 17.SS-Panzergrenadier-Division "Götz von Berlichingen" and were planning to break through American lines and recapture St-Côme, thus driving a wedge between Carentan and Ste-Mère-Église, forcing the 101st Airborne back to the beaches.

The following day Colonel Sink instructed the regiment to set up defensive positions west of Carentan, and moved 1st and 2nd Battalions into the area. By early afternoon, the Germans launched an unsuccessful counterattack, and as a result, Sink decided to go on the offensive. He brought 3rd Battalion out of reserve in readiness for a regimental attack that he had planned for 0500hrs on June 13.

By the evening of June 12, 3rd Battalion had been relieved by the 502nd PIR and its 200 remaining men gathered by the church in St-Côme-du-Mont's main square waiting for their transport to arrive. The place was cluttered with abandoned German horse-drawn carts, clothing and equipment, and looked like a rubbish tip. Ammunition was in short supply and some of the guys did their best to obtain anything they could from the drivers. As we were waiting to board the trucks, I felt a tap on my shoulder. "Happy Birthday buddy, how's it goin'?" It was Joe Madona. Overjoyed to see him safe and well, I thanked Shorty for the sentiment before telling him that my 22nd wasn't until the following day.

Joe explained to Ed that he'd landed near DZ A in the 82nd Airborne Division's area of operations at Ste-Mère-Église. Although Ed was relieved to hear that George Retan was also OK he was shocked to hear that I Company had been decimated by two plane crashes. Gerry Howard and the entire communications team were all killed during the run into the DZ and Jim Japhet was also missing, and now presumed dead. Jim's plane had been hit by antiaircraft fire and had crashed into the Channel off Pointe du Hoc, leaving only three survivors.

Lost for words, Ed listened intently as Shorty recounted events until they reached the safety of the bivouac area. Lieutenant Nye was nervously sheltering in a foxhole shouting orders to what was left of

I Company who – unlike Nye – were quite casually moving around in the open. As he was the only officer around, one of the boys handed over a covering note given to them by Colonel Sink explaining where they had been for the last few days. Nye flicked through the letter and burst out laughing. Sneering, he accused them of being malingerers, and still ranting, crumpled up the letter and threw it away.

"Jeez," I said to Shorty, "I knew he could be difficult at times but that really was going a little too far."

Bloody Gully – When things go wrong

At 0230hrs on June 13, the battalion was dropped off near the northern outskirts of Carentan, which was still burning following 24 hours of relentless bombardment, and continued their journey by foot. The men had been trained to freeze when the enemy fired flares into the sky, but because of the urgency of the situation the battalion was ordered to keep moving through the dense smoke that was drifting across the town. A circling German aircraft saw the column silhouetted against the flames and dropped several bombs. Luckily, although the bombing shook everyone up, nobody was hurt.

The outfit was ordered to wait in a field close to Colonel Sink's CP, where the men were informed that there would be no ammunition resupply. Meanwhile, Sink told his company commanders to report.

As I was being attached to H Company for the mission, First Sergeant Gordon Bolles and myself were asked to be present at the briefing.

This was also attended by members of the 501st, which was on the battalion's left flank, plus 65th and 397th Artillery Regiments which were attaching observers to the 506th. Intelligence sources had discovered that the 17.SS-Panzergrenadier-Division had deployed two regiments (six battalions) plus tanks from the 6.Panzer-Division in the area. The Shermans from 2nd Armored Division were still being offloaded at the beachhead and were expected to arrive before the attack got underway. However, nine M5 light tanks from D Company, 70th Tank Battalion, each armed with a 37mm cannon, were present and had been assigned to the regiment. The attack would commence at first light following an artillery barrage, which was intended to neutralize enemy positions.

Someone, perhaps Captain Harwick, decided I should be paired up with a radio operator and keep battalion and regiment appraised of the situation on our right-hand flank.

The briefing broke up around 0200hrs and a number of men, including most of 3rd Battalion's new company commanders, set off to establish contact with 1st Battalion and make final plans for the attack. With Captain Harold van Antwerp from G Company now known to be dead and John McKnight captured, Shettle had replaced them with First Lieutenants Joe Doughty and John Kiley.

It was dark and misty as the officers, accompanied by Shames and Bolles, walked down the RN803 road (now D223) toward where they thought 1st Battalion might be located. Suddenly a motorcycle dispatch rider appeared out of the mist and rode slowly past Joe Doughty, heading toward Carentan. The man was stopped and asked how far ahead 1st Battalion was. As he jumped off his machine everyone were amazed to discover that he was a German. Doughty decided to abort the mission and return to Carentan with the prisoner and they never found the whereabouts of 1st Battalion.

When all the company commanders had returned, it was decided that moving across country would be far safer than using the road. The paratroopers were told that 2nd Battalion would be on their right flank and the 501st beyond a road to the left. Orders came down the line to move out in company order and advance to contact.

The rifle companies moved forward in columns echeloned to the right, and G Company headed the advance led by Joe Doughty. The "start line" was about 1,400 yards away on some high ground, east of a sunken drovers' road that would soon become known as "Bloody Gully."

The gully was a little over 1 mile long and on average 15ft wide and 9ft deep. It was lined on each side by high hedges and stretched northeast from La Croix de Méautis in the south to the Carteret-Carentan railway line. The RN803 road dissected the gully at about its midway point between La Croix de Méautis and the railway. As dawn broke the battalion followed a hedgerow and moved into fields on their right. Within minutes the men's legs were soaked with heavy dew from the long grass. Several platoons lost contact with each other after encountering the thick hedgerows, and a number of squads were late getting to the start line. Among those was G Company's 1st Platoon, commanded by Second Lieutenant Tom Kennedy.

West of the gully, the land rises to a height of about 80ft, which gave the enemy a clear tactical advantage over the 506th. The 3rd Battalion's area was divided into three fields, all bounded by thick hedgerows. For ease of reference we have numbered them 1 through 3, with the battalion's left or southern flank being field number 3.

The enemy's plan was to advance on the left flank along the Carteret–Carentan railway line and then break through American positions and head for the northern outskirts of Carentan with artillery and assault gun batteries supporting the attack. The troops of the Fallschirmjäger-Regiment 6 and 17.SS-Panzergrenadier-Division were well trained and highly disciplined, unlike some of the enemy soldiers previously encountered by the 101st Airborne Division.

By first light, Corporal Bobbie Rommel and his machine-gun team from HQ Company were in position on the high ground 220 yards west of the gully. Their orders were to provide covering fire for the battalion and they set up their guns beside a hedge that bordered the RN803. One of the other gun teams thought they saw movement in the hedge up ahead and fired a short burst. A figure jumped down onto the road and ran off. Moments later, M5 light reconnaissance tanks from the 70th Tank Battalion arrived, in support of 2nd Battalion, 506th, and mistook the machine gunners for the enemy. As the tanks moved along the road, Rommel could see their turrets above the hedge. Ed Shames looked on in horror as the lead tank fired its heavy machine gun, hitting a couple of men behind Rommel.

Because of the shortage of ammunition, the much-anticipated barrage did not last long. However, about 12 rounds landed short, showering everyone in the gully with dirt, branches and leaves. By now G and I Companies had been deployed across several enclosed fields that coursed away to the south. Some members of I Company had been attached to H Company, whose orders were to attack alongside the road on the right flank. After their earlier mistake, which had wounded several machine gunners, three of the M5 tanks remained and moved along the road, giving H Company direct fire support. First Lieutenant Dick Meason and his company HQ group had orders to move forward independently on the left side of the same field.

First Lieutenant Ken Christianson was leading the main H Company attack. Ed Shames and his radio operator followed him out of the gully and started slowly moving along the hedge.

I looked across the road beyond the adjacent hedgerow to another field over on my right where F Company should have been and realized that they weren't there. They were supposed to be protecting 2nd Battalion's left flank so I just thought at that moment, they must've been late getting into position.

The open area to Ed's left [field 1] sloped upward and was the size of a football field. As H Company's scouts reached the crest, the enemy opened up with a ferocious mortar and artillery barrage that continued, on and off, for the next 2 hours. The men split up and dropped to the ground. A German machine gun was trained to fire through a gate opening just in front of Shames and had everyone pinned down. The gun had been set up on the northern side of the road and its murderous fire split H Company in two, preventing all forward movement. Everyone who was close to the right side of the field took cover in the hedge line.

Shrapnel was flying everywhere. Over to my left, one guy was hit by machine-gun fire and fell to the ground. I ran over and discovered it was Lonnie Gavrock. He'd been hit in the chest and was completely unresponsive. One bullet had left an enormous exit hole in his back, big enough to put my entire hand into. I thought he was dying and called for a medic before making my way back to the hedge. As I moved away the same gun began to target me. Peering through the thick bushes, I looked to see if F Company had arrived, but still nobody was there – 2nd Battalion's left flank was totally exposed!

After encountering a number of German self-propelled guns (SPGs), F Company had been forced to withdraw, jeopardizing 2nd Battalion's advance. Separated from the rest of his platoon, mortar sergeant Ralph Bennett was with Ken Christianson about 25 yards from the western boundary of the first field. Bullets began flying diagonally across the field into Dick Meason's group. They immediately returned fire but soon realized they were endangering Christianson's men and stopped. Suddenly, a German Stug Sturmgeschütz 40 armed with a powerful 75mm gun came lumbering along the road from Douville and stopped directly opposite Bennett. The chassis took up the whole width of the road.

Heading toward the German SPG, but completely unaware of its presence due to a bend in the road, were the three M5 tanks supporting H Company's advance. As the tanks came up alongside him, Ed Shames rose to his feet and trotted alongside, using them as a shield from the German machine-gun fire.

I was still trying to locate F Company and had been shadowing the tanks for about 20 seconds. Suddenly a couple of 75mm rounds slammed through the lead vehicle and into the tank directly behind it. The shots had been fired at point-blank range and the lightly armored M5s didn't stand a chance. The explosions were terrific and a blast of searing heat threw me to the ground, scorching my face and eyebrows. As the third tank started backing out I picked myself up and ran. My clothes were smoldering and ears ringing but other than that I was OK. Making my way back to the radio operator, I realized that, yet again, I'd been very lucky.

As the Stug reversed away from the action, the enemy sent a couple of their men forward with a machine gun to where the tanks were blazing, in an attempt to bracket and outflank H Company. Bill Galbraith was watching through a small hole in the hedge and managed to shoot one of the soldiers. Machine-gun fire started pouring across the road and Galbraith tried to throw a grenade over the hedge toward it. Unfortunately his arm became caught up in an equipment strap and the grenade fell and rolled a few yards in front of him before exploding. Shortly afterwards, Shames dashed past Galbraith, who was uninjured by the grenade blast, and got straight on the radio to battalion.

I told them that there was nobody on our right flank. The response was, "Are you sure? That doesn't sound good – you'd better speak to regiment." After a few moments I got through and Hank Hannah answered. "We've got a problem," I said. "There's no one on our right flank – repeat NO ONE." Hannah was astonished and replied, "Are you kidding me? Who in the hell did you say you were?" Once I'd explained, Hannah told me to sit tight and wait for Colonel Sink to call. Within 10 seconds my handset rang, "Sink here … Shames, do you know what the hell you are talking about?" "Yes, sir," I replied. He then said, "Get your ass back to my forward CP and give me a situation report – NOW."

The Kraut machine gun started up again and increased its rate of fire. The noise was overwhelming. I slapped the radio guy on the shoulder and shouted in his ear, "Don't move. Stay right here." Forcing my way through the hedge, I dropped down onto the road. Smoke was pouring from the knocked-out tanks and I thought I was safe from the enemy machine gun. I was wrong and stepped directly into its line of fire. The asphalt seemed to come alive as bullets peppered the surface. I started to run, zigzagging my way out of the killing zone and sprinted down the road to Colonel Sink's forward CP, which was really no more than a ditch. The first thing the colonel said was, "Shames, do you know what the hell you are talking about, boy?" I couldn't believe it. "Yes, sir," I replied. Sink responded, "Show me on the map." Colonel Chase looked on as I began pointing out the problem areas, doing my best to convince both men we didn't have much time. "We are wide open and taking extremely heavy fire from the northern side of the road, sir," I said. "Are you sure?" Sink responded. "Yes, 100 percent, sir." Finally Sink said "OK, Charlie, get up there with Shames and give me a full situation report."

The pair set off and took the fastest route along the RN803.

I told Chase how dangerous this was but he ignored me. I was muttering "Born June 13, died June 13…" On the way Chase kept saying, "Where's Harwick? Where's Harwick?" Of course I didn't know but it made me think that there was more to this mission than just a situation report on the right flank. Much to our relief, my radio operator was still waiting in the same place I'd left him. He was very scared and became quite emotional when he saw us. Colonel Chase got straight on the net to Sink and said, "Shames is quite correct, there's nobody on the right flank. Get any unit you can up here quickly to fill the gap." He then went back down the hedge line and disappeared through the trees into the gully.

Without doubt Ed's quick thinking helped to change the outcome of the battle. About an hour or so later, around 1030hrs, Sink had placed 2nd

Battalion, 502nd, in the gap on 3rd Battalion's right flank and ordered in antitank guns and air support.

Earlier that morning, in Carentan, Brigadier General Maurice Rose, the 2nd Armored Division's commander, and General Taylor had worked out a plan of attack using Rose's tanks and airborne infantry reserves. Starting at 1400hrs this new force, supported by heavy artillery, was sent in to relieve the beleaguered 506th.

Meanwhile the German machine gun on the northern side of the road in field 1 briefly stopped firing. Bill Galbraith broke cover and dashed forward toward the hedge where Jim Brown had set up their machine gun. As he slammed into the ground, he noticed two wounded men to his right – Ken Christianson and Leo Lecuyer from H Company. Both men had both been shot by another enemy machine gun some 250 yards away across the field in front of them. As Jim Brown engaged the enemy gun, Galbraith moved along the hedge to see if he could help the wounded. Christianson had been hit in the shoulder and Lecuyer was in very bad shape. As Bill was applying a field dressing, a bullet hit Lecuyer, tearing him out of Bill's arms and killing him. Galbraith then turned his attention to Christianson and doctored him up. As Ken crawled away, Bill prayed that he would make it back to the battalion aid station.

Then a small group of soldiers from 1st Battalion approached Galbraith and Brown from the right flank. As they were expecting the enemy from this direction, Brown opened fire, thinking they were Germans in American uniforms. Thankfully the burst went wide. Galbraith and Brown learned that these troopers had been stuck in a kind of no-man's-land and had pulled back during a lull in the firing.

The struggle to advance had been just as difficult for G Company in field 2. Due to lack of ammunition the company did not deploy its 60mm mortars. Before moving forward the men were ordered to fix bayonets and had just started up the slope when the intense shelling started. Most of 2nd Platoon was in the center of the field but quickly dispersed to the hedges on either side. Shrapnel was flying everywhere and caused many casualties.

Machine-gun fire from the enemy gun that was causing problems in field 1 was passing through the hedgerow on G Company's right. Its bullets were slowed by the hedge's dense earth bank, saving several people from more serious injury. An officer from another unit, perhaps one of the artillery observers, gave the order to pull back and shouted "Every man for himself." Everyone fell back into the gully under terrific artillery fire, with mortar shells air-bursting high in the trees above.

Some of the enemy fire was coming from an apple orchard on the left flank just beyond field 3. This was 440 yards southwest of where Captain Shettle had set up his position in the gully. Shettle sent an artillery observer up onto high ground to the east to direct fire onto the enemy positions. When the barrage failed to materialize, I Company had to deploy its two 60mm mortar teams. The gunners, Private Harold Stedman and Private First Class Jim Shuler, did not have enough ammunition to support a counterattack although they were successfully able to engage the enemy machine guns in both the G Company's and H Company's areas. The short barrage seemed to do the trick but Shettle and the I Company commander John Kiley both felt that the German positions in the fields on the left flank beyond the front line still needed to be dealt with. Shettle ordered a number of men from G Company, led by Second Lieutenant Linton Barling, to attempt a counterattack by joining forces with I Company. By 0745hrs they were ready to go.

Privates First Class Lloyd Rosdahl and Wilbur Fishel were ordered forward with their machine gun to provide covering fire. No more was heard from them and Captain Shettle sent Private Lenny Goodgal – a survivor of the aircraft that crashed in the Channel killing Jim Japhet and 14 others from I Company – to find out where they were.

Using the hedgerow for cover, Goodgal advanced up the field and bridged the rise to the next overgrown hedge. The natural barrier covered the area to his front and began to follow a ditch that ran alongside it to his left. Someone caught his eye up ahead. As he was now getting small-arms fire from his front he assumed the man was German and ordered him to surrender. After getting no response, Goodgal fired a burst from his Thompson submachine gun before realizing it was First Sergeant Gordon Bolles. "Pop" Bolles was with a couple of H Company men and had been scouting southwest from the next field (1) along the hedgeline toward the orchard.

Clutching his side, Bolles screamed at Goodgal to watch out for a nearby sniper who had them pinned down. Horrified at what he had just done, Goodgal ignored Bolles' warning. In a state of panic, Goodgal pulled up Bolles' shirt to check the wound and could not believe his eyes – by some miracle the bullets had only grazed the side of Bolles' body. Snapping back to reality, Goodgal asked for Bolles to pinpoint the sniper. After firing a couple of rounds into some nearby trees, Goodgal took off looking for Rosdahl and Fishel.

Eventually Goodgal found them and explained that Shettle wanted to know why they were not giving supporting fire. It turned out that they could not hear anyone firing and had decided to wait and see what would happen. With that, Goodgal turned around and started back toward the gully. During his return a piece of shrapnel hit him just above the left knee, making walking difficult. After reporting to Shettle and Kiley, Goodgal was ordered to join I Company medic, Bill Kidder, who was taking wounded back to the aid station.

As a result of I Company's short but highly accurate mortar bombardment, the Germans in the orchard area stopped firing and readied themselves for an American counterattack. This lulled Shettle into thinking that the enemy had successfully been knocked out.

The counterattack, comprising some 50 men, started around 0900hrs. As they entered the orchard, I Company came under heavy fire from a concealed enemy machine gun. The men had not gone more than 20 yards when German mortar shells began to burst in the tops of the densely planted trees, showering everyone with branches and leaves. Kiley was desperately trying to find a way to neutralize the enemy fire. Lieutenants "Sandy" Santarsiero and Barling and another man from G Company tried to circle around the enemy gun. The overwhelming mortar barrage forced Kiley to pull back and Santarsiero was hit in the thigh.

At 1030hrs several Sherman tanks from 2nd Armored arrived via the dirt road east of the gully. They attacked a German command post at Les Six Chemins (500 yards southwest of Baudoin farm), losing one tank and vital time. I Company was pleased to see them and watched as the Shermans' 75mm rounds slammed into the western side of the orchard, temporarily breaking the enemy's grip. This was the opportunity Kiley needed to withdraw his men, and the tanks eventually forced the Germans to pull out.

I Company made its way back along the hedgerow 200 yards west of the gully. There they ran into the same group of soldiers from 1st Battalion that Jim Brown had shot at earlier in the day. Santarsiero recognized First Lieutenant Eugene Knott from C Company and briefly spoke to him. At that precise moment a burst of machine-gun fire cut through the hedge, killing Knott instantly. By 1130hrs most of I Company had scrambled back to the gully. The wounded were lying about everywhere. Much later, Dr Barney Ryan and Staff Sergeant William Roots, the medical supply sergeant, arrived with Bill Kidder to assess the situation and decide which cases should be evacuated directly by jeep.

As Second Lieutenant Tom Kennedy's platoon finally reached the gully, the men found G Company in disarray. Immediately Joe Doughty told him to resupply Dick Meason with bazooka rockets in field 1. Kennedy ordered his platoon runner, Private Alfred Summerfield, to assist. They could see Meason positioned in the hedge up ahead, and set off cradling the rockets. Crawling toward them looking very pale was Ken Christianson, who was trying to support his wounded arm. Using a path that ran beside the hedgerow Kennedy and Summerfield continued forward, but came under intense German artillery fire. During the barrage Summerfield was hit badly, forcing Kennedy to abandon the mission.

By 0730hrs, 3rd Battalion's right flank was in danger of crumbling and attack had been turned into defense. Later, Colonel Chase would sack Bob Harwick for his part in these events, clearly believing that he had been negligent in the way he commanded the situation. However, despite what Chase may have thought, his sacking of Harwick was considered by many to have been a very harsh decision.

Owing to the acute convex slope, general radio contact amongst the members of 3rd Battalion was at best intermittent, especially for those like Ralph Bennett, who was now trapped in the hedgerow at the top of field 1. Precious time and vital information was being lost, as Bennett soon discovered. Bennett ordered Tech Corporal Harvey Holcomb to get on the "net" and give a situation report to "Kidnap Blue" (Harwick's call sign), but the handy talky was unserviceable. Bennett had no choice but to send a runner back through all the machine-gun fire and let the boss know how desperate the situation was. At around 0830hrs several 60mm rounds were fired by I Company from the east of the gully, so Bennett assumed that his message was received and understood. The shells landed in the woods across the road to his right and the enemy machine gun temporarily stopped firing. This gave Bennett the opportunity to get back to Private First Class Sam "Dud" Hefner, who had his 60mm mortar, and knock out the troublesome machine gun. The German gun crew was only 20 yards away so the mortar tube had to be elevated into a near-vertical position. Despite having only two 60mm shells at his disposal due to the shortage of ammunition, Ralph managed to silence the German gun. Sergeant Bennett's actions allowed most of H Company to escape and regroup.

Although the Germans had withdrawn, there was still an enormous amount of activity across the road to H Company's right as the men headed back to the gully. German artillery was exploding behind them as Bennett began regrouping his men. In the gully there was nobody in authority to tell him what to do, as the rest of the battalion was still fighting a rearguard action in fields to the south. All Bennett and his men could do was wait by the aid post for new orders.

Two hours later, Staff Sergeant Jerry Beam (I Company) found Bennett and told him the battalion was being withdrawn. At the same

time, Nye sent a runner across to Bill Galbraith and Jim Brown who were still on the far (western) side of field 1 with the remnants of H Company. Galbraith was told to shift over and rejoin I Company, who were gathering behind a hedgerow in the next field (2). Brown and Galbraith set up a defensive position halfway along the hedge to give covering fire. By the time they got into position, 20 or so men from I Company were making their way toward them. Nye sent Jim Brown to help Private Bob Penner, who lay wounded over in field 3. Using the sloping terrain for cover Brown just walked out to Penner like he was on a Sunday stroll. There was still a lot of ordnance whistling about at hedgerow height and the enemy was putting down a walking blanket barrage. A short while later Galbraith was told that I Company was pulling out and he headed back to the gully.

At 1130hrs, as Galbraith approached the gully, he noticed someone drop down behind him. Leaving the machine gun he went back to see what he could do for the wounded man. Private First Class Sam Porter from H Company had been hit in the throat, but by some miracle he was still breathing. Galbraith was acutely aware of the danger he was in but knew he was safe from enemy fire so long as he did not stand up. Dragging the casualty down the slope, he eventually found a safe spot. He attempted to pick Porter up but just could not lift him and ran down into the gully looking for assistance. Clambering over the wire fence he found Sergeant Ernie Mann and Private First Class Johnny Edwards, who had both fallen back with the rest of the company. The three ran back into the field to fetch Porter, who survived and was evacuated to the United States. Although there were a few more casualties, most of the firing had now died down and except for occasional small-arms fire, it was comparatively quiet. The 506th PIR had been ordered to hold its current position, but the men were still pulling back. Several Sherman tanks arrived via the D443 road east of the gully and this helped relieve the pressure.

"It turned out that the Germans had commenced their attack simultaneously with ours," recalls Shames. "It was a bizarre chain of events which could have gone either way." By mid-afternoon, after 11 hours of battle across the gully, 1/502 arrived with more tank support and 3rd Battalion was ordered to withdraw.

The battalion now formed part of a divisional reserve, and began digging in on the western edge of Carentan. Colonel Sink set up his regimental CP in the town's courthouse, near the port area, which had previously been a German HQ. That evening he requested Ed to meet him there.

I reported to Sink, who ordered "Parade Rest" [legs apart hands behind back]. "Shames, your conduct today was truly superb. I've spoken to division and would like to offer you a battlefield commission, the first BC for the 506. Congratulations: you are now a second lieutenant. I'm very proud of you. However, you'll have to wait until we get back to England before the paperwork can be officially sanctioned. Until then I'll put the word around about your promotion and why we've given it to you. I will expect people to treat you as an officer despite the fact that you're still wearing your old rank."

Sink also informed Ed that F Company had not been where they should have been because they had been forced to withdraw after encountering more of the German SPGs.

Later that evening at our farmhouse CP, G Company executive officer, First Lieutenant Jim Morton, dropped by to congratulate me. During the conversation, I learned that he was now taking over HQ Company from Shettle who was being transferred to 2nd Battalion as Strayer's executive officer. As Morton's ankle had been fractured on the jump, he needed some reliable help and asked if I would consider becoming his first sergeant. This was very flattering, because to me, up until his death, JP Shirley had been one of the finest senior NCOs I'd ever had the pleasure of working with. Morton had already spoken to Sink, who felt that a temporarily posting like this would help ease the pressure at least until we returned to the UK. Detecting a little reticence, Jim suggested that being "retired" from the service as a first sergeant could be very advantageous to my discharge papers and therefore any postwar pension rights. I had to laugh, as the idea of a pension seemed a little optimistic given what we'd just been through! That being said, June 13 was a very special day, not only for me personally, but also the regiment. Had the 506th lost the battle at "Bloody Gully," I'm almost certain that the enemy would have pushed us back into the sea and ultimately prevented our tanks from gaining a foothold on the peninsula.

It was the battle where Ed Shames' fighting reputation was first formed, and from a 101st Airborne Division perspective the battle of Bloody Gully was one of the most important and decisive engagements of its entire Normandy campaign.

Before Shettle was transferred to 2/506 he informed Ed that he had recommended him and Chaplain McGee for the Distinguished Service Cross for their actions at the bridge during the air attack on June 7.

Of course I was savvy enough to realize that it would be Alex Bobuck who under the circumstances would most likely be writing up the paperwork … which didn't bode well for me.

The following morning (June 14) the 502nd and 3rd Battalion, 327th, pushed southwestward from Carentan, mopping up German resistance as they went. By 1600hrs the 502nd had successfully linked up with the 82nd Airborne at Baupte, removing any possible enemy threat to the 506th's western flank. Meanwhile back in Carentan, soldiers from the regiment were lining up for haircuts in the town's reopened barbershops!

5

"FIVE SECONDS TO FORGET"
England, August 1944

Before the regiment returned to the UK in early July, standing on top of an abandoned enemy pillbox at Tollevast, Major General Taylor addressed the 506th PIR, "You hit the ground running toward the enemy, you have proved the German soldier is no superman – you have beaten him on his own ground and you can beat him on any ground." Despite these fine words the 101st had lost many good men during the liberation of Normandy. The division in total had suffered around 4,000 casualties, with 3rd Battalion, 506th, experiencing the highest percentage. Out of the 575 officers and men who jumped alongside Ed Shames, 93 were killed, approximately 75 taken prisoner and even more wounded.

When the fleet of buses carrying 3/506 drove into Ramsbury, the entire village turned out to greet the battalion. In the days that followed, the unit was completely restructured, including the S3, where John Kiley took over the section.

"Returning with a new serial number, 0-887950, quite literally signified a kind of rebirth for me," Ed reflected. "For those lucky enough to survive, the last six weeks in France had made us all grow up, myself included."

That being said we still wanted to have fun and to celebrate our return, I was tasked to organize a regimental party for the officers on Friday July 14 at Marlborough Town Hall. Upstairs, a bar was installed in the main function room and Colonel Sink kindly agreed that I could leave it in place for 3rd Battalion, so the enlisted men could hold their post-Normandy do. Hell, for good measure he even threw in a barrel of liberated cognac. The following night, fueled by a potent mixture of beer and brandy, the boys got a little out of hand, smashing windows, fighting and generally letting off steam. Someone called the MPs [Military Police], who calmly handled the situation without any further collateral damage. Some kind of Sunday service was planned for the next morning and when the local vicar arrived, the hall was still in a filthy state with half-empty glasses and bottles lying everywhere. I was in charge of the cleanup operation and was trying to figure out where to start when the priest asked if he could possibly use the stage. As I pulled back the curtains his face changed from a smile to one of total shock! Hidden behind the drapes were about a dozen comatose semi-naked men and women! I just shrugged and started to laugh. But the clergyman however, was most definitely not amused and stormed off in a huff.

After receiving a sizable amount of back pay, the men were given seven days' leave. However, as he was waiting to receive his commission from US First Army commander Lieutenant General Omar Bradley, Ed was told to remain behind, along with Master Sergeant Lloyd Wills (regimental operations sergeant), and George Retan, who had also been recognized for his leadership skills in "white tree field" on June 7.

The three of us reported obediently every day to Sink's adjutant, Captain Max Petroff, at Littlecote House. Every time we turned up he told us the same thing, that General Bradley was still busy in France and we should come back tomorrow. On the morning of the 21st, Petroff gave us a small interim wage payment and told us to take the weekend off. As we had nothing better to do, George and I decided to visit the NAAFI up at Ramsbury Airfield.

The two men were in deep conversation as they crossed the bridge over the River Kennet.

We passed by a young girl leaning over the rail sobbing her heart out. A short distance further along the road my conscience got the better of me and I turned to Retan, saying, "Dammit, she looks pretty upset. Let's go back and see what's wrong." Through floods of tears she told us that she'd just gone to see her fiancé at the airfield only to be told that he'd been killed on operations. The young woman was devastated and wanted to go home to her parents. "Where do they live?" we inquired. "That's the problem," she replied, "my mum and dad live in Llanelli, South Wales, and I don't have the money to get there." Retan and I looked at each other, shrugged, wished her luck and carried on. "Awhh, we gotta do something, George. Come on, let's take her home." After more cajoling he finally caved in and we took the young woman to Hungerford railway station, purchased three tickets and escorted her to Wales! After tea and cake, the girl's father invited us to stay the night but we politely refused. Instead, on his advice, we headed to the Gower coast, booked into a bed-and-breakfast and spent the rest of the weekend exploring country pubs and walking in the Mumbles hills. The battlefield commissions had kind of brought us both back together again and we really made the most of our unexpected "mini vacation" to Wales.

Eventually a day was selected for Ed and George to receive their long-awaited commissions. In the end Bradley was simply too busy to make the trip to Littlecote, so Sink stepped in and the men were presented with their rank bars beneath the crossed regimental standards in the great hall. The elegant hall with its enormous open fireplace was also the 506th RHQ Officers' Mess. A portrait of Civil War parliamentarian commander Alexander Popham was hanging above the hall's entrance and the dark oak paneled walls were adorned with a collection of original Civil War armor, buff coats and weaponry, all dating back to the 1650s.

Despite the opulent surroundings, it wasn't quite the grandiose occasion the regiment had hoped for. But we were pleasantly surprised when each of us were given $500 cash with which to purchase new uniforms.

After the ceremony we were driven from Littlecote to the main PX, serving SHAEF HQ in London. The uniforms on sale here weren't really that good quality and I quickly noticed some of the SHAEF officers walking around in much better outfits. A British member of staff told me that these were made to measure in the West End. George and I decided to split up and shop around before meeting back at the PX two hours later. Many tailor's shops were using the same government-issue cloth but I managed to find one establishment in Savile Row offering a full dress uniform made from a very high-quality privately manufactured material all for only $350. Plus they could deliver by 4pm the following day.

By the time I got back, George had already purchased his uniform at the PX so we got a cab to Piccadilly Circus and booked into the Regent Palace but this time it was my treat. Late the following afternoon, I went to pick up my outfit. Standing in front of a mirror I admired the superb cut from every angle. The tailor inquired if everything was to my satisfaction. "Yep, just perfect. The forage cap, the eagle patch, the insignia… I can't fault it. Many, many thanks." I left the shop with my old uniform folded neatly into a shopping bag and had a picture taken at a nearby photographic studio before heading back to collect Retan at the Regent. On the train home, we excitedly discussed our new postings. George was going to A/506 as an assistant platoon leader and I was off to 2/506 to become their assistant intelligence officer (S2).

When I got back from London, I was told to go over to the supply department and hand back some gear including my old steel helmet, which obviously still had the white painted 3rd Battalion identification symbols and horizontal NCO stripe. Before the supply guy issued me with a pistol, he asked for my M1, as he wanted to exchange it for the lighter M1A1 Folding Stock Carbine. I flatly refused to hand over my baby, which had been with me since Toccoa. Eventually I got my own way and my trusty old M1 was reissued back to me. At that point John King came in and we got chatting. John made a comment about my new government-issue Colt and how effective he thought they really were. "Let me ask you a question, Shames. Do you think that your .45 would penetrate a steel helmet at close range?" "Sure, of course," I replied, "you'd have to be nuts to think it wouldn't." "OK, I'll bet you fifty bucks it won't go through!" I figured what the heck and shook his hand, "You're on." John said something to the officer in charge, picked up my old helmet and asked me to follow him out back to a dilapidated storage shed. Pulling a couple of spare .45 ACP rounds from his pocket he loaded my pistol and handed it back to me. Placing the helmet on the ground a few yards away, he said, "Go on then, in your own time." Carefully taking aim, I put a little pressure on the trigger and fired. That SOB was right, the round just bounced off leaving a big dent – so that took care of my $50!

My first day with 2nd Battalion also didn't go quite the way I'd imagined. While they were supposedly sorting out my accommodation, Colonel Strayer told me to go get some lunch at the Officers' Mess. The place was packed and the only available seat happened to be next to Jim Nye, who'd just been transferred to D Company. Nye made it quite clear that he didn't want me sitting next to him. "You don't recognize me, do you?" I remarked. He just carried on as though I didn't exist … so I gave him a piece of my mind. The place fell into total silence and everybody stared as he stormed out of the canteen. I looked around, grinned sheepishly and continued eating my lunch! Then this big guy came over, and as I was getting ready for another argument, he inquired about what had just happened. It turned out that First Lieutenant Joe MacMillan, who was Nye's boss, had also taken a dislike to him, so we kind of hit it off right away.

Joe took me at face value when many of the others just about closed the door. I happened to mention that I was going to be working for Captain Lewis Nixon. "Do you know who that guy is? He's from one of the richest families in the States. I'm not kidding, Ed, ask anyone." Ironically it transpired that Joe's family was also fairly wealthy and owned several large cotton mills in South Carolina. After lunch, as we were leaving, MacMillan turned and said, "We're gonna wet ya down tonight and celebrate good and proper. I'll pick you up around 7:30."

Walking across the street, I was directed to a decent-sized house overlooking the green across from the church. Subsequently, I learned that this was Nixon's privately rented pad. It was an eye opener for me, I mean, I'd never heard of anybody doing anything like this before. It was as if he was on some sort of bizarre foreign vacation. The place was in a total mess with empty bottles everywhere. So much for my room, which didn't even have a damn bed. But at least it gave me somewhere secure to keep Joe Gorenc's money until I could figure out what to do with it.

That evening, as promised, MacMillan picked me up in his jeep with Bob Moon – both intent on "prop blasting" me. After a pub crawl through Swindon we ended up going to a party at the hospital in Wroughton. I soon learned that Joe could be quite a handful after a few drinks. Toward the end of the night they ran a cowboy film on an old projector. For some reason Joe managed to get into a fight with one of the male nurses. What I remember most about the brawl was the projector being knocked over and the film shakily playing at right angles across the walls! It was one heck of a night and I think after all the trouble we got into, Bob Moon wished he'd stayed at home.

The following morning Joe and I were hauled up in front of Strayer who wasn't impressed at all, but Sink, after speaking to Moon, dismissed it as just high spirits. I knew Strayer wasn't going to let it go that easily, especially after what I'd said previously to Nye.

However, Ed put the incident behind him and prepared to go on backdated seven-day leave with George Retan.

Once again we stayed in London at the Regent Palace and met up with a couple of lovely young nurses, mine was from Michigan. Returning to the hotel on the last day, as our train pulled into Piccadilly Circus underground station and the doors opened, I couldn't believe my eyes. There, waiting on the platform to board, was Lonnie Gavrock! Thinking I'd seen a ghost, I immediately grabbed hold of his jacket and dragged him off to the toilets, mumbling, "You're dead, you're dead, I was right there… Christ Almighty, you're dead!" George and the girls walked in behind me wondering what was going on? Still in a state of total shock I began to explain what had happened at Bloody Gully.

Lifting up Lonnie's uniform, we could see his wounds had healed beautifully. He told us that one of the bullets had lodged dangerously close to his heart and was therefore inoperable. "What are they gonna do with you?" we asked. "Well," he said, "for the time being I'm off the active duty roster. Beyond that I dunno. Gotta go boys … by the way, congratulations on your promotions. See ya later." George and I just shook our heads and looked at each other in utter amazement.[*]

Back in Aldbourne, things were not working out with Captain Nixon, who expected Ed to keep the house in order and also look after the daily running of the S2.

---

[*] Lonnie did return to active duty and jumped in Holland. Two months later, while at Mourmelon, he began to suffer from a recurring high fever and spent the rest of the war in hospital. Fifteen years later the bullet (which was still lodged near his heart) was removed, and Lonnie died on Labor Day, September 7, 1987 after being diagnosed with lung cancer and suffering a series of strokes.

As an enlisted man I expected my officers to lead. After being commissioned, I did my level best to live up to my own expectations, which in all honesty back then were probably far too high.

The final straw came in mid-August when Nixon left Ed to plan and organize S2 section briefings for a proposed operational parachute insertion at Rambouillet, 20 miles southwest of Paris. Luckily the operation (codenamed *Transfigure*) was canceled, as it was later discovered that a Panzer division had been waiting in the forest adjoining the drop zone.

Joe Madona, now a sergeant, was still billeted at the stables next to The Bell in Ramsbury. Many of the old familiar faces were gone, including Jack Brown who had been captured in Normandy and Bill Galbraith who had been promoted and transferred to battalion S3 under John Kiley. When things started going from bad to worse, Ed turned to Shorty for stability and advice. That was until Colonel Strayer found out.

It shouldn't have been a problem but that bastard chose to make it one and fined me $50 for fraternizing with an enlisted man, and I never forgot or forgave him for that.

As the weeks passed, several men who had been captured in Normandy arrived back in the UK, including Raymond Calandrella and Joe Gorenc. Once Joe found out that Ed was still alive, he made his way to Aldbourne. A lot had changed since they last saw each other on D-Day, but Ed had kept Joe's winnings safe in the hope that he would come back. Ironically, it had been the thought of his money that had kept Joe going as he escaped through France. Owing to his transfer, Ed had not heard much about Don Ross or Ben Hiner. Gorenc explained that Ben had just returned to work as 3rd Battalion supply sergeant and Don was now officially listed as a POW. He also went on to say that despite having two new "lodgers," the Blains were still deeply upset about Paul Simrell. Joe also announced that he had now been made up to operations sergeant.

I was pleased about his promotion and knew he would get on well with Galbraith as his assistant. We discussed the new 3rd Battalion CO, Major Oliver Horton, who'd previously been Colonel Sink's intelligence officer. Although Horton didn't possess the same tactical ability as Bob Wolverton, I must say that there was a little nostalgic envy on my part but I tried to remain positive.

In early September, the 506th was alerted for a number of operations in Belgium. However, George Patton's Third Army captured all the objectives before the airborne missions could ever get off the ground. It was during this time that Ed got to know Lieutenant Ron Speirs, who was an assistant in the 2nd Battalion S3 section.

We really hit it off, and quickly became friends. Ron was a straight shooter, and like Joe MacMillan, accepted me without prejudice or hesitation.

After the last alert, for Liège, Shames was dismayed that Lewis Nixon had seemingly abandoned him to organize the S2 missions and went to see Lieutenant Colonel Strayer.

Strayer threw me out of his office which came as no surprise. A couple of days later, I plucked up courage and went to see Sink at Littlecote. Firstly, I had to convince his adjutant, Major Salve Matheson, who told me that I should've known better and used the official channels to get a proper hearing. However, he relented and showed me into Sink's office. "I have a flock of work to do, Shames. What on God's earth do you want?" Taking a deep breath I said, "Sir, I'm so sorry but I just cannot work with Captain Nixon. He is in my opinion totally unprofessional and I'm getting very little support from Colonel Strayer. I'd rather turn in my commission and go back to 3rd Battalion than continue to work under these circumstances." Sink was horrified and almost blew his stack before sending me outside to wait in Matheson's office.

When the boss called me back, I marched in, stood smartly to attention and snapped a salute. "OK, Shames … Parade Rest." At that moment, I smelt the alcohol on his breath and realized he must've had a quick slug to calm his nerves while he thought things over. Then suddenly his voice raised, "God dammit Shames, I didn't give you Parade Rest, stand to attention when I'm talking to you!" Somewhat confused, I obeyed.

Sink recognized the fact that there were several differences of opinion between Shames and Nixon but nevertheless was still anxious to keep Ed within 2nd Battalion.

Sink told me he was thinking about creating a regimental patrols platoon and would I consider taking on the role as commander? Sink then ventured, "You think you're the meanest SOB in this outfit don't you?" Slightly taken aback, semi-sarcastically I responded, "Er no, sir, I'm sorry but I really don't like the term *mean*, but I do think that I'm the toughest SOB in your outfit," which thankfully made him smile. Of course I was delighted with the offer and while waiting, Sink assigned me to assist Major Clarence Hester, who had just taken over as regimental S3 from Hank Hannah … which to be honest suited me perfectly as an interim measure. Hester's office was located in the billiard room behind the old private puritan chapel at Littlecote.

I heard that after Normandy, Sink actually refused a promotion to division because he loved the 506th that much. On the whole our regiment was a very cohesive force, partly due to the support and understanding Charlie Chase brought to the table. Chase was the perfect foil for Sink's maverick way of command and did a huge amount of "missionary" work behind the scenes. It's funny but after I was commissioned, Chase never expected me to come to attention when I spoke to him … such was his paternal attitude towards me.

Dragon's teeth

Late on the morning of September 14, Colonel Sink alerted his battalion commanders during an emergency staff meeting at Littlecote.

We received packets from SHAEF through the British containing a huge amount of material with a rush designation and we knew this was for real. The initial preparations for the invasion of the Netherlands (that we really knew as Holland) seemed to me to be more or less a joint regimental effort as Hester and I worked through the battle plans in the billiard room.

The mission was codenamed *Market Garden*. *Market* was the airborne phase, led by Lieutenant General Lewis Brereton, commanding the newly formed First Allied Airborne Army. The *Garden* portion of the mission would be the ground assault led by British Lieutenant General Sir Brian Horrocks and XXX Corps. Due to poor weather and the constantly changing tactical situation, existing British plans had been modified to include the US 101st and 82nd Airborne Divisions. Lieutenant General Frederick "Boy" Browning was appointed deputy commander of the First Allied Airborne Army, to assist Brereton in synchronizing all three forces for the mission.

If all went well, over 16,500 paratroopers and 3,500 glider men would be on the ground in less than 90 minutes. The British 1st Airborne Division and 1st Polish Parachute Brigade were ordered to remain at their departure airfields, while the Americans were mobilized. The 82nd Airborne was marshaled around Nottingham, while the 101st deployed to airfields throughout the Newbury area such as Chilbolton, Membury, Ramsbury and Greenham Common.

As overall commander of the invasion force, General Bernard Montgomery was determined to take several key areas in the Netherlands and advance north across the big rivers of the Maas, Waal, and Neder Rijn (the Dutch name for the Rhine). The aim was to form a strong bridgehead around Arnhem, before striking east into the industrial heart of Germany and ultimately Berlin, thus – crucially – ending the war in Europe and saving millions of lives. It was a bold, audacious plan that fundamentally relied upon the main arterial roads to Nijmegen and Arnhem being kept open by the American, Polish and British airborne forces. The main ground route for XXX Corps was to be Eindhoven, Grave, Nijmegen, and Arnhem. As soon as the drop began, the Guards Armored Division, ahead of XXX Corps, was to lead the advance to Eindhoven, the main objective of the 506th Parachute Infantry Regiment. The 101st Airborne Division was to seize bridges along the main axis of advance, ensuring that the British had expedient passage northeast toward Grave and the 82nd Airborne Division's area of operations. When it was time to leave, Shames was reassigned back to 2nd Battalion and joined Ron Speirs in the S3. Fifteen hundred men from 1st and 2nd Battalion, along with 506th Regimental HQ, departed later that afternoon to their designated marshaling area at Membury … *Market Garden* had begun.

6

"BULLETS FROM THE SUN"

The invasion of the Netherlands

Fundamentally the mission for the 506th PIR was to capture the city of Eindhoven and four small but vital bridges over the river Dommel by 2000hrs on Sunday, September 17. Eindhoven was a large industrial city in the province of North Brabant. By the early 1940s, Greater Eindhoven was made up of a series of *wijken* or suburbs. The northern *wijken* of Woensel and Vlokhoven merged into Centrum (city center), with the suburb of Strijp to the west, while Tongelre and Gestel made up the southern part of the city. At the beginning of the 19th century, the Philips Corporation started to develop Eindhoven as an important electrical manufacturing center that affectionately became known as "Philipstown."

Just before the German invasion, the directors fled to the USA and set up a new operation called the North American Philips Company. The only member of the family to remain behind was Frederik or "Frits," whose loyalty and respect toward the people of Eindhoven would result in his being later elevated to saintlike status by the city. In September

1944, out of the 113,000 people living in the city, 25,000 were working in the Philips radio works and lamp and valve factory at Strijp.

Eindhoven straddled one of the principal road routes to Nijmegen. Due to the Allies' previous mistrust of the Dutch resistance, little was really known about enemy forces around the city. However, the regiment was aware of a small number of German security, pioneer, and headquarters troops garrisoned in Eindhoven and a Luftwaffe officers' candidate school situated somewhere in the village of Son.

The assault was to be spearheaded by 3rd Battalion, which would jump onto DZ B, 2 miles north of Son, shortly after 1300hrs. They would be followed by 1st Battalion, whose first objective was to capture three bridges over the Wilhelmina Canal supported by Regimental HQ Company and 2nd Battalion. When both battalions had completed their primary tasks, the entire regiment was then supposed to attack south, capture Eindhoven and wait for the British tanks.

On September 17, 90 aircraft from the 436th Troop Carrier Group transported 1st and 2nd Battalions into battle from Membury in Berkshire. At 1043hrs, Ed's formation joined around 400 other aircraft flying at 1,500ft along a designated "southern route," codenamed *Miami*, toward Ghent. An additional 1,033 planes were flying the longer "northern route," codenamed *Tampa*, carrying paratroopers and gliders from the 82nd Airborne and the British Airborne Corps to their targets at Grave, Nijmegen and Arnhem. On the ground in England, thousands watched for almost 90 minutes as the greatest air armada in history passed overhead. Hundreds of ships and barges moored in Kentish ports blew their sirens as the southern formation turned southeast over the Thames Estuary to fly out over the North Sea towards Belgium.

Breaching the Belgian coast, the flight was joined by a fighter escort, which furnished high and low protective cover. The journey over Belgium to Ghent was uneventful until the planes crossed enemy lines near Rothy and antiaircraft fire began to burst through the formation. No further evasive action could be taken for the C-47s after they reached

Geel – at the same time fighter-bombers set about neutralizing ground targets. Maintaining a vulnerable northeasterly heading about 10 miles out from Son, the transports began to reduce air speed in preparation for the drop. As red lights flicked on, the paratroopers clambered out of their seats to begin the usual safety checks and pre-exit drills.

Approaching the DZ, flak grew in intensity, emanating from antiaircraft positions around Best, Valkenswaard, Eindhoven, and a barge moored along the Wilhelmina Canal.

Over the canal, one of the guys on my plane got hit in the buttocks from ground fire coming up through the floor.

A few moments later, the light inside Ed's aircraft switched to green, signaling the start of the momentous drop. Altogether 2,195 paratroopers from the 506th PIR descended in three waves, spaced 3 minutes apart.

I was in the third wave and didn't realize that our plane had been seriously damaged until we began losing altitude. We jumped low, probably under 400ft.

Ed was lucky – four of the C-47s that took off from Membury either crashed or made forced landings on or near the DZ. From the air the vast 400-acre site at Son seemed to reach out to infinity. Being the first to jump, 3rd Battalion was assigned to secure the DZ. The entire regiment was expected to be assembled and clear of the area within one hour. Ten minutes after Shames landed, another 2,000 men from the 502nd PIR arrived and began their drop onto DZ C over on the far side of the jump field.

Initially 1/506 failed to fully reorganize but headed off to Son anyway. Colonel Sink recovered his glider-borne jeep and drove over to 2nd Battalion's assembly point to inquire why they had not yet moved out. Sink was perplexed to discover that they were still waiting for Lieutenant Colonel Strayer. Thirty minutes later, there was still no sign of him.

Eager to get things moving, Sink ordered Charlie Shettle (who was now Strayer's executive officer) to take command and First Lieutenant Fred Heyliger, commanding officer of the 81mm Mortar Platoon, to lead 2/506, plus the remainder of the regiment to Son.

Collection points for ammunition and supplies were located in woods adjacent to a wide track on the southern edge of the DZ. It was somewhere around here that resistance fighter John van Kooijk was directed toward Ed Shames. Armed only with a pistol, John spoke superb English and was wearing an orange armband stenciled with the word "ORANJE" in black letters. It was not luck that brought John to the woods outside Son to offer assistance. Like many other resistance people, earlier that morning van Kooijk had listened to the public information broadcasts on Radio Oranje and noted that Allied aircraft were strafing and bombing the area around Son in preparation for the landings.

The freedom to fail

On September 5, 1944, many of the larger resistance groups in the Netherlands combined to become the Nederlandse Binnenlandse Strijdrachten (NBS), or Netherlands Interior Force. The NBS was under direct control of Queen Wilhelmina's son, Prince Bernhard. To satisfy international law, the Prince requested that official armbands displaying the word "Orange" be worn by the NBS and all other "legitimate" resistance personnel. After the Dutch Army was decommissioned in 1940, the regular soldiers were sent to prisoner-of-war camps, while reservists like John van Kooijk simply went back to work, hopeful that one day their military training would once again be needed. By the summer of 1940, a group of ex-Dutch Army officers came together to create the Binnenlandse Strijdrachten (BS, Domestic Forces). The idea was to recruit and train a covert army that would eventually rise up and fight alongside the Allies. As the occupation progressed, the national press was taken over by the Germans who then forbade any alternative publications that criticized the regime, reported on the royal family (who had evaded capture by escaping to the UK in 1940), or printed news of the war. Every month, the British printed millions of copies of *De Vliegende Hollander* (*The Flying Dutchman*) that were then dropped into occupied Holland by the Royal Air Force. These leaflets were often copied by the resistance and redistributed by other paramilitary groups such as the Knokploegen (KP). Each KP cell was made up of six to ten people and eventually developed into a more cohesive national organization, the Landelijke Knokploegen (LKP or National Paramilitary Group). Expert forgers, KP units also provided "safe houses" for escaped political prisoners, refugees, and Allied airmen. The German occupiers regarded all resistance fighters as "terrorists" and more than 700 were executed during the four years of occupation.

Anton A. Mussert, the leader of the Dutch National Socialistische Beweging (NSB, National Socialist Movement) welcomed the occupying German forces as liberators and protectors of the Dutch people, who by and large disliked him even more than they did Adolf Hitler. During the first few months of occupation, the NSB recruited 20,000 new members, who were mainly opportunists looking for better jobs or higher social status. As the dynamic of authority began to shift, so did the freedom of the people. One of the largest unions in the Netherlands, the Socialist Trade Union, collapsed after Nazi infiltration and many others followed. The Germans quickly cracked down on all political parties, meetings and demonstrations, by replacing many mayors, town councilors, police officers, and even teachers with German-friendly members of the NSB.

Ed takes up the story of how he worked with the Dutch resistance:

John van Kooijk, who was around 32 years old at the time of the Allied invasion, was deputy underground chief for the southern part of Holland. As van Kooijk seemed exceptionally well informed, I decided to leap-frog Strayer (who was still nowhere to be seen) and introduce him to our regimental intelligence officer, Captain Bill Leach.

Van Kooijk quickly explained to Leach that the two bridges east and west of Son had already been destroyed. The new information meant that the regiment would now have to focus its full attention on the remaining, intact swing bridge. Sometime around 1500hrs, 1st Battalion was forced into a flanking maneuver around the western side of town, while 2nd Battalion attempted a bold direct assault on the bridge. There were at least two antiaircraft guns in Son. The first was located in fields 200 yards northwest of the bridge, between a tuberculosis hospital and the canal. This 88mm gun seriously delayed 1st Battalion's advance, firing point blank into the oncoming paratroopers from A Company.

Another had been placed 300 yards from the canal, in a previously prepared position in front of the Aloysius Boys' School. From here the crew had a commanding view along the main road in both directions. Despite the preparations and fine fields of fire, the gun was quickly overrun and knocked out by a bazooka crew from D Company. At around 1620hrs, as both battalions were converging on the bridge, most of the remaining German forces retreated across the canal to the southern bank before blowing up the objective. Several mines were detonated beneath the central turning mechanism, tearing the bridge in half. The huge explosion threw debris hundreds of feet into the air, showering the Americans with dozens of wooden planks.

Under supervision of General Taylor and Colonel Sink, the engineers from C/326, assisted by Regimental HQ Company, began clearing the twisted remains. As the bridge repair work got underway, all three battalions were deployed in defensive positions around the area.

It was around this time that someone told me George Retan had been killed while attacking the "88" behind the hospital, doing what he loved best, leading from the front. I just couldn't believe it, that man had so much potential and now he was gone and we hadn't even damn well started … what a waste.

By 1730hrs a temporary bridge structure had been fashioned and the regiment began to cross the canal in single file. The original plan to take Eindhoven by 2000hrs was now completely out of the question, despite the city only being 4 miles away. A Company remained to protect the temporary crossing, while the rest of 1st Battalion went into reserve. Both 2nd and 3rd Battalions moved to a defensive position astride the road at Bokt, a tiny hamlet 1 mile further to the south. The night was cold, misty and wet and cut with sporadic enemy artillery fire. At approximately 0130hrs, the men heard several enormous explosions as the Germans blew up a number of important installations in Eindhoven. Shortly afterwards, 3rd Battalion was told that they were going to lead the attack into the city, which was scheduled to commence at dawn. The following morning the first jeeps and horse-drawn carts began to arrive after being ferried across the Wilhelmina Canal on makeshift rafts.

At 0600hrs on Monday, September 18, 3rd Battalion kicked off the regimental assault. At the time the enemy was still withdrawing from the city to the southwest in an attempt to stem the British XXX Corps' advance. The regimental move along the main road known as Eindhovenscheweg had been split into four phase lines with the fourth being Vlokhoven, a suburb of Woensel. Bringing up the rear were Ed Shames and John van Kooijk with 2nd Battalion. Up ahead 3rd Battalion was spread out along both sides of the road. At around 0730hrs the advance party led by John Kiley came under accurate small-arms fire north of Vlokhoven and called for backup.

An intense battle raged for about 30 minutes causing the advance to temporarily fragment into chaos. Several accidents occurred as the soldiers misunderstood what they were being told by the Dutch, many of whom were wearing non-regulation white armbands, which only served to confuse everyone. To make matters worse, as he moved forward Kiley lost radio contact with Major Horton. Ed Shames and John van Kooijk were now only a short distance behind as Kiley's battalion HQ passed by the local girls' school and established its CP beside a burnt-out German halftrack.

Two hundred yards beyond the abandoned vehicle, on the eastern (left) side of the street was a church known locally as the Vlokhoven Tower. Everyone including Ed looked on in horror as Kiley walked across the road, and stood obstinately in full view, studying the church and the route ahead. Even though the captain's bars on his helmet had been painted over, he could ill-afford to be so reckless. From where Ed was kneeling he could hear Bill Galbraith from the 3rd Battalion S3 section shouting at his boss to get back into cover. Moments later Kiley was struck in the neck by a single bullet and collapsed, his wound pumping out blood. Although the perfectly aimed round was fired from the church shrubbery, initially everyone thought it had come from the arched openings high up on the northern side of the bell tower. A volley of shots followed and about a dozen paratroopers ran forward to clear the building but the shooter was long gone.

When the firing stopped the entire neighborhood came out to welcome the Americans. It was quite a surreal scene, with Kiley's body still lying in the gutter, covered by a blanket. Ersatz tea was served to the "liberators" in bone china cups. After four years of German occupation the Dutch could barely contain themselves. However, pockets of enemy resistance were still being mopped up and every time shots were heard, the locals quickly disappeared back inside their homes. During the cleanup operation, 3rd Battalion captured about 50 Germans, some of whom were wearing civilian clothing. In the meantime, the men were overwhelmed with gifts of fruit, flowers, sandwiches and kisses in abundance. It soon became almost impossible to conduct the advance safely with people running everywhere trying to touch the paratroopers.

One hour later, at around 0900hrs, the leading elements of 3rd Battalion along with Regimental HQ were pinned down by machine-gun fire as they struck the German main line of resistance (MLR) a few yards into Woenselsestraat. It was not long before the battalion encountered two more 88mm cannons. The first, a Flak 18 standard antiaircraft version was located on the eastern side of the street outside the Firma

AA Notten grocery store. The second, a static Flak 18 AT variant was located 150 yards behind the first, in an open area between two houses opposite a road called Kloosterdreef. Both guns were boldly sited, firing on a flat trajectory along the two streets. Almost all of the houses and stores in Woenselsestraat had front doors that opened onto the sidewalk and harassment from enemy machine guns forced many to seek shelter in the recessed doorways.

Ed Shames and John van Kooijk were busy interrogating a group of German prisoners near Kloosterdreef, when Charlie Shettle came over with a local man named Henk Staals, looking for advice on the best way to attack the guns. It was soon decided that Staals and another resident, Piet Pulles, would guide Shettle and two squads from D and F Companies in an assault. The guns were quickly outflanked and silenced but not before they had caused a huge amount of damage and injured a number of people including Bill Galbraith, who almost lost a leg.

Meanwhile 2nd Battalion was sent forward around 3rd Battalion's left flank and into Eindhoven. A friend of John van Kooijk's volunteered to guide Colonel Strayer, who had now caught up, through the city to the bridges over the Dommel. Van Kooijk also happened to mention a telephone service network operated by the Philips Corporation to Ed:

John asked if we knew about the telephone lines, which of course we didn't. I was amazed to learn that the Germans were also unaware and that the southern command had been exchanging sensitive information via the system for the last couple of years! I didn't waste any time and took "John the Dutchman" straight to Sink.

In the early 1930s, Philips had purchased several large power stations and manufacturing companies. Many of the sites continued to operate under their original names, including The Nederlandsche Seintoestellellen Fabriek (NSF) at Hilversum and the Metaaldraadlampenfabriek NV Volt factory at Tilburg. Each factory had its own independent power plant for generating electricity, with its own direct, secure telephone service link back to Eindhoven, operated by the Philips engineers, which was not part of the German-controlled national Postal & Telephone Company network. Frits Philips shared the service lines with resistance groups across the region and in return used the subsequent intelligence to guard against factory inspections and searches. This resistance line of communication would come into its own in the ensuing battle.

Colonel Sink was keen to exploit any opportunity and immediately attached Shames and John van Kooijk to Captain Bill Leach (regimental S2) and Bob Moon as "unofficial" liaison officers.

To be honest, I never really liked Leach, and thought he was never really suited to intelligence, on account that he lacked any common sense. Before long John and I arrived in the center of town beneath the awesome twin spires of St Catharina Church, where we were quickly swallowed up by the joyful crowds.

More civilians joined the American force as the 506th moved deeper into the city. Some were wearing official resistance armbands, while others just wanted to be involved in the fight. Many were destined to become scouts while those who could speak English offered their services as translators. Leach and Moon set up a temporary office at 109 Stratumseind, which was then home to the Vosters family.

Information supplied by Ed, John and other groups was then plotted and relayed via radio to the rifle companies. Capturing buildings intact such as post offices and telephone exchanges was vitally important although some, like the Deutsche Reichspost, had already been destroyed. By 1215hrs 2nd Battalion was in control of the Dommel bridges. Two hours later, as enemy resistance began to collapse, 2/506 was sent to guard the eastern sector of the harbor near the gasworks at Nachtegaallaan. The remainder of the regiment moved into town following the disused tramlines, establishing their own defensive sectors to the southwest.

With 3rd Battalion now controlling the bridges at de Wal and Van Abbe, Major Horton and Colonel Sink occupied Den Elzent, an imposing property diagonally across the street from the art museum. The three-story townhouse had previously been the German military headquarters. The regiment settled into the wealthy suburbs of Elzent and Villa Park and Regimental HQ Company established its base at the nearby Catholic community center.

At 1500hrs, over 400 gliders landed on the landing zone (LZ) at Son, bringing with them much-needed artillery and medical support. The following morning, Colonel Sink and Major Hester visited areas held by the regiment and were pleased to see the steady stream of Allied vehicles moving northward through the city and beyond. Captain Leach was doing his best to disseminate the information coming in from the resistance regarding enemy troop movements. As a result he asked Ed and John for assistance with this task.

One of John's friends was a local doctor from Veghel, who volunteered to drive us around in his sumptuous black Opel Kapitan, which was originally intended for Colonel Sink.

Eindhoven was still in a celebratory mood but all that changed during the afternoon of the 19th. Orange bunting around the city suddenly vanished when forward elements of the German 107th Armored Brigade were seen in the vicinity of Nederwetten, 2 miles east of Woensel. Supported by a contingent of Mk V Panther tanks and self-propelled guns, the brigade had recently been rerouted by train from Aachen. The unit had orders to capture Sint Oedenrode and cut the Allied supply route to Grave. Unbeknown to the Americans, the immediate threat was not aimed at Eindhoven but the newly completed Bailey bridge at Son.

Colonel Sink ordered 2nd Battalion to reposition eastwards through the suburb of Tongelre to protect Nuenen and Helmond from the German tanks. That evening Ed and John were stuck in a traffic jam of military vehicles trying to get through Eindhoven when the German air force struck. John and Ed were very lucky as several men from RHQ based in the city died in the ensuing inferno.

When the first flares appeared above the city at 2030hrs, the streets were flooded with tanks and trucks, and civilians trying to express their gratitude to each and every Allied soldier. A few minutes later the bombers arrived. The markers grew brighter and brighter until the city was covered in a yellow light that hung suspended like some kind of giant chandelier. Before long the southern part of Eindhoven was in flames, telephone lines were down, and the mains water pressure had failed. Streets close to Sink's CP were badly hit. The city's public air defense platoons were completely overwhelmed when buildings began to collapse, burying dozens in the rubble. The AB Theater and part of the municipal gasworks were totally destroyed. Over the next 20 minutes two more raids struck Stratumsiend and Vestdijk, annihilating the Van Piere bookstore, damaging St Catharina Church and blocking vital roads.

A British ammunition truck exploded and set fire to a number of homes in Hertogstraat. It was virtually impossible to evacuate the residents of the affected areas. The worst tragedy occurred at the entrance to one of the public shelters on the northern edge of the city at Biesterweg, where almost 50 people were killed. In total 227 civilians lost their lives during the raid and 800 were wounded. Afterwards the regiment returned to Eindhoven and 2/506 established its CP at Tongelre on the eastern edge of the city from where two roads led directly to Nuenen and Geldrop. It was obvious that the Germans might attempt a breakthrough toward their forces fighting at Best so the regiment was keen to gather more intelligence about what was happening to the east.

Another friend of van Kooijk's, Mr van Lierop, who lived along the Nuenen road, volunteered to supply information to the 506th. Early on the morning of September 20, acting on intelligence provided by van Lierop, Ed and John visited Nuenen. John's family was living in the center of Nuenen at the time but they were unable to reach his house because the German Panzer brigade was closing in from Eckart. After leaving Nuenen, Ed and John attempted to make their way to Schijndel but were forced to withdraw at Sint Oedenrode due to the continued heavy fighting around Best. The various airborne task forces sent out to stop the enemy were unsuccessful and as darkness fell, the troops returned to Eindhoven to protect the city. "For us every night was spent in a different CP, but always in houses belonging to John's friends." The two men reported back to Eindhoven if they had any important information that shed light on the chaotic situation. Ed and John were constantly on the lookout for local NSB politicians and officials such as Eindhoven's mayor, Dr Hub Pulles. Other than that, any spare time was taken up interviewing people whose stories were somehow suspect, especially if they were claiming to be "divers," individuals who had gone into hiding to avoid the compulsory labor program when over 600,000 men were sent to work in German factories.

After the 506th finally departed from Eindhoven, British forces moved in behind them. Although combat operations were generally successful elsewhere in the region, Best would not be liberated until October 24. When the Allied battle lines were drawn along the corridor to Arnhem, nearly 300,000 German troops were trapped in the Netherlands with a seemingly inexhaustible supply of tanks, SPGs, and 88s at their disposal. By September 21, the German 107th Armored Brigade had joined forces with two other fighting groups to focus its attention further north, launching a series of attacks along the "corridor hubs" at Sint Oedenrode, Veghel and Uden.

Veghel was crucial to the enemy due to its position on the road and railway networks and close proximity to the Zuid–Willems–Vaart Canal. The constant German activity along the 40-mile stretch of road between Eindhoven and Arnhem meant that it was almost impossible to keep open, and came to be known as "Hell's Highway" by the 101st Airborne Division.

7

"DEAD MEN'S SHOES"
Zeeland and Tilburg

On September 20, intelligence reports were received by the 506th from one of the resistance groups east of Veghel that a sizable enemy force was planning to attack Uden. Colonel Sink believed it might be possible for the enemy to launch an assault from the industrial town of Tilburg, 12 miles northwest of Eindhoven. Once Sink had settled into the idea of using the Philips telephone lines, he started to make plans for a very special reconnaissance mission.

Naturally John and I were elected to go to Tilburg and assess the situation regarding enemy armor. John's doctor friend from Veghel was now on the team and had a medical colleague, Frans de Sain, who lived 2 miles east of the city in the village of Oisterwijk, close to the main railway line, where several large German ammunition and medical supply depots were located.

From Eindhoven, the doctor drove Shames and van Kooijk to Nuenen, where John was briefly able to meet up with his family.

John wanted to introduce me to his wife, and we were there no more than 5 minutes before having to leave. It was here that I learned he'd owned a sporting goods company and was really quite well to do. Oddly, at the time, I still had some reservations.

If John had been working for the Germans, it would have put Ed and the 506th in terrible danger but as a genuine resistance officer John's help proved invaluable to the Allied cause.

After saying goodbye to his two sons, we made our way to Uden for a meeting with John's resistance group. The doctor parked up on the outskirts of town, where we rendezvoused with John's commander, Milo, and a couple of his men who decided to escort us to the village of Zeeland, 3 miles away to the northeast. Milo had heard that the village was temporarily free of enemy forces but wanted to double check before we did anything else.

Reaching Zeeland, on instructions from Milo, the doctor parked his Opel outside the unisex hairdressers on Kerkstraat 50, which bizarrely still appeared to be open. Situated on a corner with the main road, the barbershop was diagonally opposite an imposing church. John and Ed went into the shop to confirm if it was true about the Germans. Somewhat dumbstruck by the unexpected visit, the owner of the salon, Martien van Ganzewinkel, told John that the Germans had gone and, as far as he knew, Ed was the first American paratrooper to enter the town.

I just couldn't resist the temptation and there and then decided to have a shave and a haircut! John couldn't believe what I was doing and went outside to wait in the car, just in case the Germans returned.

Trying to converse, the 32-year-old barber went quiet for a moment when Shames mentioned "Virginia." Pointing at Ed, Martien shouted excitedly, "Ah Virginia, Virginia, Virginia!" and then without warning ran to the back of the shop.

At that point I grabbed my M1, which was leaning against the front window and dashed outside to get John. Martien followed me out holding a letter that turned out to be from his brother Piet, dated April 1940, which he'd received just before the German invasion. It was the postmark that got my attention – Franklin Street, Portsmouth, Virginia. I couldn't believe the coincidence because – incredibly – my sister Anna also lived on Franklin Street! I asked John to come back inside and translate as Martien was going loopy with excitement. John explained to me that Martien was the youngest of five brothers: Jan, Antonius, Piet, Henricus and they also had a sister, Elisabeth. Piet had become a Catholic priest and immigrated to the States in 1931 … amazing eh?

Before we left, I promised that at the first available opportunity, I'd write to Anna and ask her to try and make contact with Piet to let him know that his brother and family were all still alive and doing fine. Waving and hugging everything that moved, the boys said goodbye to Martien and we headed for Oisterwijk. The following day, I heard the Germans returned to Zeeland, thankfully unaware of our incursion and contact with Martien.*

The team headed back to Veghel and reported what they had seen to Bill Leach.

Afterwards I told the doc that although we were going to use his car, he wouldn't be coming with us to Oisterwijk – the risks were just too high. Before we departed, John asked me to leave my M1, pistol, uniform and even dog tags with the doctor for safekeeping. Despite the Dutch boys all being armed, when I asked what would happen if we got stopped, they simply handed me some forged documents and said, "Don't worry

---

* In May 2013, Ed revisited the salon on Kerkstraat 50, where Peggy van Ganzewinkel was able to finish the haircut started by her grandfather almost 69 years earlier.

about it." In fact that's all they ever said! Nervously, I stripped down to my underwear and pulled on a set of old coveralls and a pair of work boots. The others were all dressed the same. While I realized it was important for the mission, what if I were to be caught like this ... Christ Almighty!

During the late evening of September 21, Ed and the boys arrived at the spacious home of 56-year-old Frans de Sain, which was situated on the junction with Kerkstraat and Bayerdijk. The Opel was parked next door at a Catholic junior boys' school, out of sight in an old garage. The friars who taught at Sint Hermanus were sympathetic and had been sheltering several local resistance people wanted by the Germans, who had also been billeted at the school.

Ignoring the side entrance to the surgery we entered the doctor's house through a courtyard at the back and were quickly ushered upstairs to the attic.

Two dormer windows gave the men a clear view in either direction down onto the neat suburban tree-lined brick-paved street. Ed learned that after several previous attempts, the resistance had successfully blown up an ammunition train at Haaren only a short distance away from de Sain's house on the day before the invasion. The massive explosion completely destroyed the line, blocking access to Oisterwijk's station, causing havoc for later German reinforcements.

De Sain ran a medical practice from consulting rooms on the ground floor. As a representative of the local Red Cross, he had volunteered to work with the German medical services and a surgeon from the nearby evacuation hospital was staying at the house. This did nothing to deter Frans from covertly treating wounded Allied airmen and anyone else needing his help. Allied aviators were hidden in an adjacent attic, belonging to Sint Hermanus, connected by a small hole through which supplies could be passed.

When we were in that house, although we never saw the German officer downstairs, I was frightened. I kept wondering what I was doing there and how I'd got myself into this position. I didn't know Milo or the other Dutch guys and still wasn't entirely sure of their motivations. Despite having John around, not being able to understand the language was a big issue. As van Kooijk was so much older, I truly believe that the confidence he exuded gave me the strength to put any negative thoughts behind me and keep on going.

As it turned out, Ed had no need to doubt because Milo and the boys had everything planned.

Dead set on living – Tilburg

The following morning, Shames and his six-man team set off on their reconnaissance mission as ordered by Sink. As they walked away, toward the church, Ed glanced to his left at the statue of Sint Hermanus, situated over the main entrance to the school and superstitiously crossed his fingers in the hope that he would see it again.

The Volt factory manufactured copper filaments for light bulbs produced by Philips and was situated in a district known as Broekhoven. Like many others, the facility at Tilburg had its own small independent power plant furnished with a direct private secure telephone service link to corporate HQ in Eindhoven.

It now quickly became apparent to Ed why he and the boys were dressed in coveralls as they merged with thousands of workers, all walking along the main road, known as Oisterwijksebaan, towards Tilburg.

Several enormous buildings lined the route. At one point we passed by a leather factory and the smell of tannin running into an open sewer was completely overpowering. We did notice some sort of military hospital with a red cross painted on the roof but there didn't seem to be any enemy troops around to bother us, although we'd been warned that they could well be present here as well as the leather place.

Eventually the path converged and followed the railway for a short distance before connecting to a tarmac road that led to a swing bridge over the Wilhelmina Canal. The bridge here was virtually identical to the one demolished at Son. Usually there would have been two sentries on duty but due to the chaotic fighting they were absent, most likely sent to Best, leaving the crossing rigged for demolition. Even the local police, known by the Dutch as the Grün Polizei, were nowhere to be seen.

The Volt factory was located on the outskirts of the city and Ed boldly entered the premises through the main gate, which was overlooked by a 140ft-high clock tower. The men cautiously made their way across the compound, toward a large chimney, which to Ed looked uncannily similar to the one he had seen in Carentan on D-Day. The group then turned left behind the paintshop and entered the machine room, designated building E, through a set of double doors at the rear.

Shining through a row of skylights, the early morning sunshine filled the room with light. Ed looked around at the enormous electric motors and dynamos bolted to the black and white tiled floor.

The space was wide open and if compromised, there was absolutely nowhere for us to hide. After a briefing, I was left with an engineer whose only English seemed to be "No problem, no problem." Each two-phase motor had its own transformer powering the factory's lighting system. All of these had cabinets next to them but only one, belonging to the largest generator, contained the Bakelite handset. This phone was used to monitor any faults and maintain the unusual voltage output that was specific to Philips.

The engineer then began to unbolt the faceplate using a special tool. The phone was next to a secondary cover that appeared to protect a large wiring loom and complex pulley system. I anxiously waited while the others went out to scout their designated sectors, only returning every now and then to deliver information that I relayed back to Leach – who was waiting for me at the other end of the line. Due to the earlier sabotage at Haaren, the tactical situation at Tilburg was virtually non-existent with regard to any tank, vehicle or troop concentrations. As the haunting clock chimes from Broekhovense church echoed hourly across the courtyard, I don't recall ever feeling so scared or alone and the noise from the bell only added to my anxiety. In my mind all I kept imagining was one of those old spy movies when a guy just walks in and starts shooting. Thankfully, the mission ended around 1700hrs and we were able to head back to Oisterwijk with the returning workforce.

The following day, Shames and van Kooijk reported to Leach at his CP in Eerde for a debrief:

Captain Leach then ordered us to Veghel and assigned First Lieutenant Russell Hall from 2nd Battalion HQ to our team. Hall was a relative stranger to me but our job was to interview any locals and gain information on the enemy. Hall seemed more scared than me as we went about our business. We hadn't been in Veghel long when he was shot in the head by a sniper, right there in the street, and died instantly.

Shortly afterwards, approximately 40 German tanks from the 107th Armored Brigade attempted to seize Veghel and destroy the bridges over the Zuid–Willems–Vaart Canal and river Aa. Intermittent poor weather over the next three days severely hampered effective air support. Because of information provided by Ed and John, the division, sustained by British armor, was able to block the German tank assaults against Uden and several other places along the 4-mile stretch of road.

Eventually Uden returned to American control, whereupon Colonel Sink relocated his CP and RHQ to the Mariaschool and a nearby community center in the town. A lucky break in the weather meant that the 101st was able to coordinate air strikes on another enemy force gathering nearby. Charged with holding Veghel at all costs, the Divisional Artillery Commander, Brigadier General Anthony McAuliffe, threw together a task force and was successfully able to beat off the attacks. Over the next 48 hours, the enemy managed to deploy a much larger force around Koevering. Supported by British tanks, the resulting Allied punches on the right flank dislodged the enemy from all but a very small pocket to the south and despite two further attempts, Hell's Highway was never cut again.

General Taylor regarded the assistance given by the Dutch underground as crucial to the liberation of Eindhoven, Son, Sint Oedenrode, and Veghel. Although the 101st Airborne had taken over 3,500 prisoners since September 17, the Germans were by no means beaten. For the 506th PIR, the battle ended quietly in Uden with Ed and the others believing their job was now finished. But at the beginning of October, the 101st was both surprised and disappointed to learn that it would not be going to a rest camp in France. Instead they would now be moving forward to a place called "the Island," near Arnhem, 30 miles further north – taking over from the British XII Corps.

8

"THE BUCKET LIST"
The Island – Fall 1944

In 1944, the civilian population of the Betuwe, known to the Allies as "the Island," numbered around 40,000 people. Situated northwest of Nijmegen, the Island is bounded by the Neder Rijn (Lower Rhine) and the river Waal. The area measures a maximum of 30 miles wide by 8 miles deep and is split in the west by the Amsterdam Rijn Canal. The canal was built at the end of the 19th century and today still connects the port of Amsterdam to the main shipping arteries of the Rijn. Many towns and villages, including Opheusden, Zetten, and Valburg, comprised deeply religious farming communities; while others, including Randwijk, Dodewaard, Heteren, and Driel, depended on shipbuilding, tobacco and jam production. Brick manufacturing was another important industry, with at least a dozen factories situated along the banks of Neder Rijn to the north and the river Waal in the south. Dissected by three main railway networks and the Linge Canal, the Island had superb transportation links to Arnhem and Nijmegen in the east as well as the larger industrial cities to the west.

On September 17, 1944, Allied fighter planes attacked German antiaircraft sites, which at that time were located on the Island (Betuwe), as the first British gliders passed overhead and began landing north of the Rijn along with thousands of paratroopers.

The 82nd Airborne had successfully completed their original mission to capture and keep open the bridge at Nijmegen over the Waal – the gateway to the Island and a branch of the Rijn. During the early afternoon of October 1, the 506th PIR were alerted for a possible move to the city. Seemingly unnoticed by the British now occupying the Island, over on the Veluwe, the high ground across the Rijn, the civilian populations of Wageningen, Bennekom and Ede were being systematically evacuated by the Germans. The Grebbeberg – which at 165 feet is the highest and most densely wooded part in the Veluwe – had formed part of the Dutch defensive line in 1940. The imposing hill was dissected by the main trunk road between Arnhem and Utrecht, and was also close to a vital railway bridge crossing the river at Rhenen.

On the morning of October 2, the 506th was moved by truck from Uden across the Nijmegen Bridge in support of the 82nd for what was to become perhaps the toughest phase of the entire campaign for Sink's paratroopers.

The next day, the regiment replaced the British 214th Infantry Brigade at Opheusden. As with many other places on the Island, the land around this small town was made up of reclaimed floodplain, consisting of open pastures, numerous apple and cherry orchards, all enclosed by deep drainage ditches and dijks.

For the depleted and fatigued paratroopers their time on the Island would be a brief succession of defensive stands, fierce fighting and continuous flanking movements. The 2nd and 3rd Battalions took over the main line of defense (LOD) while 1st Battalion went into local reserve. The consensus among British soldiers coming out of the line was that the area was quiet and boring. Although the LOD was blocking the important western approach to the Island, the sector had been undeniably peaceful for the last week. The 2nd Battalion moved up onto the Rijn to defend a wide front along the dijk from Opheusden to Heteren. Forming a right angle, 3rd Battalion took over another sector facing west from the northern edge of Opheusden, extending south through the railway station toward Dodewaard and the Waal. Shockingly most of the deployment took place under the watchful eye of the Germans on the Veluwe.

Before dawn on October 5, the 363. Volksgrenadier-Division launched a ferocious attack advancing from the west via the towns of Kesteren and Ochten, aiming to break through and seize the bridge at Nijmegen. The 3rd Battalion bore the brunt of the initial assault and suffered many casualties, including Major Horton who was killed by machine-gun fire. The German division was almost bled dry during the epic two-day battle and while 2nd Battalion remained static, they successfully beat off several full-scale incursions from the enemy forces who boldly tried to cross the river opposite their positions. The tactical situation was not helped by the superb observation afforded to the German artillery from high points such as the Grebbeberg and Wageningen. As a stalemate set in across the front line, the Allies evacuated thousands of women and children from Dodewaard, Hemmen and Zetten to Eindhoven and Tilburg, which had only just been liberated by Scottish forces.

During this period the bulk of the 506th dug in on the MLR behind the dijk road, overlooking the Rijn. They were also sending out regular night patrols across the river to Wageningen. During the day, enemy artillery was still a problem, along with heavy mortars and rockets. On October 14, 2nd Battalion was finally withdrawn from its positions along the river and moved into divisional reserve on the southern side of the Island.

3rd Platoon, E Company – Driel

A week or so after the battle for Opheusden, Major Hester brought Ed Shames to his new CP at the Baltussen factory, situated on the extreme left flank of the 501st at Driel. Split into two areas, Marskamp (north) and Grietenkamp to the south, the village was dominated by two churches and a number of large orchards. A fruit processing plant owned by Josephus Baltussen was located on the southern edge of Driel along Honingveldsestraat. The village had previously been occupied by elements of the Polish 1st Independent Parachute Brigade who had been dropped near Driel in a desperate attempt to relieve pressure on the 1st Airborne Division, fighting for their lives across the river at Arnhem. In fact, Major General Stanislaw Sosabowski, commander of the Polish 1 Independent Parachute Brigade, had had his headquarters at the Beijer house in the heart of the settlement along Molenstraat, a few hundred yards due north of the Baltussen factory.

The platoon sergeant of 3rd Platoon, E Company, Staff Sergeant Amos "Buck" Taylor was not particularly welcoming as he explained to Shames that their last platoon leader, First Lieutenant Robert Brewer, had been wounded during the early stages of the campaign. By rights, Ed should have been the assistant to First Lieutenant Ben Perkins, who took over from Brewer, but he had recently been transferred out on charges of misconduct. Truthfully, Buck felt that the platoon was in fine shape and believed Ed lacked the experience needed to run this little gang of talented misfits.

Shames recalls:

Word had already gone around that some "hard-ass" former first sergeant was taking over and the men were intent on showing me who was boss. After making myself at home in the only office that was still virtually intact, I decided to call a meeting and around 20 percent of the platoon didn't even bother to show up. I couldn't believe what was happening and made it clear that we would reconvene the following morning when I expected "ALL," repeat "ALL," to turn up or else. The next day everyone was in attendance. "Guys … trust me when I say that I'm a perfectionist and although it isn't always possible to attain I'll bust a gut trying. Firstly I want us to accomplish whatever mission we are given and secondly, if we completely understand our role then we will, me included, have a better chance of getting home. I didn't come here to be loved but I do want your respect … if I earn it. Likewise, I expect you to prove yourselves in the same way to me!"

After the meeting, Buck Taylor introduced Shames to his new squad leaders, Corporal Walter Gordon, Sergeant Art Youman, Sergeant Paul Rogers and Corporal Darrell Powers, known to everyone as "Shifty."

Shifty Powers was from 2nd Squad and seemed adamant that he didn't need me or any other officer to tell him what to do. In fact the entire platoon was really quite antagonistic toward me, but good, bad or indifferent we still had a job to do.

With so many new people it was hard for Ed to remember their names, although one guy did catch his attention, perhaps for all the wrong reasons:

Very abrasive, Private First Class Frank Mellett was a New Yorker who fancied himself as a bit of an insubordinate smart arse and therefore most definitely one that I needed to keep a close eye on.

It took a few days but Shifty, Mellett and some of the other guys soon realized that I was on their side. Shifty was very friendly with Paul Rogers from the mortar squad, and for some reason I took a shine to both of them. Paul was a few years older than me and had a natural way with the men, who playfully called him "Hayseed" because he came from Kansas and was very much a country boy at heart.

Paul had taken over the mortar squad after Sergeant Clarence Tridle was seriously wounded in Normandy. Rogers never raised his voice but had a presence very similar to Paul Simrell, which did not go unnoticed by Ed.

I understood that Shifty got his nickname while running bootlegged whiskey around Virginia. When he started to call me "cap" I knew things were changing. The term came from the coalmines of the Appalachian Mountains where all the charge hands were known as "cap." Anyhow, it caught on and pretty soon everyone started using the term – I wasn't complaining, in fact I kinda liked it!

Buck Taylor was fantastic. That guy possessed real authority and would've made a great officer. From the outset, with more than a little help from Buck, we created our own cadre at the factory to enhance and teach patrol skills. One of the things we focused on was something called "marking." Marking is the ability to recognize and remember any feature that had an unusual look or stood out for some reason. This way an individual could assimilate and be more aware of their surroundings, essential to any advanced map reading that was now being taught to the team. My old S3 knowledge was useful, especially when it came to lessons on mission planning and model making.

At this time, due to lack of manpower, E Company was operating a rotational policy with regard to its three platoons on outpost and patrolling. When Ed arrived, 3rd Platoon was already tasked with outposting the dijk between Heteren and Randwijk.

During this period another two guys came to my attention, my armorer Tech Corporal Forrest Guth and Private First Class Rod Strohl. "Gutty" [pronounced Goud-ee] and Strohl were both "Pennsylvania Dutch" from Fogelsville, a suburb of Allentown, where Rod's father owned a Chevrolet agency, the very first of its kind in the state. Rod was well educated and intelligent, as of course was Gutty, but his hands were like gold to me. Guth could repair anything and was incredibly useful to have around. All subsequent operational planning took place at the factory where we received many of our patrol instructions direct from regiment. I don't think our battalion executive officer, Captain Winters [who had only recently taken over from Ed's old boss Charlie Shettle] was ever fully consulted by Sink regarding my posting, which I'm sure caused him some concern.

Better than any invasion currency, our new home was filled with jars of preserved cherries … so we collectively opened the European branch of Shames Provisions! At the time we were living on British rations and had to virtually beg for everything, including cigarettes and chewing gum. I was lucky to have Private Robert "Mac" McArdle as my runner. McArdle was a resourceful man who could "borrow" virtually anything. Due to the abundance of cherries, 29-year-old "Mac" turned out to be brilliant at trading them for all manner of supplies.

Buck, Paul and Ed ran the "store" and kept in constant radio contact with their men up on the dijks. During the day those members of the platoon who were on deployment remained hunkered down out of sight behind the 20ft-high dijk wall. The higher ground on the Veluwe, especially near Heveadorp at Westerbouwing, provided the enemy with a commanding view across the Rijn, allowing them to target any daylight movement with devastating efficiency. Subsequently the area between the factory and the dijk, which was also the MLR, became a no-man's-land that could only be patrolled under cover of darkness.

The sector assigned to the company was quite a large area that ran from my CP to a windmill at Heteren, then along the river to a brick factory near Randwijk.

Because of the distances between observation posts (OPs), Mac managed to procure a step-through moped. We called the windmill "At Will," due to the heavy shelling it constantly received from across the river. That old "putt putt" came in mighty handy, especially for dropping people off at OPs, the closest of which was "At Will," and that was almost 3 miles away!

Often German artillery spotters on the high ground at Westerbouwing would try to zero in as Ed hurtled toward the river.

All I could do was grit my teeth and squeeze the last ounce of speed out of the moped! One time I happened to be out in daylight when the shellfire came so close it nearly got me and "Smokey" Gordon who was riding pillion!

Back at the factory, one person in particular, Private Don Moone, always seemed to be trying to get one over on me. I called him "Cosmetic" [although to the enlisted men he was more commonly known as Moonbeam] because he was constantly applying moisturizer to his face and hands, but despite that he was a superb scout. I would often catch Moone wandering about with a clipboard trying to look like he was doing something useful but I knew the score.

Private First Class Robert "Popeye" Wynn was similar in nature to Don Moone. Popeye was an intelligent and smooth operator. I soon learned that alongside his half-Indian buddy, Earl McClung, Popeye could almost smell the Krauts. Subsequently, I often had them working together as scouts in our six-man patrols.

Like Shifty and some of the others, Popeye did not take kindly to Ed when he first arrived. Although Wynn was one of the most genial and fun-loving men in the company, Ed often joked, "the way Popeye carried his Thompson sub-machine gun [TSMG] it sometimes made me wonder if one day he was gonna shoot me! Two rounds from that Tommy gun and he was on target. Shifty and McClung were probably the best shots in the platoon but I think Earl had the edge, maybe because of his Native American background."

Once I started to get to know the boys I began to realize what a crazy bunch of bastards they were, especially Private First Class Wayne Sisk. One of the guys told me that, while the regiment was in training at Toccoa, Wayne, aka "Skinny," got into a bit of bother. Skinny had this girl and they were making love on the tracks when the driver of a locomotive was forced to do an emergency stop and called the police. Apparently when Skinny appeared in court, the judge asked what on earth he thought he was doing on the line and I understand that his reply was, "Well sir, she was cummin, I was cummin and the only one who had any control over the brakes was the damned engine driver!" Yep, old Skinny was quite a character alright, and I was glad to have him on my team.

Utrinque Paratus – "Ready for Anything" – The rescue of the British Paras begins

On the night of October 15, a man swam across the river and came ashore directly opposite one of the listening posts in the 3rd Platoon sector.

A couple of my people near the brick factory challenged the guy, who was wearing just a shirt and underpants, only to be told that he was a British paratroop officer with an important message for 2nd Army. Initially I found it hard to believe because due to early winter flooding the river was faster flowing and bitterly cold. I explained who we were and after a short "interrogation" the officer requested a meeting with Colonel Sink.

The swimmer was Lieutenant Colonel David Dobie, Commanding Officer of 1st Battalion, the Parachute Regiment. Thirty-two-year-old Dobie had been captured at Arnhem on September 19, along with his adjutant, Major Nigel Grove. Wounded by shrapnel, both men were taken to a German military hospital at Appledorn from where Dobie made good his escape. After being picked up by the Dutch underground he joined around 80 British paratroopers who were being hidden in private dwellings around the town of Ede. At the time Ede was full of refugees, who had been evacuated in early October from Wageningen. This chaotic situation made it much easier for the British to blend in. Several weeks later an escape plan was hatched during a meeting with Brigadier Gerald Lathbury, commanding officer of the 1st Parachute Brigade – at a safe house in Ede, where the brigadier had been recovering from wounds sustained at Arnhem.

According to the original plan, the paratroopers were to be reequipped, which would enable them to carry on a guerrilla war until the Allies crossed the Rijn. A Belgian Jedburgh agent named Gilbert Sadi-Kirschen ("Captain King"), along with his team (codenamed Claude), who had parachuted in with the 1st Airborne Division, arranged for airdrops of weapons, ammunition, rations and uniforms through his Special Forces radio link to London. There were four bespoke highly specialized teams, known as Jedburghs or Jeds, assembled for Operation *Market Garden*. For the most part these four-man units were made up of Dutch expatriate soldiers who had been selected in the UK from the Special Operations Executive (SOE).

There were now approximately 2,500 enemy troops belonging to the 363.Volksgrenadier-Division stationed in the area, with their headquarters in Ede! However, with the Island offensive now reaching a stalemate, Lathbury decided that he had no choice other than evacuate the small airborne force in order to protect the lives of the local population, who would be at serious risk if the British remained and were captured.

Lathbury and his officers were well aware of the service telephone from the PGEM power plant in Ede to Nijmegen but preferred to use "Captain King's" secure radio link to the UK. However, when the need arose for more expedient communications, Lathbury turned his attention toward the telephone at the power plant. It did not take long for the brigadier to decide that David Dobie, with his natural ability to improvise, would be the best envoy for the proposed escape. On October 14, after several intensive briefings Dobie, accompanied by his Dutch guides, said a few last farewells and headed for the river. Before leaving Ede, the colonel settled on a time with Major Allison Digby Tatham-Warter (officer commanding A Company, 2nd Parachute Battalion) that they would talk via telephone after Dobie reached Nijmegen on October 16.

Shortly after arriving at Sink's CP in Zetten, Dobie was dispatched to XXX Corps HQ in Nijmegen. Over the next 48 hours, the telephone link between Tatham-Warter and Dobie became vital in developing a basic evacuation plan. Subsequently after talking to Dobie, Lieutenant General Sir Brian Horrocks visited the 506th CP during the morning of October 18 to pitch Dobie's ideas to Colonel Sink. Initially, Sink was not overly optimistic about the possibilities of rescuing the British. But because Dobie had come ashore in Ed Shames' sector, he naturally asked Colonel Strayer for assistance.

From his CP at Lonkhuyzen farm (opposite Hemmen Castle) Strayer and Clarence Hester met with the 2nd Battalion company commanders and intelligence staff. Later that evening Ed was ordered to Lonkhuyzen, along with the new E Company commander, Moose Heyliger, and First Lieutenant Harry Welsh, who was in temporary command of 2nd Platoon. "A Bedford lorry arrived at the factory to collect me. One of the GIs from 2nd Battalion HQ was giving directions to the British driver. From Driel we went to pick up Welsh and Heyliger from their locations and returned to the battalion CP. Here the GI got out and handed over to Strayer, who immediately ordered the three of us into the back of the vehicle. At the time nobody, except Strayer and the driver, knew where we were going. Even Moose, who was a happy-go-lucky kind of guy, didn't have much to say, we just sat, smoked and stared out over the tailgate as the light faded into darkness." The vehicle soon crossed Nijmegen Bridge and headed southwest. Once the Bedford reached Grave, the driver turned off and followed the dijk road alongside the River Maas. The rough unpaved track twisted and turned under the bridge before winding its way to Eindsestraat and the tiny hamlet of Nederasselt.

It was pitch dark by the time we stopped outside a large barn. Entering the dimly lit interior we were surprised to see around 70 people sitting in rows on benches and made our way toward the back. For the most part they were British but we also noticed some Polish troops, Dutch civilians and eight or nine Americans. A couple of British soldiers came in through an outside door over to our right carrying a wooden platform. Someone called attention. Jokingly, I whispered into Harry's ear that Strayer had inadvertently invited us to some kind of floor show! We obediently stood as a British brigadier walked in and stepped up onto the podium. He told us to sit and relax, then without any formal introduction explained, "Gentleman, at this precise moment several trucks are en route from Belgium, carrying 25 collapsible canvas boats, destined for the river Maas here at Grave" …so at least we now knew where we were!

The brigadier was most likely Sir Harold Pyman, the British Second Army Chief of Staff whose headquarters were also in Grave.

I remember the brigadier saying that he'd called us there to discuss the possibilities of mounting a mission across the Rhine to bring back a number of British paratroopers who had recently escaped the fighting at Arnhem. He then confirmed with Colonel Strayer, as part of our battalion was holding the section of river in question, if it would be possible to supply some of our men for the job? Strayer nodded politely as the brigadier continued by saying that the operation would not be without risk, and that he needed about 20 or so men to support British forces. We were required to form a bridgehead on the northern bank of the Rhine near Wageningen.

Sir Harold then outlined some of the logistics such as boat handling and how prior to the mission a pair of Bofors antiaircraft guns would be firing 40mm tracer shells across the river to guide the evaders toward the waiting craft.

I felt that there was no question that the British had come up with a top notch plan, but as the brigadier began to wind up his briefing, he told

Strayer that he was also required to supply several of his NCOs to lead the mission. After everything that I'd been through as an enlisted man, I couldn't just sit there and remain silent. So I raised my hand and asked if the operation was that important surely one of us officers should be going with them. The brigadier responded by asking if I was volunteering. "No sir, I never volunteer for anything." He asked me again, and this time I felt obliged to accept. The brigadier then asked if perhaps my colleagues would care to join me and of course they had little choice other than to say yes.

Directly after the meeting, Strayer designated Heyliger to lead the mission, now codenamed Operation *Pegasus 1*. The following morning Moose ordered a company formation for all those able to attend. In total 24 men were selected, who were mostly from 2nd and 3rd Platoons. Ed was to be accompanied by Smokey Gordon and Frank Mellett (who had just been promoted to corporal), Skinny and Popeye, Walter "Blackjack Lou" Hendrix and several others from 3rd Platoon.

Practice makes perfect

The next day Heyliger, Welsh and Shames returned to Grave with their "chosen" men. Royal Engineers (RE) from the 43rd Wessex Division were on hand to teach and oversee the boat handling on the Maas. "I didn't realize the river was so close until we came back to the dike in daylight."

The area north of Nederasselt was still strewn with gliders that had been part of the 82nd Airborne post-invasion resupply mission. From here the dijk ran parallel to the river and underneath the bridge, which had been captured intact by the 504th PIR on September 17.

To prevent anyone from drifting away in the strong currents, the RE had safety boats with outboard motors positioned either side of our training area. Below the embankment, a steep grassy slope descended down to the clear water where a natural indent on the bank provided mooring for our canvas boats. Here the British had rigged a series of pontoons which had been covered by heavy fiber matting to form a small pier.

Over on the far southern bank, directly opposite the jetty, Ed could see a concrete bunker and a large building, both of which became the group objective.

The river here was ideal for training because it was quiet and they could keep us contained. The engineers were located on both banks with megaphones, yelling instructions, while we paddled back and forth across the river. Smokey was constantly bitching about the Brits as they bellowed "Pull right!" or "Pull left!" The flat wooden hulls on the collapsible boats proved particularly challenging and despite spending most of my childhood rowing around Chesapeake Bay, the powerful eddies just off shore in the Maas kept sending us spinning around in circles. It took all day before the engineers thought we were ready to begin the second phase, which was to combine our newly acquired boat skills with assault training.

The idea was for a combined force from 2nd and 3rd Platoons to form a semi-circular bridgehead about 75 yards wide on the northern bank of the Rijn, with a machine-gun team on each flank.

In charge of one .30cal, it was Mellett's job [on the right flank], if we were ambushed, to provide interlocking arcs with the other gun controlled by Gordon, which would give us time to withdraw and form a skirmish line along the riverbank.

Meanwhile, using the telephone at the PGEM power plant in Ede, Major Tatham-Warter was able to communicate with David Dobie in Nijmegen to further develop the plan, now set for the night of Monday,

October 23. It is likely that Dobie advised Tatham-Warter to utilize the same route that he had previously taken down the shallow valley between Renkum and Wageningen toward the river.

Much to the amusement of Digby Tatham-Warter, the final evacuation point was given the codeword "Digby." The signal indicating that the group had reached the river was to be a red torch, flashing a "V" for victory sign. During their third communication, Tatham-Warter announced that the Germans were planning to evacuate the nearby town of Bennekom on Sunday 22nd, so it made good sense to bring the operation forward by 24 hours and maximize the ensuing chaos.

On October 21, to get things moving Dobie and his intelligence officer, Lieutenant Leo Heaps, a Canadian who had also recently escaped from Arnhem, moved into Strayer's CP at Hemmen (leaving Tatham-Warter in the capable hands of SAS Major Hugh Fraser and intelligence officer Major Airey Neave). Strayer and Dobie were no strangers as they had previously worked together in the UK during several exchange visits.

Operation *Pegasus 1* – October 21–22, 1944

Preparations were now underway across the Rijn. Maarten van den Bent was a resistance worker living in Renkum and well aware of the risks he and everyone else involved were about to undertake – two weeks earlier his brother Simon had been captured and executed by the Germans. During the evening of October 21, Maarten made a final reconnaissance with Major Tom Wainwright (officer commanding Support Company, 156th Parachute Battalion) and Dunkirk survivor Company Sergeant Major Robert Grainger (D Company, 10th Parachute Battalion). Earlier that day, after checking the road near the empty tuberculosis sanatorium at Oranje Nassau's Oord, the three men visited a nearby dairy farm belonging to Jan Peelen.

Peelen was a friend of Maarten's, whose local knowledge had been invaluable to the recent preparations. At the same time, Hendrikes van der Pol (codenamed "Flip") and Major Tatham-Warter – codenamed "Dr Peter," were looking around Peelen farm for a suitable final assembly point. Leaving Wainwright and Grainger at the farm, Maarten and Jan headed north through the woods toward a large hotel called Nol in 't Bosch, to scout a shorter route, and afterwards waited along Molenweg for Flip and Tatham-Warter to arrive. After a brief discussion they all agreed the troops would leave the road at a nearby bend, which offered clear views in either direction. At 2015hrs, after a brief map orientation session, Grainger and Wainwright changed into their military uniforms in the cellar of Peelen farm, before heading off to reconnoiter the route to the river.

On Sunday afternoon, together with the commander of the Ede resistance, Dirk Wildeboer aka "Bill" (who had previously arranged civilian clothing and ID cards for many of the soldiers), Tatham-Warter and Brigadier Lathbury met up with van den Bent, to give him the go ahead for the operation. Before going home Maarten was briefed by Captain Tony Frank (A Company, 2nd Parachute Battalion) who told him to expect an additional group of around 40 armed and uniformed British soldiers, led by Major Tony Hibbert and Dutch truck owner Piet Kruyff. The group of 40 was to arrive from Oud Reemst, near Arnhem and that it was Flip's job to make sure the two lorries arrived at Molenweg on time.

About 90 men, including 30 airborne medics, came in during the day, guided predominantly by nurses from the Red Cross and local boy scouts. Dressed as civilians, the soldiers spent the evening at a central rendezvous point, operated by Tony Frank, in a copse of trees opposite the sanatorium at Dennenrust. Later that same evening a wagon delivered weapons and uniforms to Oranje Nassau's Oord, previously procured through "Captain King." Major Tatham-Warter asked Maarten van den Bent to meet the vehicles that were expected to arrive around 1900hrs.

Later that evening, disguised as a lumberjack, Maarten returned to Molenweg where he was horrified to see two men waiting in a parked car. The occupants were part of a local neighborhood watch scheme and their presence forced van den Bent to relocate to another position further down the road. Not long afterwards, Jan Peelen arrived, carrying an old axe, and reported to his colleague that the vehicle had gone. As the area now seemed clear the two men began to chop and stack wood as they waited for the two lorries from Oud Reemst to arrive.

All systems go...

In the meantime, along the southern bank, members of H/506 were assigned outpost positions across a two-mile front. The first OP, over to the west, was located next to the brick factory at Wolfswaard, with the second centrally located opposite Wageningen, by the ferry crossing. The third outpost was situated 900 yards further east on the dijk near Randwijk. For a couple of nights before the operation, the two Bofors antiaircraft guns, half a mile apart, fired tracer shells across the river for several minutes every hour. The tracers were marking the left and right parameters of "Digby," the embarkation area, and as long as the escapees kept between these limits, they would be headed in the right direction. It was hoped that by firing the Bofors on a regular basis, they would not arouse suspicion or alert the enemy when the time came to evacuate the British.

By Saturday night all the boats had been placed under apple trees in the 3rd Platoon, E/506 area adjacent to the river. Night routes were laid out using engineer tape and additional artillery placed on alert just in case anything should go wrong. Throughout the evening of October 22, constant enemy mortar and artillery shells landed immediately behind the operational area. A barrage of rockets fired from a Nebelwerfer battery seriously wounded three men when they hit Colonel Sink's new regimental CP, located at Christine Hermine School in Zetten.

Back on the northern side of the river, as the paratroopers from Oud Reemst were unloading at Molenweg, a platoon of German soldiers came pedaling by on bicycles! Luckily it was dark and the British were partially hidden from view and the Germans continued on their way completely oblivious to what was happening. A group of about 10 resistance men were also on board the trucks, including Charles Douw van de Krap (a Dutch naval officer) and two recently escaped Russian POWs.

Shortly before midnight, after several small mistakes, Tatham-Warter began to seriously doubt Jan Peelen's ability as a reliable guide. It was never van den Bent's intention to take over but, keeping Jan by his side, he moved the group downhill in single file through the woods, onto a track densely lined with tall pine trees. They soon reached Peelen's cattle barn, where the soldiers changed into military uniforms and were with issued weapons.

At that point the column split into four groups. Flanked by two smaller sections, the main body, with Brigadier Lathbury, Tatham-Warter and Tony Hibbert, followed the advance party led by Major Wainwright and CSM Bob Grainger. Maarten van den Bent moved through the meadows west of Oranje Nassau's Oord, with Wainwright's group, and crossed the elevated main road from Wageningen to Renkum.

V for Victory

Earlier that evening Airey Neave and Hugh Fraser joined Sink, First Sergeant Carwood Lipton, Buck Taylor and the southern shore party down by the riverbank. Covering the actual crossing point with their machine gun were Private Edward "Babe" Heffron and Private First Class Jimmy McMahon from 2nd Platoon. Leo Heaps and David Dobie were part of the first phase and went across with Heyliger and Welsh. Dobie was given a field telephone, the cable of which was spooled into the water as he crossed. An area on the northern bank some 400 yards wide and 500 yards deep had been "boxed" for protective artillery and mortar fire. If anything should go wrong, it would be down to Dobie to call in protective fire.

Nearby, Ed Shames and his men anxiously awaited the order to embark. Suddenly from somewhere across the river a German machine gun opened up – quickly followed by several others. The firing continued for about 3 minutes before the night fell completely silent. At that moment everyone on the southern bank thought that the operation must have been compromised. Even Ed, by now a hardened combat soldier, felt nervous.

I did my best to remain calm but was so nervous that I kept regurgitating bile. This was not a good thing because during the course of the mission the acid actually damaged the fillings in several of my teeth.

Just before midnight a red flashlight was seen across the river, about 500 yards away to the east (right), blinking a "V" sign signaling the start of the operation. Moments later the two Bofors guns opened up to identify the embarkation area. The Americans, guided by the white minetape, quietly carried their boats into the water and proceeded to paddle, while enemy artillery flashed somewhere in the distance, silhouetting the men as they rowed across.

Because of the strong current a couple of the wooden framed craft collided during the slow and deliberate 5-minute crossing. Upon reaching the northern bank, Ed began to set up the defensive bridgehead on the left flank. Moving away from the river, Shames placed his men in a wide semicircle 10–15 yards apart, with the two machine guns placed on either side protecting the flanks. Ed then took up a prearranged position at the apex and waited. At the same time Harry Welsh and six men from 2nd Platoon, accompanied by Mellett and his gun team, spread out to cover the right. Leaving the riflemen to guard their immediate front with the beachhead now secure, Tech Corporal Ralph Stafford moved out on point, ahead of Heyliger and his team, who were mainly from 1st Platoon and Company HQ.

Before he departed, Moose half-jokingly said to me, "Shames, we are relying on you to still be here when we come back – good luck." While we were waiting for the search party to return, I sent Smokey around to check on the men.

Moments later Stafford nearly gave himself a heart attack when he spooked a nesting bird in the undergrowth. Shortly afterwards just as they were calming down, Heyliger was welcomed by Brigadier Lathbury who good-naturedly told him that he was the finest-looking American officer he had ever seen.

Tension began to mount amongst the rescuers when, as a diversionary tactic, British artillery started to shell enemy positions east of Arnhem. About 10 minutes later, much to everyone's relief, Heyliger reappeared with Brigadier Lathbury and his men. Immediately a signal was flashed across the river for the other boats, which were crewed by the sappers from the Royal Engineers, to come across. The British paratroopers came through the right-hand flank in single file as Welsh and Shames steered them toward the boats. It was hard to keep everyone quiet, as each man greeted them with "Thank you Yank" or "God bless you Yank."

Once inside the bridgehead, it took about 30 minutes and several trips to evacuate all 149 people (including approximately 130 British paratroopers and seven American airmen). At around 0120hrs, Shames was told by a British officer, "All present and correct, last man sir." Strictly speaking he was not the last man, as one of the two Russian POWs had disappeared during the journey. With that, the signal was given for the perimeter to implode and exfiltrate back to the river. "I think we were among the last to leave and from my perspective the patrol went like clockwork, both in its planning and execution."

Despite the obvious noise restrictions, the trip back was fast and furious, and each time a paddle came into contact with the wooden boat frame, it sounded like a large kettledrum being struck. "We had suffered no casualties and I believe to this day that it was one of my proudest moments in World War II."

Ironically most of Ed's men never got to see any of the British soldiers, who were whisked away before they had reached the southern bank. In fact, by the time Shames got out of the boat even the shore party had all left for a debrief. After arriving at Lonkhuyzen farm, each escapee was given a cup of coffee laced with rum and a complimentary carton of cigarettes, before being taken by truck to Nijmegen. Tragically as he was leaving Hemmen, Tony Hibbert's legs were crushed when the jeep on which he was sitting collided with another vehicle in the pitch darkness. As the main group was leaving, Sink invited Brigadier Lathbury, Lieutenant Colonel Dobie and a couple of other British officers back to his CP in Zetten, but they soon changed their minds after seeing the damage done by the recent Nebelwerfer attack.

The following day, Colonel Sink commended Heyliger, Welsh, Shames and most of the enlisted men who took part in the operation. For some reason, perhaps due to poor record-keeping, several names were omitted from the published citation, which read:

On the night of 22–23 October 1944 in the vicinity of the Neder Rijn about 1,000 yards north of Randwijk, Holland, First Lieutenant Frederick T. Heyliger and a force of 24 men of his company were selected to act as a covering force to effect the passage of 130 British Army Parachutists from enemy territory north of the Rijn to the south side of the Rijn. At about 2400 hours, 22 October 1944, this force crossed the river by collapsible boats with the utmost secrecy and efficiency. They immediately contacted the British Army Parachutists and by timely disposition of their forces carried out their duties with outstanding bravery. So exact was their planning and execution that although there was limited enemy fire, not one single casualty occurred. By 0130 hours the entire party of marooned British Parachutists and covering force as well returned to the south bank of the Neder Rijn. The courage and calmness shown by the covering force was a major factor in this successful evacuation. So well organized and executed was this undertaking that the enemy never knew an evacuation had taken place. All members of this covering force are commended for their aggressive spirit, prompt obedience of orders and devotion to duty.

No rainbow without rain

On Thursday October 26, the entire regiment was reassigned to Driel to defend the northeastern sector of the Island. Two days later, Colonel Sink switched areas with the 501st and relocated his regimental CP to Landgoed Schoonderlogt, a complex of three beautifully appointed farmhouses three-quarters of a mile northwest of Valburg. The largest house, previously owned by the Mom family, became Sink's CP, while another became the headquarters for 2nd Battalion. Close to Schoonderlogt were several batteries of 105mm guns, belonging to 321st Glider Field Artillery (GFA) Battalion, ready and waiting to support the 506th PIR.

For some time the enemy had been sending propaganda leaflets across the Rijn, packed into specially modified artillery shells. The projectiles gave off a peculiar sound as they exploded, alerting the men, who liked to collect the literature as souvenirs. As a response the regimental Interrogation Prisoner of War team (IPW) made a broadcast in German across the Arnhem–Elst railway embankment near Driel on the night of November 2.

The embankment, called Schuytgraaf by the Dutch, was over 50 feet high and marked the boundary at that time between 2nd Battalion and the Germans, who were now holding the ground on the eastern side of the tracks. The message asked for the enemy troops to give themselves up as further resistance was futile and no relief was in sight. When a prearranged barrage from 321st GFA began at 2130hrs, a number of enemy troops tried to desert but were shot by their own NCOs.

However, four did manage to make it across the embankment, and revealed amongst other things, that they had been fighting for fear of the more serious consequences of not fighting.

All three battalions were deployed around Driel on a regular basis with each rotation lasting four days. This had no effect on Ed Shames and 3rd Platoon who, along with the rest of E Company, continued to patrol the river. However, the open farmland situated to the east of the Baltussen factory and facing the railroad embankment became the new battle area. The regiment was deployed west of the imposing feature that led to the now demolished bridge, which had spanned the Neder Rijn near Oosterbeek and Arnhem. Taking advantage of the stalemate, Colonel Sink left Bob Strayer in charge of the regiment and headed to Brussels for three days' leave. Around the same time, Moose Heyliger was accidentally shot and wounded several times by a nervous sentry during a visit to 2nd Platoon one night out on the line. Moose was evacuated back to the UK and was quickly replaced by First Lieutenant Norman Dike, who had previously been working at Regimental HQ.

By late November the 506th prepared to be relieved and replaced by the 2nd Battalion, Seaforth Highlanders, who belonged to 152nd Infantry Brigade. At the time constant rainfall caused the Rijn to flood, forcing the MLR at Driel to be withdrawn by almost 500 yards. There was a rumor that the enemy might take advantage by demolishing part of the dijk wall in their sector. As a precautionary measure the paratroopers were briefed on Operation *Deluge*, the army's plan to evacuate all Allied troops to higher ground.

Thanksgiving came and went but the rain continued. As the flooding grew more widespread, it became obvious that the populations of Valburg and Andelst would have to be evacuated. For this the authorities created a secondary plan codenamed Operation *Noah*. Hundreds of women and children were sent across the Waal to reception centers in north Brabant. During the early hours of November 25, the regiment handed over control to the Seaforth Highlanders. At long last, after

71 days of hell, the 506th was being sent to a rest camp in northeastern France, at Mourmelon-le-Grand near Reims.

In total during *Market Garden*, the 101st Airborne Division lost over 900 men killed, nearly 4,000 wounded and 1,000 captured or missing. On December 3, under cover of darkness, as feared, the enemy demolished a section of the main dijk about a mile behind the railroad embankment at Driel. The massive explosion ripped a 150ft-wide gap and flooded the land east of the railway between Elden and Elst. Seeping through culverts and drainage ditches, the floodwater soon found its way across the Island, forcing British and Canadian forces, and the few remaining civilians, to migrate along the Waal toward Zetten and Dodewaard. By January 1945, Zetten had been virtually destroyed by an unexpected German counterattack. The vicious tank and infantry battle raged in the snow for several weeks until the enemy finally gave up and withdrew. Much of the Island became a "no go" area, a wasteland scattered with ruined buildings and corpses, which would not be declared "safe" for the civilian population to return until May 1945.

One Sunday, 58 years later, Ed was hosting a family barbecue in the backyard when the phone rang and he asked his granddaughter to answer.

I told Sarah to tell whomsoever it was that I'd call them back, but the man on the phone wouldn't take "no" for an answer. "Hello. Who is this?" "Erm, you don't know me but my name is Clyde Remy, and I've been looking for you for almost six decades." "I didn't know I was lost – what are you talking about?" "Well, you saved my life! You probably don't recall but I was in your boat when we came back across the Rijn." "You were in my boat? No that can't be, they were all Brits in my boat." "No, no, sir, there were also two American airmen and one of those pilots was me!" "You're kidding, I never knew that. Where are you from?" "Fort Collins Colorado." "Hey listen, Clyde, we are having an E Company reunion later this year, here in Norfolk. Would you come?" "I'd love to," he said, "but I'm dying of cancer and have maybe two months left at best." Sadly, Clyde passed away shortly before the reunion, and although we subsequently spoke several times on the phone I never did get to meet him in person.

9

"AND THE RAIN DRANK CHAMPAGNE"

Mourmelon-le-Grand, France

Situated outside of the garrison town of Mourmelon-le-Grand, Camp Châlons had been used by the French Army as a barracks and training area since 1857. Mourmelon was a dreary, long-suffering town some 20 miles from Reims, which for centuries had endured the embrace of soldiers from many nations. Caesar was said to have quartered two divisions of infantry and several squadrons of light horse here during the latter stages of his Gallic campaign. Despite its name, Mourmelon was really no more than a long street dotted with a few shops and cafés but was not to be confused with nearby Mourmelon-le-Petit, which was, as its name suggests, even smaller!

During the occupation the Germans had used the adequate facilities at Camp Châlons as a tank depot and airfield. As soon as the 506th PIR arrived, plans were commissioned by Charlie Chase to build a new set of toilets and washrooms to replace the existing French-style latrines.

Accommodation was basic but clean, with all junior ranks sleeping 32 men to a room. The senior NCOs fared better and were quartered in a communal barracks equipped with stove and basic amenities.

The camp became synonymous with reconstruction and cleaning as it was expected that the division would be here in winter quarters for at least three months' rest and recuperation. The first week was marked by incessant rain, which soon turned the ground into thick mud. In desperation gravel was "borrowed" from local roads, and bricks recovered from ruined buildings to create proper company streets and sidewalks.

The bad sanitation and poor food hygiene led to many cases of stomach cramps and dysentery. Despite these worrying issues, a belated Thanksgiving dinner was held and shortly afterwards the men began to receive mail from home. Miss Polly Baker arrived from the American Red Cross to open a new club, which was invaluable in rebuilding comradeship and esprit de corps. The only topic of conversation on everyone's lips was Paris. Backdated leave passes from Holland slowly began to filter through. Despite the fact that there had been several reports of a sniper taking potshots at Allied troops in Reims, the city was still popular, but ultimately everyone dreamed of Paris. Four years of German occupation had not seemingly changed the French capital in any way except for the fact that it now cost a small fortune to purchase anything. Many began their leave at the Café de la Paix or "Caffay De La PX" to meet up with old friends and decide which places to visit, while Parisians struggled by, clutching old scuffed briefcases containing family heirlooms they were hoping to sell to the new occupiers.

After what everyone had just been through, the three- or seven-day passes could not come fast enough. It was planned to send the regiment to the queen of European cities one company at a time. In the meantime many received passes to Mourmelon, which made Phoenix City, Alabama – nicknamed "Sin City" at that time – look positively Presbyterian.

Ed Shames was luckier and managed to get a 72-hour pass to Reims:

We had an impromptu officers' party at the Café du Palais, which was known by all as the Lyon Bar. I guess because of its art deco styled ceiling, which was similar to many of the Joe Lyons restaurants in London. While the champagne was flowing, this French guy came over and introduced himself as the Deputy Mayor of Reims! For a moment we thought he wanted to join us for a drink and told him to sit down. However, when he asked for penicillin, it kind of took us all by surprise. Apparently he needed the antibiotics for his daughter who was gravely ill and had been going from bar to bar begging for help. By the time he got to us, the poor guy was almost at the end of his tether, and we could clearly see the utter desperation, which was quite sobering. So taking our bottles of fizz with us, Joe MacMillan, Bob Moon, myself and a couple of others, commandeered a jeep and drove to the nearest medical facility where we set about trying to bribe the gate guard. An hour or so later a small box of penicillin appeared and we headed back to the Lyon Bar, where the mayor was patiently waiting for us. Of course we had no idea what happened after that, as we were due back at camp, but I sure hope that the Frenchman's daughter survived.

Things were getting back to normal with the usual drill and camp duties. The superb recreational facilities meant that those who showed any sporting prowess competed for positions on the regimental football, basketball, or boxing teams. Naturally Joe Madona was back playing right guard for the "Sky Train" football team, and he was looking forward to "The Champagne Bowl" trophy – a big match scheduled for Christmas Day against the 502nd PIR, "the Screaming Eagles," in Reims.

Five hundred and forty enlisted men and 38 officers were flown into Mourmelon from the UK as replacements The 506th PIR had suffered around 60 percent losses in Holland. Despite the enormous influx of new soldiers, the most radical changes were experienced among the officers. This was not surprising: 17 commissioned men from the 506th had been killed during Operation *Market Garden*.

At this time Shames was still getting to know his new company commander, First Lieutenant Norman Dike (who had replaced "Moose" Heyliger), as well as First Lieutenant Tom Peacock and Second Lieutenant Jack Foley. Jack was Buck Compton's new assistant in 2nd Platoon. Tom Peacock had just taken command of 1st Platoon and his assistant was none other than Ed's old friend from I Company, Ernie Mann, who had recently won a battlefield commission in Holland.

Their platoons being so badly understrength, Buck Compton and Tom Peacock had already made their selections by the time Shames was informed that replacements were still available. However, Second Lieutenant Richard Hughes, Privates Stephen Grodzki and Edward Stein were all transferred across from 2nd Platoon.

Hughes was a wealthy and exceptionally well-connected New Yorker. I believe that his grandfather had been Governor and later Chief Justice to the US Supreme Court. I'm not really sure why he was assigned to 3rd Platoon because we were expecting someone with slightly more experience. Perhaps Strayer or maybe even Dike may have figured that as our next assignment wasn't due to start until the spring, Hughes had plenty of time to settle in.

As luck would have it Shames, together with his inexperienced replacements, were about to be thrust into some of the fiercest fighting of the entire war.

After the transfers, Shames and Taylor were left with replacements Private First Class Henry "Hank" Zimmerman and Privates Levi Harkins, Patrick Neill, Frank Soboleski, Herbert Suerth and a couple of others. "They all looked so damn young, especially Suerth, who I nicknamed 'Junior.'" Shames himself was still just 22 years old.

Harkins, or "Big Chief" as we came to know him, was a Cherokee Indian from Tulsa, Oklahoma, and became one of my scouts. Somewhat unpredictable, Grodzki, because of his large forehead, was nicknamed "The Brow," after one of the villains in the Dick Tracy comic strip series. "The Brow" was posted in as an assistant machine gunner.

Despite the influx of new men, the platoon still only had enough manpower to field three squads, which were respectively led by Corporal Smokey Gordon, Sergeant Shifty Powers and Sergeant Art Youman.

By early December 1944, the Allied military commanders were growing uneasy about a possible German threat in Belgium. It had not gone unnoticed by many of the paratroopers that the nearby airfield had been unusually active, with scores of P-47 Thunderbolts constantly landing, refueling, and taking off. The enemy had attacked US forces along the German border with Belgium and the 101st was being sent in behind the 82nd Airborne to plug the gaps made by the enemy tanks.

Word filtered down from regiment to prepare for the worst. Shortly after 2200hrs on December 17, the 101st began to mobilize and prepare for movement. Hundreds of troopers who were still on leave in Paris had to be recalled to Mourmelon. The camp was in total chaos. All available equipment and supplies were secured and placed on transport provided by the logistical center at Oise near Paris. Nearest to Mourmelon, Oise was one of several enormous support bases belonging to the Southern Command Section.

The divisional advance party, consisting of B/326 Airborne Engineer Battalion, 101st Reconnaissance Platoon, and a detachment from divisional HQ were the first to depart. The 506th PIR had less than one day to get organized for the mission and everything had to be done at the double. Most of the weapons were being repaired by the 801st Airborne Ordnance Company and their small workshop had been overwhelmed due to an earlier decision by division to assess and repair just about everything unless it was in near-perfect condition.

When the order came for mobilization, the 801st went into overdrive and took on extra armorers; in the next 48 hours, around 5,000 firearms were overhauled. Those soldiers who went to the front unarmed – and there were many – were told that their personal weapons would follow within a few hours. When that did not happen many joked that they had been equipped with nothing more than a hangover and a pair of silk stockings! At best, the average rifleman, if he had a rifle, was issued no more than 12 rounds, and 100 rounds per machine gun.

The following day at 1500hrs, lacking any kind of pre-mission briefing and still with only a pitiful quantity of small-arms cartridges per man, the regiment, accompanied by the 321st Glider Field Artillery, clambered aboard 40 10-wheeler semi-tractor vehicles parked outside divisional HQ. Every rear-wheel-drive truck in the column was towing an open trailer weighing 10 tons. In total 380 trucks were used to transport the division.

As the convoy headed northeast across the battlefields of World War I, the men huddled together for warmth. "We had no winter clothing or overshoes and even RHQ didn't have a clue where we'd finally end up," recalled Ed. As the vehicle lights went on, some tried to sleep, while others like Ed stared into the night, lost in their own thoughts.

Originally heading for Werbomont, 30 miles north of Bastogne, the movement order was changed en route and the 101st Airborne was redirected to Bastogne. Lacking snow chains, the rear-wheel-drive prime movers were not suited to the icy road conditions meaning that the 107-mile journey there was fraught with delays. Finally, during the early hours of Tuesday, December 19, the 506th and 321st GFA de-trucked at a crossroad in the village of Champs, 3 miles northwest of Bastogne. Half-jokingly the drivers were told, "We'll be right back, so keep the engines running." Attached to the 506th was a team of four specially rigged evacuation jeeps from the 326th Airborne Medical Company, whose job was to transport casualties from the front-line aid stations to the divisional clearing hospital at Herbaimont.

It was an unusual way to begin a large-scale combat operation but this mission would become the most brilliant and courageous chapter in the history of the 506th Parachute Infantry Regiment.

10

"FAITH AND JUSTICE"

The Battle of the Bulge – Bastogne

On December 16, 1944, Heeresgruppe B (Army Group B), under the command of Generalfeldmarschall Walter Model (nicknamed "Hitler's Fireman"), made an unexpected thrust northwest across the German border into the Belgian Ardennes, jeopardizing the entire front of the US First and Ninth Armies.

At the time, the Allied footprint across this part of Europe was maintained by three main US groups. The forces covering the central Ardennes included the 4th, 28th, and 106th Infantry Divisions plus the 9th Armored Division constituting VIII Corps, led by Lieutenant General Troy Middleton, which, along with V Corps and VII Corps collectively formed First Army. The 9th Armored was on its first deployment and had never been in combat, while the 4th and the 28th Infantry Divisions would be reduced by around 50 percent after two weeks of bitter fighting in the Hurtgen Forest.

The German plan was to drive a wedge between the British in Holland and Americans in France, and to capture the Belgian seaport of

Antwerp. Known as Operation *Wacht am Rhein* (*Watch on the Rhine*), this "last hope" offensive was the brainchild of Commander-in-Chief for the West, Feldmarschall Gerd von Runstedt. The 88-mile-long Allied front ran due south from Monschau in western Germany along the Belgian border to Echternach in eastern Luxembourg, and encompassed a total force of 250,000 troops, who had over 2,000 artillery pieces at their disposal. Heeresgruppe B, 5. Panzer-Armee, commanded by SS-Oberstgruppenführer Josef "Sepp" Dietrich, and 7. Armee, led by General der Panzertruppe Erich Brandenberger, were tasked with the northern and southern flanks. The breakthrough was launched with the support of over 1,000 Stug self-propelled guns (SPGs). The German armor – Mk III, IV and V Panther tanks – penetrated over 50 miles in three days, taking the Allied defenders completely by surprise. It was the most serious defeat of US armed forces since Japan invaded the Philippines three years earlier.

Major General Norman Cota's 28th Infantry Division (ID), nicknamed "Keystone," fought a rearguard action to the north, allowing the 10th Armored Division time to occupy Bastogne and deploy its tanks. A town of 4,500 people, Bastogne was central in the province of Luxembourg in the southeastern corner of Belgium, close to the independent Grand Duchy of Luxembourg and the border with Germany. The town was a major transit hub, sitting astride the meeting of seven major roads and a railway. Taking Bastogne and gaining control of the road network was vitally important to the Germans and their ultimate goal to capture the seaport at Antwerp.

From the important road junction at St Vith, 18 miles northeast of Houffalize, the "Keystone Boys" were initially tasked with defending a 21-mile front extending south along the German border to the confluence of the rivers Sûre and Our. Concurrently, the 106th ID fought a bloody six-day battle in and around St Vith against 5. Panzer-Armee alongside the 7th and elements of the 9th Armored Divisions.

The 2nd and 99th Infantry Divisions from Major General Leonard Gerow's V Corps carried out another essential blocking maneuver at

Elsenborn Ridge. The battle caused serious delays to 6.Panzer-Armee and their attempt to reach the river Maas (or Meuse) beyond Verviers in the west. Despite the overwhelming situation facing V and VIII Corps, the troops from First Army did an incredible job, and their actions made a valuable contribution to the successful deployment of the two US Airborne Divisions.

At the time, the 46-year-old Divisional Artillery Commander Brigadier General Anthony McAuliffe was in charge of the 101st Airborne, after General Taylor had been recalled to Washington, DC, for a conference with the War Department. However, when word reached Taylor of the German breakthrough, he immediately made plans to return. Taylor's assistant, Brigadier General Gerald Higgins, had just arrived in Belgium from the UK and sensibly acquiesced to McAuliffe who had a better understanding of the situation.

McAuliffe had left Mourmelon on December 18, ahead of the divisional advance party. While on his way to Werbomont, McAuliffe decided to visit Bastogne and get an impromptu situation report from Troy Middleton at his HQ in the Caserne Heintz on Rue de la Roche. During this meeting, Lieutenant General James Gavin – deputy commander of the 82nd Airborne Division and temporary commander of XVIII Airborne Corps (part of the First Allied Airborne Army) – appeared with vitally important news. Gavin had just come from Werbomont, where Major General Gerow and V Corps were clearly in trouble. After some discussion it was decided to assign the 82nd Airborne to V Corps and let them deploy around Werbomont.

Intelligence revealed that Heeresgruppe B and 5.Panzer-Armee, led by General der Panzertruppen Hasso von Manteuffel, were now well on the way to Bastogne. After advising Mourmelon of the change in plan, McAuliffe sent his operations officer, Lieutenant Colonel Harry Kinnard to a crossroad, codenamed "X," near Herbaimont, along the N4, 7 miles northwest of Bastogne. Upon arrival Kinnard instructed the MPs to direct all traffic belonging to the 101st straight to Bastogne.

The first unit to arrive, 1/501, was ordered to take up positions in the village of Neffe, 2 miles east of Bastogne, where a number of German tanks were known to be massing. At that point the expected destination for the enemy armor was the river Maas and the garrison town of Namur in southern Belgium. The Panzer-Lehr-Division (an inexperienced training division) under the command of Generalmajor Heinz Kokott, and 2.Panzer-Division had already been forced toward Bastogne. Collectively these three main enemy assault groups made up the 47.Panzerkorps and would ultimately be tasked with the capture of Bastogne, while further north the 116.Panzer-Division, supported by 560.Volksgrenadier-Division, was targeting Houffalize.

Several makeshift tank units had been formed by the 10th Armored Division (from Third Army) to defend the eastern approaches of Bastogne. The 10th Armored − known as the "Tiger Division" − had dispatched two task forces, codenamed Combat Command A and B, to the battlefront. Each command was made up of around 50 tanks, one battalion of infantry, a company of engineers, and antiaircraft units equipped with "quad fifties" (a truck or half-track mounted with four .50cal machine guns).

Combat Command A deployed to the river Sûre on the southern flank of the German advance while Combat Command B headed to Bastogne. Led by Colonel William Roberts, Combat Command B was divided into three forces and initially deployed in a wide arc, facing east, 5 miles from the city. Task Force Desobry, led by Major William Desobry (CO of the 20th Armored Infantry Battalion) was sent north with 15 tanks to Noville. Task Force Cherry, under Lieutenant Colonel Henry Cherry, headed northeast to Longvilly. The US armored groups established roadblocks in an attempt to stem the advance of the 47.Panzerkorps.

The German assault was a desperate attempt to turn the Allied tide, and now the 26.Volksgrenadier-Division, together with the rest of 47.Panzerkorps, would be at the very forefront of the battle with the 506th PIR. Many of the personnel who made up the German Volksgrenadier, or "People's Army," units were conscripted and had received only the most basic of military training. Among the Volksgrenadier infantry were teenage boys and older men. Others came from across Europe as prisoners of war, press-ganged into service under threats of retribution. Despite their relative inexperience their devotion to duty together with the support of the numerically superior German armor made them a formidable enemy.

The presence of Task Force Cherry at Longvilly actually influenced General Fritz Bayerlein, the commanding officer of Panzer-Lehr-Division, into delaying his attack on Bastogne until the following morning. Bayerlein stopped briefly at Mageret after local intelligence reported that a convoy of US tanks was heading his way. His decision to halt was a grave error, for at that precise moment Bastogne was his for the taking: despite the advancing US armored column, in reality, little in the way of Allied combat power stood in the way of Bayerlein seizing the vital crossroad town. However, the early deployment of 1/501 turned out to be crucial and in fact coincided with the attack at 0730hrs on December 19 made by the over-cautious Bayerlein. The arrival of the 101st came as no great surprise to Hitler and his senior commanders, who had simply been hoping to achieve their aims before any Allied reinforcements could be deployed.

Back at Caserne Heintz, McAuliffe decided to take over VIII Corps' basement CP, while for reasons of safety General Middleton moved his command center to Neufchâteau, located 12 miles to the southwest. McAuliffe felt he could realistically hold Bastogne for 48 hours, before needing full backup from General George Patton's Third Army, which at that moment was 100 miles away, fighting through the "West Wall" beyond Saarbrücken. While Third Army was being redirected, Patton mobilized his 4th Armored Division, which was being held as reserve in Alsace Lorraine.

As Middleton was leaving for Neufchâteau he warned McAuliffe and Kinnard not to let themselves become surrounded. Although General

Middleton would be instrumental in organizing Allied tank tactics and roadblocks during the next few weeks, luckily McAuliffe and Kinnard chose to ignore his advice. Rather than create one straight line to the north, McAuliffe decided to gamble on a defensive ring around Bastogne, 14 miles in length, thinking it would be far easier to command and maintain.

Ultimately von Manteuffel would need total control of the roads to keep 5.Panzer-Armee freely on course and moving toward Antwerp. McAuliffe ordered every man under his command in the pocket of Bastogne (approximately 11,840 paratroopers and 6,500 other troops) to form and defend the perimeter at all costs. In contrast, the enemy forces directed against the 101st at that time numbered 38,000, although due to unforeseen operational issues, this would be reduced to around 20,000 shortly before Christmas.

The road to Foy – December 19, 1944

After Sink had posted guides along the road to Mande-St-Étienne near "Crossroad X," the regimental convoy was rerouted to Champs where the Fox had already established a forward CP. It was early in the morning and still dark when the regiment began de-trucking at Champs on December 19. Nobody seemed to know what was happening. After unloading, Ed and his platoon set about digging temporary defensive positions on the northern edge of the village. The ground here was muddy and waterlogged. Barely audible in the distance, Shames could hear explosions of artillery and tank fire coming from Neffe or Noville.

A few hours later the regiment was formed into a combat team, consisting of 1st Battalion, 3rd Battalion, Regt HQ Company and 321st GFA, and marched through Hemroulle along Rue de la Roche to a large field south of the barracks. Bringing up the rear of the column was 2nd Battalion. After the 321st GFA were sent to Grande Fontaine, the 506th waited for orders while Colonel Sink established a permanent CP in one of the accommodation blocks overlooking the holding area on the northern side of the caserne. During the delay before fresh orders arrived, Ed and his men waited in the bitter rain for almost five hours. A fortunate few had overcoats but most were clad in only basic combat uniform.

The platoon commanders briefed their men as best they could on the uncertain tactical situation when word came down that the combat team had been ordered to proceed north. Shortly afterwards it was decided to place 2nd Battalion in reserve at nearby Luzery, although 3rd Platoon, E Company was to be temporarily attached to 3rd Battalion.

Ed, Buck Taylor and the boys were ordered to advance 3 miles to Foy. The city seemed quiet. Along Rue de la Roche, before the soldiers reached the N30, the main road to Foy, those civilians brave enough to remain handed out scalding hot coffee. Within minutes the men came across elements of 10th Armored Division, who had by now been fighting a rearguard action for the last eight hours. A few hours before the 2nd and 3rd Battalions moved out of the city, 1st Battalion, 506th PIR, commanded by Lieutenant Colonel James LaPrade, was sent ahead to penetrate beyond Foy into Noville in support of Task Force Desobry.

Situated in the bottom of a shallow valley, Noville was surrounded by rolling hills, making the town difficult to protect from 2.Panzer-Division. It was vital for 1st Battalion to seize Noville in order to give 3rd Battalion more time to establish and strengthen its defensive positions at Foy. Since 0530hrs, 2.Panzer-Division had been attacking along the Houffalize and Bourcy roads. In the fierce fighting before 1/506 arrived, over 12 enemy tanks had been knocked out by Task Force Desobry between the hamlets Vaux and Cobru.

As Ed and his men marched north during the early afternoon of December 19, he was perplexed to see increasing numbers of troops from the 28th ID and remnants of 9th Armored Division heading toward them. Many of the beleaguered troops were horrified when they found out the paratroopers were advancing north to close with the enemy.

These people had cold-weather clothing and seemed far better prepared for a winter war than we were. The only extra garments we had at our disposal were either discarded by the "Keystone Boys" or liberated later from the Germans!

In contrast, other armored troops belonging to Combat Command B were more upbeat and handed over whatever spare ammunition they had. Although they were exhausted these men still managed to find a few positive words of encouragement. By the time 3rd Platoon had reached a Combat Command B weapons carrier, most of the available ammunition was gone, having already been picked clean by 3rd Battalion. Ed's men were now entering a region covered by dense spruce and evergreen woodland, not unlike North Carolina or the Brecon Beacons in south Wales. Dissected by the N30 and overlooked by undulating hills, the tiny farming community of Foy was built around a crossroad in a natural hollow and therefore the perfect staging area for the enemy to launch an attack against Bastogne. Overlooking the village of Recogne, about a mile northwest of Foy, is Château d'Hoffschmidt, known locally as "The Whitehouse." Built in 1842, the beautiful three-story manor house belonged to the d'Hoffschmidt family.*

In 1944, the village of Foy consisted of 26 farms and dozens of barns with a total population of around 130 people, and the close-knit community was dominated by the Bastin, Dumont, and Koeune families. Except for that belonging to the d'Hoffschmidts there were no cars, meaning that transportation was by horse, bicycle or on foot. The N30 ran straight through Foy and at the center of the village, overlooking a

---

* The d'Hoffschmidt family still owns some of the surrounding farmland as well as the dense area of woods along the ridge overlooking Recogne and Foy known as the Bois Champay (Champay Woods). At the time, Baron François d'Hoffschmidt owned around one-third of the properties in Recogne, the front doors of which were painted in a burgundy color with a white diagonal stripe. In 1944, two large ornamental ponds adorned the grounds in front of the château, which were also planted with European beech trees to create a luxurious rural idyll for the family.

crossroad was the Chapelle Ste-Barbe. Originally built in the late 16th century, the dour gray stone church would eventually become a focal point for Ed Shames and 3rd Platoon.

Most of the male villagers over the age of 17 had already left Foy and headed west, attempting to escape the prospect of German forced labor. On December 18, the first American convoys from Task Force Desobry moved through the village en route to Noville. That evening, as the sound of battle began to draw nearer, the remaining civilians took shelter in the basement of a substantial house owned by Jules Koeune, situated on the corner of the crossroad, diagonally opposite the church. The basement quickly began to fill up and when 3rd Battalion moved into the area, there were about 45 people, predominantly women and children, sheltering there.

When Ed and the others reached Foy during the late afternoon of December 19, 3rd Battalion was deployed along a 2-mile front stretching from the railway line (that ran southeast through Bastogne to Gouvy) to Recogne in the northwest. Brigadier General Higgins was there along with Colonel Sink when Ed and his platoon arrived behind the 3rd Battalion battle group. Sink selected a handful of men from G Company to act as security while he drove into Noville for a meeting with 1st Battalion. While he was gone the rest of the company took up positions facing toward Recogne. G Company was holding the left flank on the eastern side of the N30 aligning with 3/502. It was important for the Germans to control the road between the two villages as Foy afforded a potential safe passage for their troops and vehicles, allowing them to move northwest towards the high ground overlooking Hemroulle.

The line of defense (LOD) began in the west on the edge of the Bois Champay and ran down a wide logging track known as the "Route Madame" past Château d'Hoffschmidt along the northeastern edge of Recogne, before turning due south across open ground paralleling the road back into Foy.

Colonel Patch established his CP at Detaille farm, located on the extreme right flank of 3rd Battalion's LOD. The sizable two-story house had only recently been abandoned by the Detaille family and was marked on Patch's map as "Halte Station" because in the 1920s the building had been the rail terminus for Bizory. Centered on Foy, the sector allocated to H Company followed a secondary road that ran perpendicular to the N30 for about 1,500 yards all the way to the railway embankment at Detaille farm, which in turn aligned with the 501st LOD. Because of the wide frontal area the company was expected to defend, a decision was made by Colonel Patch and the H Company commander, Captain Jim Walker, to bring elements of I Company out of reserve and send them east toward the railway line and deploy them around the 3rd Battalion CP.

Foy was quiet and seemed like a ghost town except for dozens of animals that had been abandoned in their pens and stalls. The only sound was from the troops as they dug in; 1st Platoon, H Company was ordered to create a defensive bubble around the village, and established several roadblocks facing north. The H Company line blended with G Company to create a semi-circular pocket around Foy, coursing southwest to dissect the Bizory road, before meandering in a northerly direction, through the Bois Jacques (Jacques Woods) to Detaille farm. The open ground between the woods now occupied by 2nd Platoon, H Company, had previously been used as a quarry, which meant that the area was littered with dozens of holes.

At dusk a recon patrol from Volksgrenadier-Regiment 78 appeared through the mist, walking along the N30 right into the H Company front line. As one of the enemy scouts cautiously moved forward, he was challenged and mortally wounded at close range. After a brief exchange of gunfire, the enemy patrol slipped away, leaving the wounded scout lying sprawled in the road to die.

In Foy, a faint rumble of tanks could be heard coming from the direction of Noville. Now unable to communicate with 1st Battalion, Colonel Sink was anxious to know whether the road was still open and called on Shames for assistance.

As it was getting dark, the colonel drove up in his jeep and asked me to mount a foot patrol from Foy, along the main road toward Noville. Sink explained that we should patrol beyond a field full of haystacks on the southern edge of town. During the briefing I was amused to see Clarence Hester and Bill Leach both crammed into the back seat of the vehicle alongside Strayer [who was most likely working at Regimental HQ by this time].

Among the scouts I selected for the recon were McClung, Skinny Sisk, Cosmetic Moone, Strohl and Ed Stein. The heavy fog meant visibility was down to a few yards as we carefully worked our way into the drizzly blackness along the road.

Noville is situated astride a crossroad with roads leading to Bourcy in the east and Cobru to the west. Dominating the eastern side of the junction was a neo-Gothic church. Built in 1882, the pointed steeple of l'Église St-Étienne was visible for miles on a clear day.

On the outskirts, I placed my guys in all-round defense before moving the last few hundred yards with Strohl. Ahead, Noville was smoldering and bathed in a faint yellow glow. Peering through the mist and smoke, we could just about make out the silhouettes of what we thought were the haystacks that Colonel Sink had told us about. Strohl then commented that they were the funniest damn haystacks he'd ever seen. Suddenly we heard engines being started and it was then we realized they were actually Kraut tanks [from 2.Panzer-Division]. I put my lips to Rod's ear and whispered, "Let's get the hell out of here," and we carefully retraced our steps back to the boys. Once clear we double-timed back to the northern edge of Foy and reported to Sink, who inquired, "Well, Shames, what did you find?" "We counted 18 tanks sir." Strayer then asked, "What type?" "Big ones," I spluttered, before continuing "…I don't know, sir, we didn't hang around long enough to ask." Strayer wasn't impressed and tried to order me back to physically identify the enemy armor but luckily Colonel Sink stepped in and dismissed me.

The colonel then instructed Shames and his platoon to join I Company and wait for further orders.

During the night many attempts were made by the enemy against the 1st Battalion perimeter at Noville, using two or three tanks at a time, supported by infantry. Heavy artillery and tank fire could be heard throughout the early hours. Luckily the German commander, von Manteuffel, did not order the 2.Panzer-Division to launch a frontal attack along the N30 against the southern edge of town. Instead, he opted for a three-point envelopment, which likely consisted of the tanks that Shames had seen the previous evening, and which turned out to be a poor tactical decision.

In a further attempt to close the net behind 1st Battalion, Volksgrenadier-Regiment 78 was attached to the Panzers. Their commander sent several companies of infantry, supported by more tanks, to flank Foy and encircle Recogne. Shortly after dawn on December 20, the enemy broke through the fog opposite 3rd Platoon's positions in the Bois Jacques. Over to Shames' left in the H Company sector, several haystacks were blazing, set alight by German tracer rounds. A few moments later the clatter of enemy tanks became louder through the fog and the line began to receive heavy mortar fire. A 75mm gun attached to 3rd Battalion from the 321st GFA knocked out at least one enemy vehicle. Ed and his men did their level best to support I Company on their right flank, near Detaille farm, but as the ammunition for both groups was so low it was almost impossible. Moments later a jeep, which may have been from the 501st, drove up and the driver was heard shouting "Tanks, tanks!"

A German tank was now advancing down the railway toward Detaille farm. As the mist began to disperse an enemy armor-piercing (AP) shell hit the CP and went right through the building. Another German tank shell burst into the trees above Shames' head. From his position, Ed watched the medical evacuation jeeps from the 326th hauling away the wounded, driving like lunatics down the road back to Foy.

The next couple of hours were complete chaos, until the thick curtain of mist lifted. Luckily at that moment an M10 tank destroyer (TD) arrived in Foy and destroyed an enemy tank that had been causing problems for 1st Platoon, H Company. These TDs were armed with a 76.2mm gun, mounted on a highly maneuverable well-balanced turret system that fired a powerful armor-piercing round which proved devastatingly effective against the German Panzer IV and Stug SPGs.

The mist returned and descended across the battlefield, causing all small-arms fire to stop for around 10 minutes. Once again the fog slowly lifted and the enemy was in full view, firing at the paratroopers from very close range. The fog quickly descended again. A few minutes later as it was lifting, the paratroopers could see more enemy troops coming in, and word came down the line that 3rd Battalion was ordered to fall back about 700 yards to the high ground in the Bois Champay.

While Ed and his platoon were defending the line alongside I Company, his assistant platoon leader, Richard Hughes, took a small group and headed across the road in an attempt to stop some enemy troops that H Company had observed crawling through the woods. During the morning, Sergeant "Crash" Tridle was wounded and evacuated back to Bastogne. Around 1030hrs as H and I Company were pulling out to the Bois Champay, 2nd Battalion, who had been in reserve, finally came through and occupied their abandoned positions in the Bois Jacques.

Further north in Noville, 1st Battalion was also under attack. Over 20 enemy tanks formed a U-shape and systematically pulverized the town with constant gunfire. At approximately 1315hrs, following orders from 506th Regimental HQ and division to withdraw, Major Bob Harwick (who was now in command after James LaPrade was killed) gathered his remaining forces and headed for Foy in a ramshackle convoy of tanks and halftracks.

The Bois Jacques – Mouth of the Leviathan

While this was all going on, Lieutenant Shames and his platoon received orders from 2/506 (most probably from Colonel Strayer), to occupy a sector of woodland alongside the Foy–Bizory road on the far northwestern edge of the Bois Jacques. The new area was close to the quarry where 2nd Platoon, H Company had previously held the line.

All I had at the time was a map of Foy I'd drawn by hand during our pre-deployment briefing. Thankfully the proper 1:50,000 maps were issued shortly afterwards.

This area of the Bois Jacques was scattered with bricks belonging to an old hunting lodge that had been blown up by the Belgian Army in 1940. The forest partially overlooking Foy was to be Shames' "front room" and patrol base for the next two weeks.*

As Shames and his men were digging in they could hear the sound of small-arms and tank fire as 3rd Battalion took back Foy. The counterattack started at 1100hrs. With help from two tank destroyers from the 705th TD Battalion, the Germans were driven back a couple of hundred yards into the fields north of Foy.

Supporting the withdrawal on the edge of the village, Shames watched from the woods while another tank from the 705th TD Battalion forced its way through the back of a house to engage targets between Foy and Noville.

If it hadn't been for 10th Armored, then I don't think we could've stood up to the Germans with just our bazookas. With their up-armored TDs, the 10th were crucial to the outcome of the campaign.

---

* It is interesting to note that in 2015, the woods east and west of the Bizory road have been cut back, leaving a more exposed and open landscape. In 1944, the area occupied by 3rd Platoon extended further northwest toward Foy – as did the woods on the eastern side of the road, which were then occupied by the enemy. Also of note is the fact that during World War II the forest directly behind Ed's position extended all the way back to the N30 – which afforded the platoon safe passage to 3rd Battalion's CP and the main line of resistance.

"JUMP INTO THE FIGHT!" A recruiting leaflet similar to the one that encouraged Shames to apply for the 506th Parachute Infantry Regiment. (Paratroopers Historical Center, St-Côme-du-Mont)

Ed Shames, by then a staff sergeant, pictured here at Fort Bragg, North Carolina, shortly before overseas deployment in 1943. (Bob Webb Jr)

Staff Sergeant George Retan, Third Platoon, I Company, Fort Bragg, 1943.

Pictured in 1939, Private Joseph Paul Madona, Third Platoon, I Company, was Ed's closest friend from his days at Camp Toccoa, Georgia. (Bob Duval – Winthrop American Legion Post Historian, via Kenny Gunther)

The commanding officer of Third Battalion, Lieutenant Colonel Robert Lee Wolverton. (Bob Webb Jr)

Members of G Company close to the top of the infamous Currahee Mountain while in training at Toccoa. (Jim "Pee Wee" Martin)

Recruit Tom Newell, working out at the athletics field, Camp Toccoa, Georgia 1942. In the background can be seen the outdoor exit trainer and PLF ramps used for practicing parachute landings. (Johnny Gibson via John Klein)

First part of the bone-shattering assault course at Camp Toccoa. (Johnny Gibson via John Klein)

Colonel Robert F. Sink, commander of the 506th Parachute Infantry Regiment. (Donald van den Bogert)

Regimental Executive Officer, Lieutenant Colonel Charles "Charlie" Chase, pictured here in the United Kingdom at Marridge Hill Training area. (John Reeder via D-Day Paratroopers Historical Center, St-Côme-du-Mont)

The "goofy" commander of I Company, Captain Charles Shettle.

Lieutenant Colonel Robert Strayer, the commanding officer of Second Battalion.

The "shock harness": a test of nerve and courage, Fort Benning. (NARA)

One of three 250ft high jump towers at Fort Benning used for all aspects of parachute training including the "shock harness."

Carl Fenstermaker, Rod Strohl, Forrest "Gutty" Guth, and Amos "Buck" Taylor all from Third Platoon, E Company pictured at Toccoa, kitted up with dummy 'chutes for the outdoor exit trainer, seen here in the background. (Buck Taylor via Joe Muccia)

"Red On" – trainee jumpers about to exit a C-47 as the jumpmaster checks the drift of the previous stick, Fort Benning. (NARA)

Private First Class Don Ross, pictured shortly after the war. (Kenneth Ross)

First Lieutenant Fred "Andy" Anderson, Commanding Officer of Third Platoon, I Company. (The Anderson Family)

Staff Sergeant Jimmy Japhet, First Platoon, I Company.

Members of G Company pictured during the record-breaking battle march to Fort Benning in early December 1942. (Jim "Pee Wee" Martin)

Third Battalion chief clerk, Sergeant Major Paul Simrell. (Bob Webb Jr)

Runner, Private First Class Elwood Kendall – Planning & Operations (S3). (Bob Webb Jr)

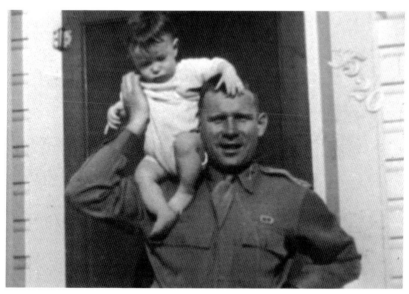

Bob Wolverton and his son "Lock", or "Lach" as he was known then, at their home in Elkins, West Virginia, 1943. (Mark Bando Collection)

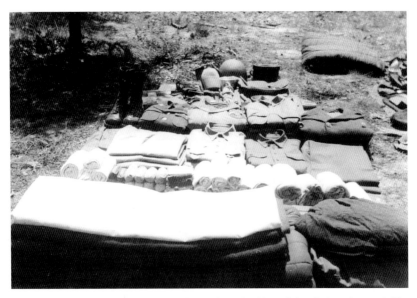

Camp Mackall, North Carolina, 1943. Layout of kit issued to each soldier including the instantly recognizable new jump jacket and trousers. (Tex Collier via Judy Gamble)

Woodrow Lee from the Medical Detachment showing off his jump suit in front of a typical barracks block at Camp Mackall. (Johnny Gibson via John Klein)

First Sergeant James "JP" Shirley (HQ Company) from Gordo, Alabama. (Bob Webb Jr)

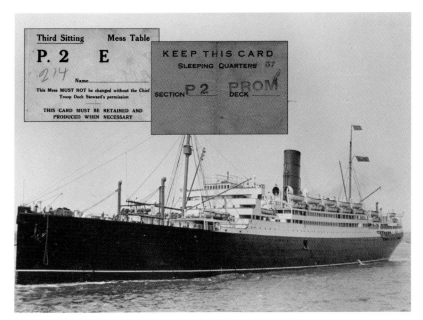

His Majesty's Troop Ship (HMTS) *Samaria* set sail for Britain from New York on September 5, 1943. The *Samaria* was an old British Cunard liner originally built to carry 1,000 passengers but was crammed with over 5,000 US troops for the Atlantic crossing, including the 506th Parachute Infantry Regiment.

Lovely view of Camp Ramsbury, England. Private First Class Jim Martin from G Company is seen here in front of the huts during the winter of '43/44. (Jim "Pee Wee" Martin)

The Blain family circa 1937. Ed and Paul Simrell were billeted with the Blains throughout their time in Ramsbury. Tom (rear), Gwen (fourth left) and their daughters, Margaret (holding cat) and Joan (front right). (Joan Smith)

1930s view from Hills Stores and the Blains' towards the Bell Hotel. The stables where Joe Madona was billeted are out of shot to the right. (Peter Mills)

An interior shot of Hills Stores where Ed helped out on Saturday mornings. The photograph was taken in 1947 and shows, left to right: May Edwards, unknown, Stanley Mildenhall, and John Lewington. (Joan Smith)

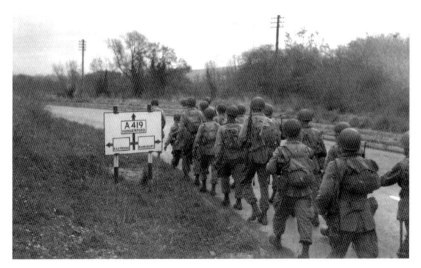

Captain Bob Moon leading the Regimental Communications Platoon on a route march while training in England 1944. (John Reeder via Roger Day)

One of several parachute drops and exercises carried out while the 506th Parachute Infantry Regiment was stationed in the UK. This photograph was taken near Ramsbury. (John Reeder via Roger Day)

Littlecote House 1944, Regimental HQ for the 506th Parachute Infantry Regiment and Colonel Sink. (John Reeder via D-Day Paratroopers Historical Center, St-Côme-du-Mont)

First Lieutenant Jim Nye, Second Platoon, I Company.

Private Bill Galbraith, Second Platoon, I Company. Bill was transferred to the S3 after Normandy and seriously wounded during the early stages of Operation *Market Garden*. (Bill Galbraith via John Klein)

Third Battalion Mail Clerk, Corporal Ben Hiner. (Bob Webb Jr)

Third Battalion Staff Officers, left to right: Major George Grant (XO), First Lieutenant James "Jeb" Holstun (S2 – Intelligence), Captain Charles Shettle (S3), Captain Stanley Morgan (Battalion Medical Officer), First Lieutenant John King (S4 – Supply Officer) pictured during a special parade at Littlecote House. (John Reeder via Paratroopers Historical Center, St-Côme-du-Mont)

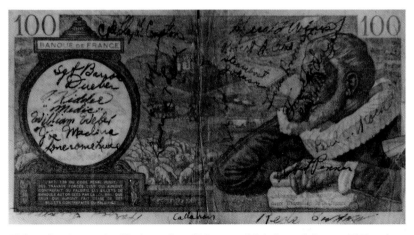

Ed Shames' invasion note signed by the members of I Company while in the marshaling area. (Ed Shames)

One of the last photographs ever taken of Bob Wolverton. (NARA via Paratroopers Historical Center, St-Côme-du-Mont)

Pilot and Commanding Officer of the 440th Troop Carrier Group, Colonel Frank X. Krebs, climbs aboard the lead plane "Stoy Hora" as an apprehensive Don Ross looks on. (NARA via Paratroopers Historical Center, St-Côme-du-Mont)

The number one stick: Joe Gorenc (second left), Bill Atlee (cigarette in mouth) and Ray Calandrella (wearing goggles) June 4, 1944. (NARA via Paratroopers Historical Center, St-Côme-du-Mont)

3/506 moving towards their designated aircraft on Exeter airfield, June 5, 1944. (NARA via Paratroopers Historical Center, St-Côme-du-Mont)

Colonel Wolverton and his number one stick at their aircraft "Stoy Hora" on June 5, 1944. (NARA via Paratroopers Historical Center, St-Côme-du-Mont)

Third Battalion Adjutant, First Lieutenant Alex Bobuck, and Sergeant Joe Gorenc (S3) at Exeter airfield on June 4, 1944. (NARA via Paratroopers Historical Center, St-Côme-du-Mont)

Third Battalion's D-Day objectives (orientated north): the wooden bridges at Brévands, May 1944, road-bridge seen here on right. (Crown copyright 1944/MOD, reproduced with kind permission of the Controller of Her Majesty's Stationery Office – with special thanks to the Air Photo Archive at Keele University, Staffordshire)

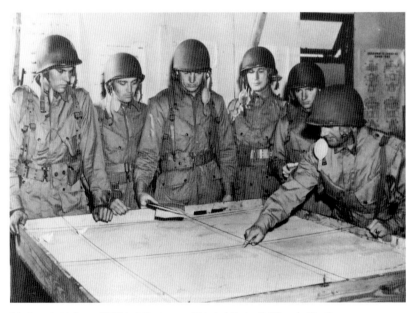

A basic sand table layout. (NARA via Paratroopers Historical Center, St-Côme-du-Mont)

The Gloria Milk Factory where Ed Shames landed on D-Day. Photograph taken in the early 1950s. (Michel Léonard)

Ed standing on top of his old position in 2005, adjacent to the Canal de Carentan, discussing D-Day with (left to right): Al Wenger, English historian, author Paul Woodadge and local French historical enthusiast, Michel Léonard. The church steeple at Carentan can be seen in the distance behind them.

View northwest across the river from the enemy-held bank toward the remains of the bridge and the aid station at Fortin farm (seen here in the distance on left). The photograph shows just how exposed and open the area was behind the bridge.

Allied aerial reconnaissance photograph taken on June 12, 1944, showing full extent of damage to both bridges and surrounding area. The vehicular bridge is seen here on right. By this time a temporary pontoon crossing had also been built and can be seen on far left next to footbridge. (Crown copyright 1944/MOD, reproduced with kind permission of the Controller of Her Majesty's Stationery Office – with special thanks to the Air Photo Archive at Keele University, Staffordshire)

The orchard at le Ferage, St-Côme-du-Mont, June 11/12 1944. A member of the 502nd Parachute Infantry Regiment is seen here standing next to what the author believes is Colonel Wolverton's helmet and liner, close to the spot where he was killed on D-Night. (Mark Bando Collection)

Chaplain Tilden "TS" McGee kindly gave assistance to Ed Shames under extreme duress, during the air attack on June 7. "TS" is pictured here on August 27, delivering a sermon at Littlecote House for those killed in Normandy. (John Reeder via Paratroopers Historical Center, St-Côme-du-Mont)

Dead Americans wrapped in body bags waiting to be identified and buried in a temporary cemetery. (NARA)

Pre-war view of the church square at St-Côme-du-Mont where 3/506 rendezvoused before the German counterattack against Carentan. The church tower was badly damaged by enemy shellfire during the early days of the invasion. (Michel Léonard)

A Stug IV knocked out near Carentan. This German SPG may well have been the one that destroyed two US M5 light tanks during the battle for Bloody Gully on June 13. (Joe Crilley via Mark Bando Collection)

This photograph was taken on June 17, 1944 and shows abandoned German equipment littering the church square at St-Côme-du-Mont. (NARA)

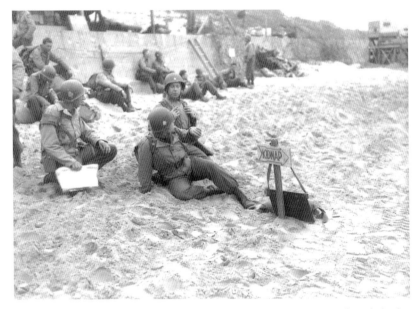

Lieutenant Colonel Charlie Chase talking to Captain William "Bill" Leach (Regt S2) on Utah Beach, shortly before returning to England. (John Reeder via Paratroopers Historical Center, St-Côme-du-Mont)

Portsmouth. The 101st Airborne Division is seen here after arriving back in the United Kingdom from Normandy. (Johnny Gibson via John Klein)

Ed had this picture taken in London shortly after picking up his new uniform from Savile Row in Mayfair. (Ed Shames)

Ed standing in the Great Hall at Littlecote House where he, George Retan and Lloyd Wills received their battlefield commissions from Colonel Sink.

Major Clarence Hester (Regt S3) to whom Ed was assigned shortly before the invasion of The Netherlands.

The Allied Air Armada turning over the town of Geel in Belgium and lining up for the drop zones. Note artillery or bazooka damage to church steeple. (Chris van Kerckhoven via Ronald Ooms)

Captain Bill Leach, Regt S2 Intelligence Officer.

2/506 jumping over Son. (Tom Peeters)

Bridge over the Wilhelmina Canal at Son, circa 1936. (Tom Peeters)

The German gun commander waiting to be questioned shortly after the two 88s were overrun at Woensel. (Tom Peeters)

Two troopers from A Company relaxing after reaching central Eindhoven at the corner of Stratumsdijk and Geldropseweg. (Tom Timmermans)

A soldier from 2/506 signing autographs in Eindhoven. (Tom Timmermans)

Captain Lewis Nixon S2 (holding map) and members of Second Battalion pictured here with a recently captured German *Umbauwagen*. This modified light truck was one of several commandeered during the invasion. (H. Teune via Tom Peeters)

Members of PAN bringing in more German prisoners. (Tom Peeters)

Typical liberation street scene in Eindhoven, showing Dutch underground members, dancing civilians and American forces in a captured *Umbauwagen*. (Tom Timmermans)

British vehicles covered in admiring Dutch children waiting to leave Eindhoven. (Henk Beens via Tom Peeters)

Dutch barber Martien van Ganzewinkel, pictured here in 1938 at his salon in Zeeland. Ed Shames was the first American serviceman to enter Zeeland, and his meeting with Martien was to prove extremely memorable. (Peggy van Ganzewinkel via Tom Timmermans)

Oisterwijk resistance worker, Dr Frans de Sain. (Peter van der Linden)

Doctor de Sain's house (left), Oisterwijk. (Peter van der Linden)

Pre-war view of the Volt N.V. Factory at Tilburg, taken looking across the courtyard from the director's house towards the machine room and chimney – E Block. Paint Shop (left) and Production Office (right). (Tilburg City Archive via Tom Timmermans)

Pre-war photo showing the interior of the power room at Volt N.V., where Ed used the engineers' service telephone line to relay information back to Eindhoven. (Tilburg City Archive via Tom Timmermans)

Soldiers from the 501st Parachute Infantry Regiment bringing in German prisoners near Veghel. (Tom Peeters)

The windmill known as "At Will" located in the E Company sector at Heteren, pictured in 1939. (Donald van den Bogert)

Corporal Walter "Smokey" Gordon, Third Platoon, E Company, seriously wounded at Bastogne. (The Gordon family via Marcus Brotherton & Joe Muccia)

Staff Sergeant Paul Rogers, Third Platoon, E Company, pictured here in Austria wearing Ed Shames' cap. (Karen McGee)

Darrell "Shifty" Powers, Third Platoon, E Company. Photo taken while at Toccoa in 1942. (The Powers family via Joe Muccia)

Captain Richard "Dick" Winters was Second Battalion Executive Officer when Shames took over Third Platoon in October 1944. (The Dick Winters Collection via the US Army Heritage and Education Center, Carlisle, PA)

Earl "One Lung" McClung, Third Platoon, E Company. (Joe Muccia)

Robert "Popeye" Wynn, Third Platoon, E Company. (Joe Muccia)

Lieutenant Colonel David Dobie, Commanding Officer of 1st Battalion, the Parachute Regiment, 1944. (Imperial War Museum via Bob Hilton)

First Lieutenant Norman Dike took over command of E Company in early November 1944 after "Moose" Heyliger was accidentally shot. Dike is pictured here with his English girlfriend at Littlecote House while working at Regiment. (John Reeder via Paratroopers Historical Center, St-Côme-du-Mont)

This picture most likely shows First Battalion preparing to leave Lienden en route for Mourmelon-le-Grand, France, at 0600hrs on November 26, 1944. Second Battalion departed the day before from Valburg. (Donald van den Bogert)

Paratroopers from the 506th Parachute Infantry Regiment advancing past Caserne Heintz (right) through the rain along Route de Houffalize (N30) towards Foy and Noville. (NARA via Reg Jans)

Ed's platoon sergeant, Amos "Buck" Taylor. (Joe Muccia via Amos "Buck" Taylor)

Pre-war photograph of the Chapelle Ste-Barbe at Foy. (Jöel Robert)

Rod Strohl was one of those selected by Shames for a night patrol towards Noville on December 19. (The Makos Family via Tim Gray & Joe Muccia)

Commanding Officer of Regimental HQ Company, Captain Gene Brown, was based with Third Battalion in the Bois Champay above Foy. Brown is pictured here before Normandy in his room at Littlecote House. (John Reeder via Paratroopers Historical Center, St-Côme-du-Mont)

Shames standing outside the basement of Jules Koeune's house in May 2014, from where in early January 1945, his patrol captured seven enemy soldiers dressed in American uniforms.

Probably the Panzer IV disabled by I Company at the crossroad outside Jules Koeune's house in Foy on January 13, 1945. (Jöel Robert)

View along the N30 north towards Foy adjacent to the "minefield" and Dr Ryan's aid station from the Collard house, showing an M18 Hellcat from 11th Armored Division, around January 14. (Currahee Scrapbook via Reg Jans & Robert Remacle)

Foy, January 14/15. This was the earlier route followed by Third Platoon into town. Note the edge of the chapel (left) and the Gaspard house (right) where McClung fired two rifle grenades at a sniper. The soldier in the jeep (right foreground) is from HQ Company, 502nd Parachute Infantry Regiment. (John Gibson via John Klein)

Post-war aerial photograph of Noville showing Third Platoon's route across open ground towards the Felton farm, seen here on the right. (Reg Jans)

View north towards crossroads at Noville littered with knocked out vehicles and showing part of the presbytery and wall (right) that Shames and Alley leapt over before the Mk V Panther opened fire. (Reg Jans)

General Taylor, Colonel Sink, General Higgins and possibly Captain Winters outside Noville church on January 15, discussing their next move. The tank seen here on left was packed with explosives and abandoned by 1/506 on December 20, in an unsuccessful attempt to bring down the church steeple and block the road. (Reg Jans)

Center of Noville after the town had been cleansed of enemy forces. (Joël Robert)

This knocked out Panther V is pictured shortly after the war along Route de Bourcy and could be the same one Shames and Alley encountered in Noville on January 15, 1945. (Reg Jans)

Ed at the E Company Memorial near Bizory and the Bois Jacques, thinking about those members of the company who did not return.

Regimental Aid Station, possibly at the schoolhouse in Ettendorf, Alsace, France. 2nd Battalion Surgeon, Captain Clements (right) hands crossed, armband on helmet. (John Gibson via John Klein)

General Maxwell Taylor addressing replacements at Château Walk, Haguenau during early February 1945. (Currahee Scrapbook)

Mourmelon – Presidential Citation Award for the defense of Bastogne. General Eisenhower, Max Taylor and other VIPs can be seen here reviewing the division on March 15, 1945. (David J. Phillips via John Phillips)

Over 12,000 soldiers took part in the parade. Note boundary lines marked out on ground as the lead column takes the first salute. (David J. Phillips via John Phillips)

In late April 1945, after being deployed to the Ruhr, the Regiment was transported by rail to Jagsthausen in Southern Germany, where Colonel Sink set up his headquarters at Von Berlichingen Castle. Left to right: Captain Knut Raudstein (CO 1/506), Major Dick Winters (CO 2/506) and Captain Fred Anderson (XO 3/506). (The Anderson Family)

Second Lieutenant Roy Gates joined Third Platoon at Mourmelon in early April 1945. (Joe Muccia)

Kaufering KZ-IV (Camp 4) had been one of ten labor camps situated around Landsberg in 1945. E Company was sent to KZ-1 to assist 12th Armored Division with the humanitarian clean-up. Both facilities were very similar in layout and emotional impact. (NARA via Gerhard Roletscheck)

The same train seen by Ed Shames and Carl Fenstermaker as they made their way towards Dachau on May 2, 1945. (NARA via Geoffrey & Gregory Walden)

The Jourhaus Gate was the main entrance into Dachau. Note that the sign placed above the arch by the occupying Allied Forces in 1946 is actually incorrect. (Geoffrey & Gregory Walden)

Dachau's *Appellplatz* or Roll Call Area viewed from the top of Jourhaus Gate, May 3, 1945. Following Ed Shames' visit, the first Jewish service took place (pictured here) and was led by US Army Rabbi, David Eichhoren. (NARA via Geoffrey & Gregory Walden)

View from the Obersalzberg road over Berchtesgaden. (David J. Phillips via John Phillips)

In the shadow of Watzmann Mountain, First and Second Battalion wait along Bahnhofstrasse for the final order to move into Berchtesgaden. (NARA via Geoff Walden)

The Berghof, Hitler's mountain home in Obersalzberg. SS annex (left) and famous picture window (right). (Collection of G.A. & G.R. Walden)

By summer 1945 regular tours were being conducted across Obersalzberg. This "tourist" shot was taken looking down from the Berghof's driveway eastwards (beyond white chair in left foreground) towards Hotel Zum Türken (far right) and Martin Bormann's house (left) top of hill. (Collection of G.A. & G.R. Walden)

Stunning view northeast close to zigzag path from the top of Kehlstein Mountain. The shallow valley seen below on left was the route taken by 3/506 on May 5, 1945, while the main body came in from the right. (Collection of G.A. & G.R. Walden)

Feldmarschall Kesselring and General Taylor enjoying the sunshine on the world famous veranda behind the Berchtesgadener Hof Hotel. (David J. Phillips via John Phillips)

Ed with the pistol belonging to Feldmarschall Kesselring.

Feldmarschall Albert Kesselring was arrested by Third Platoon, E Company at Saalfelden and is pictured here in the dining room at the Berchtesgadener Hof Hotel, around May 12, 1945. Left to right: General Taylor, Kesselring and two members of staff, Lieutenant Brown (translator) and General Jacob Devers (CO US 6th Army Group). (NARA via Geoff Walden)

Shames and Gates, Saalfelden 1945. (Karen McGee)

Ed's famous Sink Cup was one of a
limited edition run commissioned
by the Regiment to commemorate
each individual officer's service. (Sarah
Shames Ehret)

Muehlebach Reunion, HQ Company group. Left to right: Ed and Ida Shames, Jim Morrow, Forrest Troxel and
girlfriend, Ray Calandrella, and Johnny Gibson. (Bob Webb Jr)

1947 Divisional Reunion, E Company. Left to right: "Buck" Taylor, Carwood Lipton, "Shifty" Powers, Ed Shames (post-nose job), "Mac" McArdle, "Junior" Suerth and Bill Guarnere. (Joe Muccia via William "Wild Bill" Guarnere)

Ed Shames after receiving his Legion d'honneur, Bastille Day, July 14, 2014, NATO HQ Norfolk, Virginia. Left to right: Congressman Bobby Scott, French General and NATO Supreme Allied Commander, Jean-Paul Palomeros, and Norfolk Mayor Paul Fraim. (Harold Winer)

After consolidating, H and I Company dug in a few yards north of the road to Recogne and awaited further orders.

Finally the 1st Battalion task force made it back to safety and began regrouping on the ridge above Foy. With haggard faces and torn, mud-caked clothing, the men had been through a tough couple of days. Of the 600 who had originally gone into Noville, less than 400 returned to tell their tale. By 1700hrs and now in regimental reserve, 1/506 had moved into a complex of barns at Luzery on the outskirts of Bastogne, which had been recently vacated by 2nd Battalion.

That evening 3rd Platoon learned that the enemy had crossed the Neufchâteau road and the 101st was now completely surrounded and cut off from VIII Corps HQ.

More importantly this meant that if any of us were seriously wounded there was absolutely no chance of being evacuated. To make matters worse, word also filtered down that the main evacuation hospital at "Crossroad X" near Herbaimont, had also been overrun and captured! The 2nd Battalion was now holding the main line of resistance from the eastern edge of Foy through the Bois Jacques to the railway embankment at Detaille farm, which was being used as a command post by F/506.

The stressful situation began to take its toll, particularly on the more inexperienced officers and men.

During those first few days in the Bois Jacques, we all began to notice the smell of alcohol on Richard Hughes' breath. When I challenged him, he openly admitted to drinking on duty. I had no idea where the alcohol came from but to me this was totally unacceptable behavior and wouldn't be tolerated. Immediately afterwards, Paul Rogers and Buck Taylor stepped in as my "assistants"– the only difference was that the men didn't have to call them "Sir."

After Crash Tridle was hit, I also asked Paul to take over the 60mm section and remain behind in the bivouac area overseeing our defenses. Paul or Rod Strohl always made sure that whoever was crewing the mortar was up to date with range cards and any prerecorded targets. For the most part Hayseed worked with Buck Taylor to handle base administration and passwords for any 3rd Battalion CP or OP we would be encountering. This was done by either my runner Mac, or via our radio operator Private James "Moe" Alley, allowing me more time to concentrate on mission preparation and planning. Paul would often help select the men for our patrols and made sure each individual was prepared for whatever job he was expected to do. Before leaving the area our guys would go through patrol order, hand signals, time limitations, immediate actions on emergency RVs and marking.

The Twilight Zone

On December 21, 1944, 3rd Battalion LOD was no more than a single defensive belt, and at 0330hrs they came under attack once again. Enemy armor advancing through the fog down the N30 was met with bazooka fire and some well-placed rounds from the two M10 tanks still attached from the 705th TD Battalion. Due to the encirclement the artillerymen had to conserve ammunition and were only permitted to fire on specific targets, which did not help the situation on the front line. Previously the German attacks had been held back by the US artillery based at Grande Fontaine and Savy, 500 yards east of the barracks in Bastogne. Along with its own 321st GFA, vitally the 101st Airborne Division had around 130 guns at its disposal, including a significant number of M1 155mm field guns, nicknamed "Long Toms." With a range of up to 14 miles, the 155s were operated by the 333rd Field Artillery Group, whose African-American crews were part of VIII Corps and had recently been incorporated with a battery from another black unit, the 969th Field Artillery Battalion. During the first two days, artillery ammunition was in plentiful supply and no doubt helped to keep the German forces pinned down during the early stages of the battle.

Because of the heavy fog, dozens of Volksgrenadiers, supported by a few tanks, succeeded in re-entering Foy. In some instances fighting was hand-to-hand. At 0600hrs the order came from regiment for 3rd Battalion to withdraw up the ridge and back into the Bois Champay, leaving the civilians still hiding in the basement of Jules Koeune's house to their fate.

Shortly after midnight on the 21st, a patrol from 2/506, which was holding the Bois Jacques to 3rd Platoon's right, had discovered dozens of footprints near the railroad tracks around Detaille farm and traced them to a patch of woods behind the eastern MLR. The enemy troops were part of a reconnaissance group from Regiment 77, 26. Volksgrenadier-Division, who were in the process of attacking Bizory.

During the early hours of the morning, 250 Volksgrenadiers crossed the fields adjacent to the Bizory road. Avoiding the 506th CP, the enemy group slipped through the mist and swung northeast before reaching the railway embankment close to the D/501 bivouac area. Realizing the woods were occupied and with daylight fast approaching, the Germans decided to cross over and find shelter in dense woodland on the other side of the tracks. The Germans sent out recon patrols and OPs to protect their flanks. At around 0830hrs D and F Companies from the 506th heard German voices coming from the woods behind them and immediately formed a containment force with the 501st to block all possible escape routes. Thirty minutes later, 1st Battalion was mobilized and dispatched from Luzery and successfully eliminated the enemy force taking many prisoners, although it came at a high price.

After the unexpected German incursion, the next few days became a standoff with patrols from either side constantly operating through the woods. E Company soon became aware that Lieutenant Dike was not performing well and, when he bothered to come out of his foxhole, seemed unable to make the vital command and control decisions needed when the going got tough.

With Colonel Strayer still at Regimental HQ, Captain Winters was now in temporary command of 2nd Battalion. Ordinarily Winters and Nixon issued the patrol orders for the battalion but Ed believes this was not always the case for 3rd Platoon.

Sometimes I'd be briefed in the Bois Jacques for the upcoming evening by either Hester, Leach, or Captain Gene Brown, the commanding officer of Regt HQ Company, who was based with 3rd Battalion in the Bois Champay. Hester and Brown gave us grid references but left the execution of the patrols up to me. For instance Hester, sometimes by himself, would come over to specifically brief me on the map with what they wanted the platoon to do each night. The experienced men were rotated on the patrol roster, one night on, one night off, but the new people like Suerth and Soboleski, we couldn't take them out, so they remained behind with Hayseed and Buck to look after security.

According to Ed, some of 3rd Platoon's patrolling was done at Recogne, which had been badly ravaged by shellfire. Located on the southeastern edge of the grounds belonging to d'Hoffschmidt Château was a large tenant farm run by Nester Degives, from where there was direct road access to the ridge and the Bois Champay. The logging track, Route Madame, became vital to 3rd Platoon as they moved into Recogne.

Above Degives farm, lined by tall beech trees, Route Madame marked the extreme western edge of the 506th PIR operational area. The unmetalled road ran downhill for approximately 600 yards to the beautiful farmhouse, surrounded by five barns, which had been recently abandoned by the Degives family. Extending for about 250 yards and descending from the ridge alongside Route Madame was a shoulder of woodland that became part of the permanent MLR for G Company. Although partially overlooked by the château, Recogne was destined to become a no-man's-land that could only be patrolled at night by either side.

Much of the time was now being spent on improving defenses. The most lethal enemy actions were the "tree bursts" that sent shrapnel of all shapes and sizes ripping through branches into foxholes. Everyone started to cover their trenches with any logs they could find, using soil to fill the gaps.

Some of our people actually used German bodies to cover their positions, which of course froze solid once the temperature began to drop. Eventually the engineers turned up and cut bigger logs but that wasn't until much later, so until then we just had to make do with whatever was available.

When 3rd Platoon patrolled into Recogne, avoiding Degives farm, they would penetrate through the village, setting up listening posts to determine what buildings were occupied and by whom. It wasn't unusual for Shames to have several three-man teams in Recogne and Foy on any given night.

Generally Shifty, Popeye, McClung, Skinny and Smokey Gordon would lead the teams. Combat patrols were a different thing altogether and usually numbered around six people and were required to capture enemy soldiers for interrogation.

The worst winter in 50 years

In 1944, the trees covering the 3rd Battalion MLR were planted in such a way as to create two long, dense protrusions of woodland – these vitally important features are referred to in this book as the "Western Finger" and the "Eastern Eye." At the time, G Company was responsible for the largest section of the Bois Champay, covering a front 800 yards wide which ran east across three sectors before it tied in with I Company. G Company's 2nd Platoon was based in the "Western Finger," which when viewed from above formed a distinctive stepped shoulder pattern in the shape of an outstretched "W."

The "Eastern Eye" was located in the sector shared by H and I Companies and ultimately became the doorway into Foy for the 506th PIR. Being the closest point to the village, a number of forward OPs were established there. A single line of trees ran northwest midway between the lookout area and the village. At the center of this feature, directly opposite the "Eye," the tree line broke into a number of isolated clumps which, over the next three weeks, became forward listening posts for 3rd Battalion and the regiment.

Along the road south of Bastogne on December 22, a party of four Germans had approached US lines under a "white flag" of truce. It is believed that the commander of the 47.Panzerkorps, Heinrich von Lüttwitz, personally drafted a letter asking for the American commander to surrender. The original message read:

To the U.S. Commander of the encircled town of Bastogne: The fortune of war is changing. This time the U.S. forces in and near Bastogne have been encircled by strong German armored units. More German armored units have crossed the river Our near Ortheuville, have taken Marche and reached St. Hubert by passing through Hompré-Sibret-Tillet. Libramont is in German hands. There is only one possibility to save the encircled U.S. troops from total annihilation: that is the honorable surrender of the encircled town. In order to think it over a term of two hours will be granted beginning with the presentation of this note. If this proposal should be rejected one German Artillery Corps and six heavy AA Battalions are ready to annihilate the U.S. troops in and near Bastogne. The order for firing will be given immediately after this two hours' term. All serious civilian losses caused by this artillery fire would not correspond with the well-known American humanity.
Signed: The German Commander

The now famous response from Tony McAuliffe and his staff was simply one word: "NUTS." Although enemy attacks continued, the threatened heavy artillery barrage was in fact delayed due to other German operational commitments around the perimeter, and subsequently von Lüttwitz was reprimanded for ordering the artillery to refocus its attention back on Bastogne.

On December 23, when the first snow began to fall, 3rd Platoon started insulating the bases of their trenches with layers of branches and ferns. On the front line, the troops were not allowed to light fires at night, although they could melt snow or boil water during daylight if their fire was well hidden. Sourcing drinking water was always a problem. Melting the snow was often the only option available but it usually took five helmets-full of snow to melt enough water to fill one canteen, which then had to be turned upside down to stop the liquid nearer to the lid from freezing solid. Eating snow was not an effective option as it lowered the core temperature, forcing the human body to burn more energy to keep warm. As food was in such short supply, many were forced to ration themselves with one meager meal per day and pretty quickly, without some means of holding them up, it was all a man could do to keep his pants from falling around his ankles.

Most of our patrolling was designed to let the enemy know that despite the situation we were still on the offensive. I made sure my guys were well drilled – it wasn't luck that got us through but training. I don't think Norman Dike or even one or two of the other officers really gave a damn about casualties but I did. We spent our downtime honing our patrol skills, all-round defense and mission preparation. I was very hard on the guys and kept hammering it in that this was all for their safety. Some kids like "Cosmetic" Moone and Joe Ramirez just wouldn't listen and became quite problematic as they tried to constantly dodge my hastily organized lessons. Whenever we went out from the "Eastern Eye" or Route Madame we never used the same routes if we could help it. Most nights we'd move across the N30 via the woods directly behind our area and report into the 3rd Battalion CP before dispersing for our separate preplanned missions.

It was Ed's determination to prepare his men for battle as thoroughly as possible that would save lives time and time again.

Located about 350 yards south of Route Madame, the 3rd Battalion CP was well hidden in the Bois Champay behind H Company on the site of an old quarry about 250 yards west of the N30. At over 10ft deep, the ancient pit was ideal and measured about 25ft in diameter. Although covered with a thick layer of logs it was possible to stand up inside and the natural bunker provided a safe haven for Captain Gene Brown, Colonel Patch and their respective staff.

Despite the light covering of snow, the overcast weather began to disperse, and by early afternoon of December 23, hundreds of vapor trails from Allied bombers (bound for Germany) began to appear in the clear blue sky. This first day of good weather also gave the Allied air forces an unlimited ceiling and free rein across the battle area. Air panels were displayed on the ground, marking friendly positions, while American P-38 Lightnings, P-47 Thunderbolts, and P-51 Mustangs alongside Typhoons, Hurricanes and Spitfires from the Royal Air Force attacked German tanks, troops and artillery positions.

The improvement in weather also brought another surprise. A few miles behind 3rd Platoon's positions in the Bois Jacques, the first of several massive aerial resupply drops came in carrying much-needed ammunition, food and medical supplies. In total approximately 238 aircraft reached the target on December 23, with the last arriving at 1606hrs, signifying the end of a historic day for the defenders of Bastogne.

"Although the first resupply mission was wonderful it had no direct effect on me or my men," recalls Shames, "in fact 3rd Platoon's patrol tasks were still ongoing and relentless." A few of Ed's guys, including Moone and Ramirez, as well as Shifty Powers, believed that the platoon was being abused.

One of the boys, who shall remain nameless, thought we were being pushed way beyond our limits, and one night in particular, he actually refused to go out on a patrol – can you believe that? He had a bad feeling and told me he didn't want to leave the platoon area. I knew him well enough by then to empathize but I had to point out that what he'd just done could be construed as a court martial offense. I was terrified that if his attitude caught on it might cause a complete breakdown in discipline. So I quietly stood him down and before he went back to his foxhole whispered, "We'll deal with this in the morning, OK?" Luckily for me, Moe Alley volunteered to take his place.

The next day the soldier reported for duty, expecting to be punished, and we carried on as if nothing had happened. Not a single word was said. I never let the others know how afraid I was for fear that they might turn against me, and did my best to keep the incident quiet. The following evening, the platoon was tasked with a number of listening patrols and I decided to stay behind and catch up on some sleep. I tossed and turned throughout the night, worrying about the boys, especially after a couple of patrols were late returning. It was then that I realized that regardless of the circumstances I'd rather be out there than back here.

Shadows of Christmas in No-man's-land

By holding a tight and well-connected perimeter, which became known as "the hole in the donut," the 101st Airborne Division was able to keep the enemy infantry and armor away from Bastogne. During the build-up to Christmas, the divisional defense force was regrouped and the 506th PIR combat team augmented by several antitank and antiaircraft batteries and two platoons of tanks from the 705th TD Battalion. So far, the 101st Airborne's luck had held as the Germans had chosen not to focus their attacks in any one particular place but instead launched small probing assaults to try to locate US weak points. However, the regiment did not know that the enemy was planning to build up strength in Recogne, Cobru, and, more importantly, on the eastern side of the MLR. At 0830hrs on Christmas Eve, the Volksgrenadiers launched a company-sized reconnaissance attack from their positions across the road in the Bois Jacques against E and F Companies. German casualties were heavy, and although the assault failed, it showed that the enemy force which had been scaled down to fight in other areas around the Bulge was still active and ready to engage.

To counter the German propaganda leaflets, division wrote and printed a special Christmas message on behalf of General McAuliffe, stating:

The Allied troops are counterattacking in force. We continue to hold Bastogne. By holding Bastogne we assure the success of the Allied Armies. We know that our division commander [who was still on his way back to the front] General Taylor, will say: "Well done!" We are giving our country and our loved ones at home a worthy Christmas present and, being privileged to take part in this gallant feat of arms, are truly making for ourselves a Merry Christmas.

Over in the Bois Jacques, 3rd Platoon had been spending a very uncomfortable Christmas Eve fighting off one particular enemy patrol that had managed to infiltrate into the edge of their patrol base. Squad leader Smokey Gordon was shot and severely wounded while manning his machine gun during the early stages of the attack. The bullet entered Corporal Gordon's chest just below his collarbone and exited through his back. One of the evacuation jeeps from the 326th Airborne Medical Company quickly arrived and took Smokey back to Bastogne where he remained until the siege was broken. While Ed was dealing with the aftermath of the attack, Buck Taylor decided to take Shifty and another man and head across the road to check for German casualties. After searching several corpses, Taylor penetrated deeper into the woods until they came upon three or four enemy soldiers at the end of a tree line. Although they had seen each other, no shots were fired as Buck quickly returned to the patrol area. After receiving news that Harry Welsh had just been wounded over at HQ Company, Ed was not best pleased to learn that Buck and Shifty had left the patrol area without his permission.

The assault left almost 40 German dead. One of these was now lying adjacent to Ed's foxhole.

The dead Volksgrenadier made a nice addition to our "front room," and we subsequently used his frozen body as a kind of makeshift sofa! Afterwards everyone got into the habit shaking the Kraut's hand every time they moved in and out of the patrol area.

Sometime around this period a rumor began to circulate that a soldier from another company had been stabbed during a German night patrol. It was said that the Germans were specifically looking to murder or capture anyone they found asleep in a foxhole! We heard later that it was actually a guy from D Company who woke up to find the German crawling toward him. The Kraut started thrashing around the trench with his bayonet when the trooper grabbed the man's arm and pulled him down before stabbing the guy twice with his own blade. He pushed the body out of the hole, and the "corpse" spent the rest of the night moaning and died the following morning from blood loss and exposure.

The first really heavy snowfall came at midday on Christmas Eve. At the time the division was issued overshoes, but most of these never reached the front-line troops. As a stopgap, burlap sacks were issued and all available white cloth requisitioned for camouflage purposes.

Up until this point we figured that the weather couldn't get any worse – but we were in for a big surprise. Christmas Eve to us was just another cold, miserable day and brother was it miserable. In a desperate attempt to combat the falling temperatures, I wrapped burlap around my boots and managed to "liberate" a German greatcoat along with a pair of fingerless mittens. Despite looking like scarecrows, every morning no matter what, I'd have my people shave, because I figured if they looked like soldiers, they might behave like soldiers.

During the afternoon, over in the western sector, elements of 3rd Battalion went to the assistance of the 502nd which was in contact with enemy tanks and infantry attacking from the direction of Recogne. Finally, around midnight on Christmas Eve, the gunfire subsided as the German attack ground to a halt.

Was it something that I said?

At first light on Christmas Day, I was ordered to send some of our men back to Bastogne to collect parachute bundles that had been dropped the day before. Christ Almighty, we'd only just got back from a very tough night and because of all the recent enemy activity, everyone on the patrol roster had been stretched to the limit. For me personally this was a low point as I'd spent the last few hours of darkness trying to sleep on the ground behind my foxhole terrified of being knifed by a Kraut.

Shortly after daylight, Buck Taylor and Paul Rogers explained that battalion wanted me to send six to eight men back to Bastogne.

Begrudgingly, Shames sent McClung and two others over to company HQ. A few minutes later, Jack Foley came across to speak with Ed. Jack was not happy about the number of people Shames had supplied for the task.

I wouldn't budge and eventually Jack gave in and accepted my decision but he wasn't happy.

Foley was now in command of 1st Platoon after Lieutenant Peacock had been sent home shortly before the encirclement, on a "30 Day Golden Ticket" furlough lottery.

I must say, for the record, that Jack went on to become a superb platoon leader and was an incredible asset to E Company.

When the DZ party returned, McClung said there was a package for me. I was absolutely ecstatic and imagined a pair of gloves, a hat or a muffler. Enthusiastically, I tore open the small parcel sent by Ida, and was underwhelmed to find of all things a damned fountain pen along with a neatly folded letter ... Jeez. Somewhat frustrated, I threw the pen into the snow and went about my business. A couple of hours later, Rod Strohl came over and said, "Here Lieutenant, you dropped your pen." "No, no, no, I threw it away in disgust! What a piece of crap. Why in God's name did she send me that?" "Well you better take another look, cap, because this thing is fabulous and made of solid 14-carat gold." "Sure it is, sure it is" – I thought he was joking because the boys were always pulling pranks, but he was quite right. I told him to hell with the pen and that he could keep it. When I read Ida's letter it was clear that, after taking advice from my sister Anna, she presumed that we were well catered for and that the beautiful high-quality pen, manufactured by Eversharp and engraved "Lt E. D. Shames" – which cost her an astonishing $245.00 – would make an ideal Christmas gift! The next day Rod gave the pen back to me and this time I was man enough to accept the gift for what it was – a wonderful gesture from the girl I planned to marry, although she didn't quite know that at the time.

Later in the afternoon Herb Suerth decided to visit a chum in the next sector, which was under control of Buck Compton and 2nd Platoon.

It seemed to me at the time that Compton was undergoing some sort of breakdown due to combat fatigue.

Rightly or wrongly, Ed was (and even to this day still is) intolerant of Buck's situation, believing that he should have stepped down days earlier. After what had recently happened with the enemy attack everyone was now feeling the strain, although they dealt with it in different ways.

At the time, I guess I was hard to get along with but it was just my way of handling the pressure. Keeping the fear within me … if you know what I mean.

As Suerth trudged through the dense snow-covered forest into 2nd Platoon's area, Compton strode over and berated him for not following the recognized protocols when traveling between sectors.

Of course before leaving, Suerth had made sure he had permission from Buck Taylor, and as Junior wasn't on the patrol roster, it didn't really matter to me, just as long as he came back before nightfall.

Shortly after Suerth returned to his own 2nd Squad area, somewhat antagonistically McClung reported the incident to Shames.

I must say that Earl got me all fired up but when Junior explained what had happened I was livid and went across to have a few words with Buck Compton which resulted in another disagreement. Christmas Day for me and for most of my platoon was just like any other during the campaign, cold, miserable, squalid and without pity or goodwill towards anyone, friend or foe.

Between December 26 and 27, scores of gliders brought in heavier supplies and equipment, plus a specialist surgical team to help with the hundreds of wounded men now clogging the aid stations in Bastogne. Despite the weather conditions, three columns from Third Army were simultaneously converging on Bastogne from Martelange, Witre and Neufchâteau. At 1645hrs on the 26th, supported by heavy artillery, tanks belonging to 4th Armored broke through the encirclement near Assenois. Early the following morning, the road between Neufchâteau and Bastogne was officially declared open. Although supported by troops from the 35th ID, it would take another two days for the main body to clear a wider and more secure corridor along the main road from the border with Luxembourg.

The American tankers were surprised to see the countryside surrounding the city littered with hundreds of knocked-out vehicles. By late afternoon, a convoy of ambulances evacuated 260 priority patients. During the epic seven-day siege a total of 943 American and 125 German casualties were treated by the medical facilities in Bastogne. Despite bringing in reinforcements from Mourmelon, the 506th PIR was still desperately short of manpower and began to draft in troops from other units such as the 327th and 401st GIR.

We had this kid from Arkansas sent to us. After a few days, I noticed that he wasn't shaving and went over and gave him the party line "If you look like a soldier…" He stared as if I was crazy, and only really showed any signs of response when I inquired what his family did at weekends, and if they hung around looking like bums like he did? My last comment seemed to do the trick and thereafter, every morning, the kid was shaving alongside the rest of the guys.

Up on the MLR ammunition became more plentiful and the cooks from the front-line units were now able to produce a variety of hot food. In addition Major General Taylor had finally reached Bastogne and retook command of the division. The Allied Air Forces flew several missions during the day against Noville, Foy and Recogne. Taking advantage of the same clear skies that had also benefited the Allies, the Luftwaffe did the same thing and bombed and strafed Bastogne for the eighth time. Shortly after the attack, it was announced by Patton's Third Army that gas masks would be issued due to growing concerns that the Germans were contemplating the use of chemical weapons. Fortunately that fear turned out to be unfounded. The 506th was now being supported by dozens of newly arrived heavy guns from Third Army, which also provided much-needed additional firepower for their own 4th Armored Division.

The "relief corridor" into Bastogne had been considerably widened, taking the pressure off the MLR. German activity along the front had slowed down to a point where it was almost nonexistent. However, the 26.Volksgrenadier Division was still holding the area around Foy and Recogne. Information from POWs and captured documents enabled the commanders to use artillery to disorganize any possible enemy troop concentrations or potential attacks.

Despite the improvement in odds, the 506th still had to remain on top of their game to stay alive. One night in the 3rd Platoon patrol area, Shames and McClung noticed a faint glow coming from one of the foxholes.

We wondered what the hell it was. On approach, we discovered it was Gutty, my armorer, underneath a raincoat, reading a book by electric light! Trying to keep my voice as low as possible, I blurted "Jeeeeezus Christ Gutty! Have I been wasting my breath? You know the goddamn rules regarding light discipline, you crazy son of a bitch!" We made him cut the wires to insure he wouldn't compromise our position ever again. After calming down we inquired as to how he'd managed to do this. Gutty was a resourceful kind of guy, and told us that earlier in the day he'd salvaged an old generator and headlight from the wreck of a nearby German motorcycle ... all these years later, I still can't believe he did such a darned fool thing.

The Deep Six

On New Year's Day 1945, members of H Company observed several unidentified American troops drawing water from the well in Foy.

That old well near the crossroad never seemed to freeze, despite the extreme temperatures and consequently, although risky, it was used by both sides.

But it was still noteworthy that unidentified soldiers were in the area, and action needed to be taken. Shames and elements of 3rd Platoon were ordered to move west across the N30 into the 3rd Battalion MLR. Here the men split into their respective squads and waited for nightfall. As Ed's patrol was tasked with observing the well, he moved forward to the "Eastern Eye" of the Bois Champay hoping to see Joe Madona, although unfortunately he was not around.

Stepping out in single file, I led my men – who included Moe Alley, Strohl and Skinny Sisk – under the protective shield of darkness to the edge of Foy.

Using foliage for cover, carefully breaking the frozen snow, Shames pushed forward through a small orchard and positioned his patrol along a slope overlooking the well.

We lay there for several hours trying to keep warm but nothing was happening. I remember feeling peckish and struggled with frozen fingers to open a tin of corn pork loaf with apple flakes. Just as we were about to withdraw, a figure appeared and approached the well from the direction of Foy. I quietly moved ahead with Skinny Sisk, who made it clear that he would cut the man's throat if he uttered a single sound. Skinny half scared that kid to death and wanted to kill him after we noted that this Kraut was wearing an American uniform. But the real surprise came when we got him back to our bivouac area.

This was the first time we'd ever seen anything like this. Our prisoner was about my age and although he admitted to being German, spoke like any other dogface American soldier … but flatly refused to tell us anything about his unit or where his team might be located in the village. However, the kid did say he and his colleagues had all lived in the States before the war.

What happened next is unclear, but suffice to say, under extreme physical duress, the enemy soldier revealed that he belonged to an eight-man commando team and then pinpointed their location on the map. It transpired that the German commandos had moved into the cellar of the Koeune house on the crossroad a few days earlier, shortly after all the remaining civilians had been forced to leave.

In a desperate attempt to plea bargain, fearing for his life, the prisoner revealed the names of his comrades and that a Feldwebel [corporal] was in charge. When asked about the layout of the basement he described a small flight of stone steps that led to a sunken doorway and a low, brick, vaulted cellar divided into four separate areas where the owners had kept their market stock. The storage rooms were connected by a long corridor studded at regular intervals by four slit windows that faced east onto the N30 at ground level. The cellar ran the entire length of the building and at its center was a concrete staircase allowing access to the house itself – although this had been blocked for insulation.

Afterwards, the traumatized prisoner was sent to regiment for further questioning.

Orders then arrived from Hester for us to stake out the house over the next two nights. Although several of my guys were fluent in German such as Guth, Strohl and Ed Stein, I asked Ed to join us for the mission. The planning was left to me and I selected a slightly bigger team to augment the guys who'd been with me the previous evening.

As we were moving across the main road toward 3rd Battalion, an enemy flare burst directly overhead, and we had to freeze. Oddly this event is very clear in my mind, because it was the only time I could ever recall it happening, at least to me. Once we were in position we made notes on the enemy's patrol patterns and movements. You'd have imagined, knowing their colleague had just disappeared into thin air, that the men working from the basement might have suspected they'd been compromised but that didn't seem to be the case at all. Maybe because the cellar provided warmth it was therefore a more comfortable and attractive place to stay. For us, the extreme wind-chill factor on nights like this was far worse than the enemy and pretty soon everyone started going down with exposure – so I gave the order to pull out.

By the second night, we'd seen enough to know that there was no immediate security; I then gave the order to move in and surround the building. We watched the doorway for another half an hour or so and saw a couple of people come and go.

Carefully walking along the side of the house with Sisk and Stein, Ed arrived at the sunken entrance to the cellar and tapped lightly on the heavy wooden door. As previously mentioned by this stage of the campaign enemy forces fighting around the pocket had been whittled down by around 50 percent, which may explain why Shames and his team were able to access the property without challenge.

When the door was opened, speaking just above a whisper, Stein uttered a few words in German, and moments later a shadowy figure of a man came forward.

Initially the Kraut thought we were another German patrol before I told him in English that they were surrounded and we knew exactly who they were. The Feldwebel was informed that if he or any of his men didn't come quietly then we would cut their throats. We counted and disarmed the soldiers as they emerged, and after checking the cellar was clear, ordered them to keep their mouths tightly shut before returning to our MLR.

It was just getting light as we reached the Bois Jacques. The senior man [who had answered the door] arrogantly began talking to his comrades in rapid German. After telling him to shut the hell up, I called the guy forward and asked him to kneel on the ground. I asked for information but he flatly refused. The intelligence was vital and it didn't matter how we got it; after all these troops were by no means conventional.

In front of the other prisoners, Ed placed the muzzle of his .45 automatic on the man's forehead. Once more he requested information:

I made it clear that if someone didn't speak up within the next minute I'd give the Feldwebel the "deep six" treatment. The Kraut snapped at his men to remain silent so I gently squeezed the trigger and blew the back of his skull off. That really got the attention of the others, who quickly told us everything we needed to know. Any German caught wearing an American uniform would face a firing squad at some point, I just sped things up a little for this guy. Afterwards, I sent the prisoners over to regiment but was never told what became of them.

The decision to kill the enemy Feldwebel certainly did not come easily but some of Ed's men who had not been on the patrol were shocked by his unorthodox behavior. As with all Ed's wartime decisions, at the forefront of his mind was the security of the men immediately under his command no matter the price. Although shocking, his actions need to be judged by the situation in which they found themselves. Enemy soldiers in Allied uniforms could easily have spread panic amongst the American forces. After being thoroughly searched, the German Feldwebel's body remained in the 3rd Platoon patrol base, acting as a frozen reminder that these were indeed times of unimaginable stress and brutality.

Word quickly spread throughout the ranks about the capture of the German soldiers dressed as Americans. Before first light on January 2, after all US patrols had returned safely, the MLR went onto high alert. This was followed by a 2-hour window, during which any unscheduled "American" activity coming from the area in front of the MLR could be instantly targeted without challenge.

The G Company commander, Captain Joe Doughty, had been turning a blind eye to Staff Sergeant James West of 1st Platoon making regular unsanctioned trips down to Degives farm on the southern edge of Recogne. Although the farm had been abandoned two weeks earlier, Nester Degives had left the wine cellar well stocked. Despite the lockdown, West, accompanied by Private Charles Hunton, decided to make a visit to the farm. Route Madame was the boundary between G/506 and the 502nd. As usual, West informed whoever was manning the OP before passing through. However, while the two G Company men were relaxing down at the farm, the H/502 OP shift changed and the new guard was not updated with the situation. An hour or so later, as Hunton and West were returning along the beech-lined road, the soldier in the OP opened fire with a machine gun and both men were killed instantly. The stupidity and risk of West's actions almost defies belief but death and horrific injury on the front line around Bastogne were things to which everyone had become accustomed.

The thousand-yard stare

By early January, 2/506 were preparing to cross the Bizory road in preparation for a frontal attack northeast alongside the 501st, through the Bois Jacques into the Bois des Corbeaux. The object of the maneuver, which was to commence at 0930hrs on January 2, was to advance through 1,000 yards of dense forest to an old farmers' road that ran from Foy to Ourbourcy. Earlier that morning at 0600hrs, 1st Battalion moved forward from Savy to take over the MLR. Initially resistance was light until the paratroopers reached the road. By late afternoon the objective had been taken and a new MLR established with F Company on the left and E Company in the center. Ed Shames and 3rd Platoon were designated to patrol the right-hand flank of the incursion and then take up positions alongside D/501 near an old iron bridge over the Bastogne-Gouvy railway.

> We moved several times and had to deal with at least 18 inches of frozen earth before the ground became easier for us to dig.

By this time Richard Hughes was having difficulty walking. Ed requested that he remove his boots for a foot inspection:

Both of Hughes' feet were black and we tried to warm them gently over a small fire in the bottom of his shallow foxhole. The man was in so much pain that I had absolutely no choice but to call our medic John Holland, who decided to evacuate him immediately. We learned later that another day or two on the line and Hughes would've lost both feet.

The iron box-shaped bridge was utilized by local farmers for moving produce and livestock from Foy and signified the entry into "bandit country" for Shames and the men from 3rd Platoon:

We were under control of the 501st and would have to approach the bridge from the west through dense forest alongside the old drovers' road and then claw our way down the icy embankment onto the tracks.

The enemy was holding the woods on the eastern side of the railway and Shames was instructed to carry out combat patrols to keep the Germans on that side of the tracks.

The bridge was our demarcation point and the only solid visual reference we had because everything else was obscured by thick snow.

One of our jobs was to try and draw enemy fire to establish if the Germans were still around. During one night patrol, it was pitch black and you couldn't even see your hand in front of your face. Skinny Sisk became separated but managed to find his way back. By the time he caught up, he was in a terrible state, and on the very edge of panic. Lucky for him and us it was a quiet night.

That same evening regiment ordered our crew back out again and I took Popeye on a pointless listening patrol to a spot overlooking the iron bridge, that we'd visited four or five times already. Popeye had been in his foxhole all day, so I figured that some of the others could do with a break and besides, I didn't want them to freeze their tails off for nothing! My God you could really feel the chill in your bones and Popeye bitched like hell the entire time – "Why me? Why me?" It didn't matter that the spot was safely on our side of the tracks, such is the responsibility of leadership, eh?

When we returned to our position, Mac McCardle came over and told me that they had a hot meal ready! I was speechless and inquired how on earth they'd managed to prepare such a thing. Earlier McClung had found a dead jackrabbit but I just couldn't bring myself to eat the semi-cooked meat because of the disgusting smell permeating from the carcass. This was crazy because although I was way beyond hungry, I just couldn't swallow a single mouthful of that hideous concoction without retching! Of course the boys thought it was hilarious.

The following day – January 4 – the 501st took over the newly established front line and 2nd Battalion began to withdraw in several phases toward an area of woods recently vacated by 1/506. The 1st Battalion had been held in reserve directly behind the original 3rd Platoon, E Company positions; they had departed for Savy the previous afternoon.

As D and E Companies were in the process of crossing the Foy-Bizory road, they came under an intense barrage of artillery and rocket fire. The initial devastating attack lasted no more than 5 minutes. "The Germans threw everything they had at us, it was total mayhem."

The shrieking crash of shells tore open the dense canopy, uprooting trees and anything else in their path. Shrapnel skipped through the branches, buzzing everywhere as soldiers cowered, trying to dig deeper into the frozen earth. Between each barrage the plaintive calls for "Medic!" could be heard.

Somehow myself, Paul and Moe formed an evacuation chain and dragged the wounded away from the target area. Then it got worse and we had to take cover as a second, even more deadly saturation came slamming in.

First Sergeant Carwood Lipton remembered Lieutenant Dike – who was without a helmet or weapon – ordering him to get things organized while he went for help. Dike simply vanished and did not return until the following morning. After Dike disappeared, Buck Compton rushed across to the regimental CP attempting to get medical help for two of his men, Sergeants Bill Guarnere and Joe Toye, who were both horrifically injured. A couple of days later, Colonel Sink ordered Buck to be removed from the line due to combat fatigue and more importantly severe trench foot and Captain Winters asked Carwood Lipton to take temporary command of 2nd Platoon.

As 3rd Platoon was reorganizing, one of the men ran over to inform Ed of an officer from 1st Platoon who was nearby and behaving strangely. Shames went over and found Second Lieutenant Ernie Mann sitting at the bottom of a shell crater staring blankly into space.

I'd known Mann since Toccoa and socialized with him at the stables in Ramsbury. "Ernie, Ernie can you hear me? It's Ed, Eddie Shames, Joe Madona's buddy. I was in I Company with you … remember?" Nothing I said seemed to connect and he just sat there motionless like a zombie, his unblinking eyes looking right through me with their "thousand-yard" stare. There was nothing I could do except keep him warm and send word to Norman Dike.

Lieutenant Dike quickly arranged for Ernie (who had won a battlefield commission in Holland) to be evacuated and Ed never saw him again.*

Shortly afterwards Jack Foley came over to the 3rd Platoon area, probably to find out what had happened to Mann, who was his assistant. While talking to Shames he noticed a small fire burning in one of the foxholes.

Jack was not happy about the fire and asked me to put it out. After the recent rocket and artillery attack, I asked, "Lieutenant, you think they don't know where we are…?"

---

* Ernie made a full recovery and was reassigned to another unit.

After being relieved by the 501st, 2nd Battalion were finally pulled out of the Bois Jacques at 2130hrs on January 4, before rotating into regimental reserve in the Bois Champay behind H/506 and later G Company. It was during this period that Carwood Lipton privately mentioned his concerns about First Lieutenant Dike to Dick Winters.

Despite 2/506 being in reserve, 3rd Platoon still seemed to be pulling the worst of the patrolling schedule. During a two-man observation patrol, Ed Stein was badly wounded while working in the clump of trees opposite the "Eastern Eye" with Lieutenant Shames. Even though they were wrapped in blankets, the ground was so cold that Shames was almost tempted to inject one of his legs with morphine to numb the pain. Instead – as it was a moonless night – they decided to stand for a short while to regain circulation.

Suddenly the tree directly above us was hit by an enemy mortar shell. Immediately we threw ourselves on the ground and after a minute or so crawled back underneath the blanket and cuddled together. When I inquired, Stein said he thought he was OK. But a few moments later, I began to feel blood seeping against me. It was only then we both realized he'd been injured but couldn't feel a thing. A piece of shrapnel had sliced open a vein in Ed's leg and as he was losing quite a lot of blood, we dressed the wound and beat a hasty retreat. Shortly afterwards Stein was evacuated and to the best of my knowledge never returned to duty.

Before the end

Ever since the siege had been effectively broken on December 26, Colonel Sink had been preparing for an all-out assault on the enemy lines. General Patton's Third Army had been working hard for a week to widen the main arterial road and clear the route. By January 5, the 506th PIR stepped up its patrolling and small-unit activity in a determined effort to regain control of the hills and woods surrounding Bastogne.

Over the next few days, in order to keep up with the fluid tactical situation, Sink relocated his CP several times. Initially, Sink went to Sonne Fontaine farm and then Hemroulle, before moving to Colonel Patch's CP in the Bois Champay.

After being relieved by 3/501 at 0500hrs on January 9, 3rd Battalion moved through the Bois Champay southwest from the MLR to an assembly area near Sonne Fontaine. A couple of hours earlier 2nd Battalion had advanced north, accompanied by tanks from Task Force Cherry. The battalion's mission was to clear and occupy the woods at Fazone and the ground southwest of Vaux, in preparation for their forthcoming attack on Noville. By now the northeastern edge of the Fazone was already part of the 506th MLR. This area of woods had previously been the operational area of 1/506 but they were withdrawn during the early afternoon, and placed in mobile reserve behind 2nd Battalion.

A fresh layer of snow around 8 inches deep lay on top of the frozen crust as 3rd Battalion moved out toward Fazone at 1100hrs on January 9; 2nd Battalion had crossed the first phase line 10 minutes earlier, and within half an hour had overrun a German OP, capturing a small number of enemy troops. After veering northeast 2nd Battalion headed toward Noville with 3/506 to their left. As both battalions made their way into the woods they came under intense and accurate mortar fire. During the German withdrawal from the Fazone, they had booby-trapped most of the main pathways along which the 506th were now advancing, which caused many delays as troops stopped to step over endless tripwires. The ground at the far edge of the Fazone sloped away in a long undulating curve toward the German-held villages of Vaux (left) and Cobru (to the right). Beyond the two hamlets on the high ground in the distance was the final prize – Noville.

Due to the constant shelling, Sink halted the advance on the northeastern edge of Fazone and the regiment, with 1st Battalion as reserve, was ordered to dig in. As dark fell the woods came under concentrated attack by German tanks, which over the course of the evening pulverized the tree line, inflicting well over 100 casualties. One of those was Charlie Shettle, who was wounded in the foot. Until that morning Charlie had been on the 2nd Battalion staff, but he had been given command of 1st Battalion after Bob Harwick was evacuated. Shortly after Shettle left the battlefield, Clarence Hester, who himself had been lightly wounded a few days earlier, took over 1/506. The day had been somewhat of a record for 1st Battalion – three commanders in eight hours.

Mortar, artillery, and tank shells hammered into the woods throughout the night, making medical evacuation next to impossible. Because of the exceptionally high wind chill factor, the temperature on January 9 dropped to below 2 degrees Fahrenheit (–17 degrees Celsius). It was the coldest night the 506th PIR experienced during the campaign. As a consequence the extreme cold seemed to "burn" the skin on Ed's face and hands like he had never experienced before.

The temperature had dropped off the scale and I don't remember it ever being quite as cold as it was that day.

Early the following evening 2nd and 3rd Battalions were withdrawn from the front line. Although the attack was somewhat disorganized and costly in casualties, it did ultimately drive the enemy from the Fazone. As Shames was heading south he decided to stop the platoon for a few minutes and regroup. Buck Taylor thought he would use the opportunity to make contact with 1st Battalion who were now in regimental reserve, waiting to be relieved by 2/506, somewhere over on 3rd Platoon's left flank. As Buck turned to leave the 1st Battalion area, a bullet came from nowhere and hit him just above the ankle.

It was a devastating blow to the team but I'd been grooming Paul Rogers in readiness for such a situation so the reshuffle was virtually seamless. Even before Paul took over as platoon sergeant, he was coping easily with the additional responsibilities, so I knew he was the right man for the job. In fact Hayseed went on to become the best platoon sergeant and soldier that I ever had the pleasure of knowing.

After Buck was wounded, 3rd Platoon rejoined 2nd Battalion, who were now on the southern side of the Bois Champay near Savy. "One of my eternal regrets is that I didn't push hard enough to get Buck a battlefield commission." Because he had only held his commission for six months, Ed was worried that his recommendation to promote Buck would not have been taken seriously by Captain Winters or Colonel Strayer.

In a way Strohl should've applied for OCS but it never interested him. But that was the amazing thing about our regiment, guys like Buck Taylor, Rod Strohl, Jim Japhet and George Retan, who were well-educated, high achievers, were all more or less happy simply being enlisted men.

Later that night the enemy blanketed the reserve area with artillery, killing Sergeant Warren "Skip" Muck and Private First Class Alex Penkala. After dark, Ed sent "Junior" Suerth and several others back to Luzery to collect stretchers. On the way the men stopped to speak with the crew of a tank whose unit was parked in the woods. During the brief conversation one of the crewmen foolishly lit a cigarette. Consequently, moments later a number of German shells exploded around the tanks, killing four people and badly injuring Suerth, who was hit in both legs by shrapnel. "That was the end of Junior's short war as he spent the next eighteen months in and out of various hospitals."

Today is the only reality – Final attack on Foy, January 13, 1945

On the evening of January 12, after relieving 401st GIR on the ridgeline at Foy, Lieutenant Colonel Patch briefed his remaining officers at the battalion CP in the trees behind the Bois Champay. The plan was to secure the village without damaging the N30 (no artillery was to be used), enabling the Shermans, M10s and M18 Hellcats from the 11th Armored Division to pass unimpeded toward Noville. Due to the high number of casualties on January 9, the remaining senior NCOs from 3/506 were shuffled between rifle companies, which, for the most part, were down to fewer than 30 men each.

For the first phase, E Company had been attached to 3rd Battalion and would join I Company for the attack that was due to begin the following morning. This transfer occurred despite the fact that 2nd Battalion was now in regimental reserve behind the MLR. As he had been working so closely with Lloyd Patch, Gene Brown was asked to take temporary command of I Company after Andy Anderson had been reassigned to the battalion staff. I Company was split into two composite squads. The first squad was under the command of Second Lieutenant Roger Tinsley and the second, that numbered around 16 men, was under the leadership of Sergeant Harley Dingman. G and H Companies were tasked with holding the line while maintaining fire support along with the 81mm mortar platoon. Several officers, like First Lieutenant Alex Andros from H Company, thought the idea unworkable due to the lack of available manpower.

After a night of light enemy shelling, the US attack began as planned at 0900hrs. However, at the last minute it was discovered that the enemy had tapped into the communications network, forcing Sink to order a complete radio silence. While the 81mm mortar platoon was puzzling over its fire control orders (which had been intercepted by the Germans), 1st and 2nd Platoons from E Company had crossed their jump-off points and were proceeding down into Foy. Earlier, Ed Shames and 3rd Platoon had been sent across the N30 to the extreme western edge of the Bois Jacques, which was then held by the 501st, from where they were supposed to be leading a diversionary attack.

I had around 40 men in my platoon that day. Our mission was to push down to the crossroad and draw the enemy forces away from the center of town.

Simultaneously, at the Bois Champay, 1st and 2nd Platoons, led by Jack Foley and Carwood Lipton respectively, had emerged from either side of the "Eastern Eye" to begin their advance, keeping the Route de Houffalize on their right. Once into Foy, Foley and Lipton had been ordered to link up with Shames and form a blocking force along a line approximately 300 yards in length, south of the road leading to Recogne.

Ed Shames and 3rd Platoon were to employ the same tactic by capturing and holding the other side of the road leading to Bizory. Enemy forces had established a defensive firebase in the gutted ruins of the Koeune house. Located at the strongpoint was a mortar forward observer who had all entry routes into the village covered with preplanned barrages. Several machine-gun crews were located on the upper floors with uninterrupted views toward the "Eye." Another gun group operated nearby at Cardonnier farm and had superb fields of fire along the road to Recogne.

The enemy machine guns were also protecting a Mk IV Panzer parked in the dip directly outside the Koeune house. Because the road dropped sharply away, the turret was barely visible from the N30. The tank created a formidable barrier and ultimately prevented Shames from connecting with Lipton and Foley. Norman Dike was with Lipton as 2nd Platoon moved out of the Bois Champay. Within minutes E Company HQ came under heavy machine-gun fire and the platoon advance ground to a halt on the exposed convex slope. As Lipton asked Dike to get everyone moving it became obvious that his commander had no real clue what to do next. Taking control Lipton screamed across at Foley, who was by now passing on the right flank, and told him to drop off his 60mm mortar and a machine-gun team. As 1st Platoon pressed forward they came under fire from a sniper who killed Privates First Class Carl Sawosko and Kenneth Webb and wounded Private Frank Perconte through the buttock and Tech Sergeant Burr Smith in the leg. As 1st Platoon reached the edge of the village, Foley was hit in the foot by a small piece of shrapnel but was able to continue. With Foley's mortar and machine-gun team now in action and properly supported by Pete Madden's four 81mm mortars, "Lip" was able to silence the sniper and neutralize a couple of enemy Forward Observers (FOs) before rejoining the main assault.

Shames recalls that after arriving at the southeastern edge of the village, they were targeted by a sniper working from the Gaspard house, possibly the same one who had inflicted so much damage on 1st Platoon.

We took cover in the shadow of a large tree. At this point we began to receive accurate small-arms fire, and someone, maybe Shifty or McClung, spotted a muzzle flash which came from an upper window of a farmhouse [belonging to Joseph Gaspard] further along the road directly opposite the church.

McClung dashed forward into the cover of a large stable block that ran alongside the Gaspard farm, where he heard German voices coming from inside one of the stalls. Firing his rifle through a small window, Earl blasted away at the enemy soldiers before continuing toward his intended target. Stopping a short distance from the sniper's window, Earl reloaded his rifle with a couple of rounds of blank ammunition that were needed to launch a rifle grenade and waited to catch his breath. Moments later a muzzle appeared and Earl fired two carefully aimed grenades into the opening and thought he had neutralized the sniper.

The only serious casualties suffered by 3rd Platoon as it skirmished through the southeastern part of Foy were replacement Private Patrick Neill, and Corporal Frank Mellett, who were both killed. Twenty-four-year-old Mellett was shot in the heart shortly after entering a house he believed had already been cleared. Moe Alley, who was with Mellett as he fell, killed the enemy soldier. Shames continues, "Because of the German tank, the furthest we actually penetrated was up to the church, where we went firm and waited for further instructions."

Gene Brown, who had only recently taken command of I Company from Andy Anderson, was tasked by Sink to lead them for the second phase of the assault. Assisted by Tinsley and Dingman, the idea was to advance down the eastern (right-hand) edge of the N30 and link up with 3rd Platoon, E Company at the crossroad. As the only medical officer available, Captain Barney Ryan was attached to Brown along with several of his medics.

Shortly after 1015hrs, as Brown's small force got within sight of the crossroad, his drive was abruptly halted. The Germans had scattered dozens of booby traps across the N30. Moments later, the Germans brought the leading elements of Brown's column under intense machine-gun fire. This forced the men to take cover along an embankment on the left side of the road. Doctor Ryan, who was following behind, received word that a number of casualties were now gathering up ahead on the left, around a three-story house that became his aid station.

Bypassing the "minefield," forward elements of I Company were moving down the edge of the road when they became pinned down by machine-gun fire from the Panzer. Beyond this point the road dropped away to where the Panzer was waiting in the hollow at the crossroad. Shortly afterwards a member of I Company fired a bazooka round at the tank, which then seemed to lose power. The Panzer was eventually overrun after it ran out of ammunition, leaving the barrel of its 75mm gun pointing toward Bastogne. Many of the I Company wounded were now being carried back across the road to the aid station. However the casualties could not be evacuated by vehicle due to the mines blocking the road opposite the aid post. Shorty Madona arrived to check on a couple of his men and moved to the rear with Dr Ryan, hoping to get a situation report from Captain Brown.

Gene had broken radio silence and was sheltering behind a nearby stone barn. Madona and Ryan listened intently as Brown told Colonel Patch that I Company had hit a "hornets' nest" and he needed immediate backup. As Shorty and Barney walked back toward the doorway there was a sudden burst of machine-gun fire. The 7.92mm bullets ricocheted off the solid stone architrave. Barney was struck in the upper chest, but Joe, being so much smaller, caught several rounds in the face and died instantly.

Although I didn't know it at the time, Shorty was only a stone's throw away from me when it happened. This was unthinkable – like a bad dream – Joe was like me, a survivor, or at least that's what I always told myself. Paul Simrell, Jim Japhet, George Retan and now Shorty – the last of my closest friends was now gone. Added to Frank Mellett's and Pat Neill's deaths, it made me vow to do my utmost to bring every man in my platoon home, no matter what.

At approximately 1100hrs, on the MLR, just like a scene from the Alamo, Bob Sink and Lloyd Patch ordered Andy Anderson and Skunk Walker to gather all available spare manpower and join forces with 1st Platoon, F Company to relieve the pressure on Brown. The enemy shelled the woods, while the composite group was being assembled behind the "Eye" on Route Madame. The intense barrage delayed the relief mission and wounded several people in the process. Shortly before the relief force left the woods, Dick Winters ordered First Lieutenant Ron Speirs to go on ahead with a handful of troops and personally inform Norman Dike what was about to happen.

After being attached to 3rd Battalion, F/506 took over the positions vacated by H Company as Skunk Walker ordered First Lieutenant Alex Andros to take his platoon and make a flanking movement across the N30 along the outskirts of the village. This was the same route previously taken by Shames and 3rd Platoon. Walker then split his 1st Platoon equally on either side of the main road before advancing down toward Foy. But before reaching the minefield, the group came under heavy artillery fire and ran for cover.

Down in Foy it was complete chaos. Brown and Tinsley were now desperately trying to coordinate the remnants of I Company, which numbered fewer than 20 men. Nowhere was safe and another of Ed's old friends, Jim Brown, was killed after being struck in the left eye by enemy machine-gun fire. As I Company was still in the process of clearing the houses along the southern edge of town, Alex Andros and his men had made it halfway around Foy. The main relief group led by Andy Anderson headed down into the village from the Bois Champay just prior to Andros' departure.

Most likely hindered by the radio lockdown, Anderson not only became embroiled in crossfire between E and I Companies but also enemy machine-gun fire coming from the Koeune and Cardonnier farms. Both companies were now under heavy mortar fire and struggling to maintain their individual missions. Something had to be done before somebody was killed by friendly fire. Taking a deep breath, Speirs ran across open ground under fire and spoke directly to Roger Tinsley, who immediately instructed his men to stop firing. As Speirs was returning to E Company he looked round and saw Tinsley fall, mortally wounded.

During the next hour or so, 1st Platoon, F Company played a vital role in mopping up the resistance in the town. Further east, close to Ed Shames' sector, H Company came under heavy shellfire near the church. As they maneuvered through Shames' position to envelop the buildings on the western side of the road, the intense shelling suddenly lifted. Realizing an enemy forward observer or observers must have been operating from the basement of the Koeune house, Andros ordered several bursts of submachine-gun fire through the slit window near the sunken entrance. Moments later, after a surrender ultimatum was issued, approximately 20 Germans emerged and surrendered.

The wrecks of several burnt-out German tanks and fighting vehicles lay scattered throughout Foy. Although the Germans continued to shell the village the area was now clear of enemy troops. In total around 70 prisoners were taken during the seven-hour operation. By 1630hrs, shortly after 3rd Battalion regained control, Ed Shames and the rest of E Company returned to 2nd Battalion, leaving H and I Companies in defense along with F Company. At this point back on the ridgeline, Norman Dike was relieved and Ron Speirs given command of E Company. Before 3rd Platoon left Foy, they returned to the Gaspard house and found the sniper that McClung had targeted using rifle grenades, with a bullet through the middle of his forehead, prompting Popeye Wynn to comment, "You know it just doesn't pay to be shootin' at Shifty when he's got a rifle." If what Popeye said is true, it would appear that after McClung fired his two rifle grenades at the window, Powers must have followed up a few minutes later with one or two carefully aimed shots, one of which killed the German soldier at the Gaspard house.

Under cover of darkness the assault pioneers cleared the main road of mines to make way for the tank destroyers and Hellcats from 11th Armored. Despite several attempts to retake Foy the following morning, the enemy was finally beaten back by flesh and steel, never to return.

Breath of fire – Noville, January 15, 1945

Shortly after the recapture of Foy 2nd Battalion was diverted to an assembly area in the woods above Recogne in preparation for a hastily organized attack on Cobru, which they subsequently secured. With Allied armor now consolidating in Foy and Recogne, the few remaining enemy tanks were destroyed. What was left of 3rd Battalion was ordered northwest to the southern edge of Fazone near a lake to make contact with 1st Battalion and the 17th Airborne (who were scheduled to take over from the 101st).

On January 14, two platoons from E Company and one from F Company took cover for the night in an old, abandoned quarry overlooking the church at Noville. The quarry pits were covered in logs and anything else that could be procured for protection. A dawn attack was planned for the following morning (January 15) that would coincide with 1st Battalion's assault into the woods directly northwest of Cobru.

During the pre-mission briefing, carried out by Captain Winters and Ron Speirs, Carwood Lipton was again tasked to take 2nd Platoon and clear the western, left-hand side of town, while Ed Shames and Second Lieutenant Ben Stapelfeld (1st Platoon, F Company) were to come in from the east. Still under radio blackout, the force was told to expect support from 11th Armored, who were expected to be approaching from E Company's right rear. Along with their M10s and M18s, 11th Armored were also operating a number of M36 "Jackson" tank destroyers that had only just arrived in theater. With its low body shape, the Jackson, weighing 29 tons, was fitted with a long-barrel 90mm gun complete with muzzle brake and at a glance its silhouette could easily be mistaken for the German Mk V Panther.

Forward artillery observers from the 321st GFA were attached to 2/506 for the assault. As there was no evidence to suggest that the 321st communications network had been breached they were able to provide the artillery and close air support vital to the assault. Because the church was so badly damaged the enemy was unable to use its steeple as an observation post. For this reason 2nd Platoon were able to move forward to a fence line from where Lipton could just make out the rear of several large properties situated on the western side of the main road.

"Lip" was uneasy about leading his platoon into the attack without really knowing what lay ahead. As the buildings seemed unoccupied, he carefully advanced with his radio operator Tech Corporal Rod Bain (who was probably tuned into the 321st network) to a barn from where they could clearly observe the N30. From the courtyard in front of the building the main road through Noville seemed deathly quiet.

The two men headed back inside the barn to call Lieutenant Speirs. Speaking just above a whisper on Bain's SCR-536, Lipton gave their location and said that he was going to move further into town for a closer look. Speirs did not object so the two men moved out toward the crossroad. Trying hard not to disturb the frost-covered snow, Lipton picked his way into Noville. Up ahead, close to the crossroad, Lip could just make out what looked like two Shermans and a half-track but Speirs, via radio, was unable to confirm where 11th Armored were and suggested the possibility that they could already be in Noville.

Feeling more confident, Lipton and Bain moved closer and were dismayed to find that the American vehicles they had seen were all ones which had been knocked out on December 20, during Team Desobry and 1st Battalion's epic withdrawal. The two men pulled back to the barn where they reported to Speirs that it looked like the 2nd Battalion attack would still be necessary for the following morning.

Let me live till morning

Shortly before first light on January 15, the assault platoons moved out to their respective jump-off points. Ed Shames crossed the N30 with 3rd Platoon ahead of Ben Stapelfeld and moved his men into position behind the Beaujean house. This building had previously served as the 1st Battalion aid station on December 19/20 and was situated on the southern edge of Noville. "I was told to advance to the church and no further because they were expecting heavy resistance further ahead."

Once again the job for 3rd Platoon was to create a diversion and punch toward the center of town and consolidate behind the church and await instructions. Shames was somewhat concerned by the amount of exposed ground he and his men were expected to cross before even reaching the church. In front of the platoon, about 300 yards away on the other side of the field, was a line of trees that ran toward the back of the church and presbytery. Beyond the trees was a small group of farm buildings that included a milking shed belonging to Felton farm.

Almost immediately Shames and his men came under artillery fire. The shelling seemed to be coming from a nearby area of woods that overlooked the town from the northwest.

I had two guys on point, while I was in the middle of our group. I watched the shells come in and start to explode on a line, one by one, bang, bang, in front of us. As they dropped closer I thought, "This is it, I'm dead," but the last shell in the salvo failed to detonate and was still fizzing in the deep snow as we passed by. There was some machine-gun fire coming from somewhere around the crossroad which seemed to be targeting the other platoon who were now advancing in line, pinching in to the crossroad.

Although 2nd Platoon was partially protected by the buildings they still lost Privates First Class Ed Joint and Brad Freeman, who were wounded by shrapnel from a German rocket. Quickly gathering momentum Ed's platoon managed to reach the tree line on the far side of the field safely and took refuge in the milking shed behind the church. After a brief respite, 3rd Platoon went on the offensive and skirmished around the barn.

When we got to the church, we could see some enemy movement further along the road but nothing in or around our location. I think the Krauts knew that they were going to lose the town and it was just a delaying action on their part.

Next door to the church was the presbytery. Although it was badly damaged, Ed noted with some concern that the house was surrounded by a still intact 5ft-high stone wall.

Suddenly a flight of P-47 Thunderbolts arrived overhead and began to circle. Moments later Ed was somewhat surprised when a garbled message came through on the radio: "Friendly armor on the right."

Shortly afterwards we heard a terrific rumbling noise and I asked Moe Alley to come outside with me and make contact.

So as not to become targets for the P-47s, and because the radio silence was still officially in force, the two men decided to leave their helmets, rifles, and equipment behind though Alley took his radio. Shames and

Alley walked around the corner into Route de Bourcy then headed down the road a short distance to the crossroad, passing the stone wall belonging to the presbytery on their left. Upon reaching the main road, Shames looked both ways but saw nothing except for a Sherman, a German Stug SPG, and the half-track, all of them knocked out in December, outside the church.

I was expecting our tanks to come in from the left but then we noticed the back of something parked between two gutted buildings on the right-hand side of the street in the direction of Houffalize.

Thinking this might be one of the new M36s, Alley ran on ahead and yelled out a greeting to its commander.

As the two paratroopers approached, they could clearly see the NCO standing in the turret. As the man turned around, Shames and Alley stopped in their tracks. The tank was not an M36 but a Panzer V armed with a powerful 75mm gun. The vehicle and its five-man crew had been left behind, possibly due to some sort of communications breakdown.

The enemy tanker panicked and attempted to traverse his turret toward Ed and Moe.

It was a terrifying moment as we turned on our heels and ran for our lives.

The tank reversed out and lurched forward in pursuit, firing its 7.92mm machine gun as the two men sprinted back toward the presbytery. On the other side of the street, 2nd Platoon looked on open-mouthed and helpless as the 46-ton behemoth chased down their comrades. Before the tank, which had a top speed of 38mph, turned into Route de Bourcy, Shames and Alley took a leap of faith over the presbytery wall, which, luckily for them, tapered at that point into a small embankment. No more than a second later, the Panzer fired into what was left of the building. The concussive blast of the gun made everything shudder, and

the resulting explosion lifted Shames and Alley bodily off the ground…
"Christ we were lucky, so damned lucky." Second Platoon were forced
to take cover as the Panzer stopped and proceeded to fire several more
shells at very close range into the abandoned tanks and vehicles before
continuing westwards toward Bourcy.

While this was happening Ben Stapelfeld from 1st Platoon, F Company,
led his men in behind 3rd Platoon and past the hulk of a burned-out
Mk IV Panther toward the graves of eight civilians murdered by the
Germans on December 21. Passing the makeshift cemetery, Ben and his
men were pinned down by enemy machine-gun fire and forced to take
cover in a nearby pigpen. Stapelfeld ordered his 60mm mortar man to
fire onto the Panzer that had chased Shames and Alley as it moved along
the road to Bourcy. Stapelfeld hoped that one of the shells might take
out the commander, but his gunner did not manage to hit the intended
target. Just as they were about to give up, the men cheered as one of the
circling P-47s flew in low and knocked out the Panzer with a 500lb
bomb as it raced over a nearby hill.

A perimeter defense was established shortly after midday when the
clearing action was complete. At this point F Company withdrew to the
southern edge of town close to the newly established E Company CP.
Everyone was convinced that this was the final objective of the campaign,
but there was still more to come.

Shortly after Noville was taken, General Taylor and Gerald Higgins
arrived to get a situation report from Colonel Sink and Captain Winters.
Due to the continuous radio restrictions over the last 30 hours, divisional
HQ had been for the most part unaware as to what was happening.
Having had no real idea of the terrible damage previously inflicted,
Taylor was horrified by the state of the town and asked Sink what on
earth he had done to it.

From his temporary command center in Recogne, Sink began
preparations for the combined regimental attack on Rachamps. With all
radio channels now reopened, full command and control was restored.

The 506th began their main attack to push the enemy forces away to the east on January 16, after 3rd Battalion, supported by 3/501, had advanced along the road from Fagnoux to Wicourt, while 1st and 2nd Battalions assaulted Rachamps from Cobru and Noville. The following morning before leaving, Ed and the boys walked along the Bourcy road to inspect the burned-out German tank; the crew had all been killed by the air attack.

North of Noville, Rachamps was situated in a gently sloping valley. From Noville, 2nd Battalion pushed forward along the N30. On January 16, immediately after occupying the high ground north of the town, 2/506 made their advance on Rachamps, and spread out to counter any enemy artillery and small-arms fire. As the attack started, the Germans fired white phosphorus shells. Thankfully, due to the wide attack formation, there were no casualties and the town was quickly cleared. E Company moved into a school and occupied the main assembly hall. For the first time in three weeks Ed and his men spent the night indoors. That evening a choir of 12- and 13-year-old girls sang a selection of songs in several languages including that wartime favorite "Lili Marlene."

Finally, the regiment handed over control to the newly formed 17th Airborne Division. By January 18, the 506th was in corps reserve at La Petite Rosière, 6 miles south of Sibret. After a couple of days' pampering, the men were informed that they were moving to a new defensive area in Alsace Lorraine.

During the four weeks on the line at Bastogne, the 506th PIR suffered over 40 percent casualties: 119 men killed, 670 wounded, and 59 missing in action – a total of 848 troopers. The 101st Airborne Division, as a whole, lost 525 KIA, 2,653 WIA, and 527 missing or captured – a total of 3,705 troopers. Combat Command B lost 73 KIA, 279 WIA, and 116 missing or captured – a total of 468 soldiers. The Battle of the Bulge was arguably one of the most important events of World War II and signified the beginning of the end for Germany. The Wehrmacht had suffered some 110,000 casualties, while the total American losses had risen to 80,000, of whom approximately 19,000 had been killed.

It was said afterwards by Winston Churchill that no other battle in World War II had caused so much American blood to be spilt. The devastation to the civilian population around Bastogne was also immense, with around 2,500 people killed, and towns and villages, including Foy, Recogne and Noville, all but destroyed. Along with the massacres of US forces at places such as Malmedy and Wereth, 172 civilians were also murdered … and so ended Operation *Wacht am Rhein* and the now legendary Battle of the Bulge.

11

"NORTHWIND"

Haguenau and the Colmar Pocket

Alsace and Lorraine are two regions in the northeastern corner of France, which borders Belgium, Luxembourg, Germany, and Switzerland. Alsace follows the river Rhine north from Basel, while Lorraine rises from the plains of Champagne before converging with the Vosges Mountains. Historically, most of Alsace was German-speaking when awarded to France by the Hapsburg Empire. In 1871, after France was defeated in the Franco-Prussian War, Germany annexed Alsace and the Moselle Department of Lorraine and reintroduced a program of forced Germanization. At the end of World War I, the region reverted to French control, only to be reoccupied in 1940 by Germany. Over the next four years around 130,000 Alsatian men were conscripted into the German armed forces.

In early 1945, the Western Front was divided into three army groups. Northernmost was 21st Army Group, under Field Marshal Bernard Montgomery. Omar Bradley and his 12th Army Group was located in the center, with 6th Army Group, commanded by General Jacob

Devers, to the south around Alsace Lorraine and the Swiss border. Devers' group was part of a joint force comprising Seventh Army (XV and VI Corps) under Lieutenant General Alexander Patch and the French First Army commanded by Général d'Armée Jean de Lattre de Tissigny.

While the fighting was going on in the Ardennes, the French were unable to push the enemy back across the Rhine. In late November 1944, the Germans forced a bridgehead along the western edge of the Black Forest between the ancient towns of Pfaffenhoffen, Haguenau, Colmar, and Basel. Before Christmas the Nazi war machine began to threaten the rear of George Patton's Third Army as well as the Seventh Army. When Patton redirected his forces toward the Ardennes, part of Seventh Army moved south to assist the French. During the early stages of the battle, the Germans tried desperately to break out and drive north to link up with their forces around Bastogne. The threat to the Allied supply lines was real, and if the enemy had not been contained in Alsace then General Patton would have struggled to maintain his push to reach Bastogne, which lay 125 miles to the northwest.

It was here in Alsace, at the crossroad of Europe, on January 1, 1945, that Hitler decided to restart his offensive. Operation *Nordwind* (*Northwind*) was similar in execution to *Wacht am Rhein*, and generally became known to the Allies as "The Battle of the Colmar Pocket." Commander-in-Chief of the West, Generalfeldmarschall Gerd von Runstedt, who had been the driving force behind *Wacht am Rhein*, was completely opposed to this new plan. Subsequently, Hitler asked SS Commander Heinrich Himmler to take charge of the southern area of operations on the Western Front with instructions to ignore von Runstedt and report directly to him in Berlin. Hitler's idea was to cut off the regional capital, Strasbourg, with two pincer movements from Haguenau in the north and further south at Colmar. Over the next three weeks the attack shifted back and forth before finally grinding to a stalemate near Strasbourg.

On January 20, the 101st was temporarily attached to Major General Wade "Ham" Haislip's XV Corps and instructed to take over one of the more peaceful sectors of the old Maginot Line along the Moder Valley in Alsace. The regiment was mobilized and transported by truck to Diemeringen near Sarre-Union, 20 miles northwest of the small town of Pfaffenhoffen. Just like in Bastogne, the journey was cold and badly delayed by icy road conditions. With 16 inches of snow on the ground, Shames and 3rd Platoon were not looking forward to their new assignment. "With more than a little help from Bob McArdle we commandeered two civilian trucks for the platoon, one of which I drove."

With 1st Battalion stationed at Weislingen and 3rd Battalion at Diemeringen alongside RHQ, 2/506 was based in the village of Waldhambach, where they were able to take stock of weapons, equipment, ammunition, and rations.

It was wonderful just to be able to stand in a chow line without fear of being shelled. Unlike some of the other officers, I never jumped the queue by pulling rank and always made sure my guys got fed first.

Even before the regiment reached Alsace, information packs were distributed, reminding everyone that although this was "friendly" territory the area contained many civilians who spoke German as their first language, and who might be sympathetic to the Fatherland.

Five days later the 506th PIR relocated 30 miles further southwest to Wickersheim–Wilshausen near Hochfelden where the three battalions were deployed within a 2-mile radius. By January 28, the regiment was still in divisional reserve when it moved closer to the river Moder and into the villages around Ettendorf in preparation to relieve the 409th Infantry Regiment (IR) from the 103rd Infantry Division (ID), which was now led by Tony McAuliffe.

Heavily depleted, the 506th PIR was enhanced by A and F Batteries, 81st AA Battalion and C Company, 807th TD Battalion. From Ettendorf the paratroops were deployed along a 1-mile front, overlooking the river, between a set of partially demolished bridges ranging east from Pfaffenhoffen to the village of Niedermodern.

The ancient and once prosperous town of Pfaffenhoffen is situated in the Val de Moder – a shallow valley bisected by the river Moder, which at this point was normally no wider than a main road. The basic plan was to send patrols across to the northern bank and disrupt enemy forces based at La Walck, a northern suburb of Pfaffenhoffen, plus the surrounding villages of Kindwiller, Bitschhoffen, and Uberach. Uberach was nestled on the edge of the Haguenau forest, on the regiment's right flank. Overshadowing the northern banks of the Moder, the densely wooded forest covered an enormous area to the east, and stretched as far as the eye could see.

On February 1, 2nd Battalion was for the most part still in regimental reserve when 1st and 3rd Battalions deployed to the MLR. At the time Pfaffenhoffen was partly a no-man's-land and virtually devoid of civilians. One rifle company from each battalion was sent forward to maintain an "outpost line of resistance" (OPLR) beyond the raised road overlooking the river. Some foxholes had to be relocated to higher ground after they began to fill with water.

Apart from the occasional shell from a big rail gun we called Alsace Annie, life was OK and there was nothing really going on in our sector at Niedermodern. I think the fact that we were there in the first place was enough to deter the enemy, who really didn't have the resources to do anything anyway. Compared to what we'd experienced in Bastogne, the ruined buildings overlooking the river Moder seemed luxurious. As things were so quiet, I had time to sit down and write condolence letters to the families of Frank Mellett and Patrick Neill. I also wrote and told my sister Anna all about my encounter with Martien van Ganzewinkel in Holland and asked if she would be kind enough to find his brother and let him know that his family were all safe and well.

Several German units across the river had previously been identified, such as the Infanterie-Regiment 937 belonging to 245.Volksgrenadier-Division, which was predominantly made up of boys and older men. Other than that, this sector of the German West Wall was relatively peaceful apart from the rail gun, sporadic mortar fire, and occasional enemy patrolling.

> During this period, I guess because the enemy weren't particularly effective, my platoon wasn't really asked to do much in the way of patrolling, although we did set up quite a few OPs. We had a decent supply of blankets and for the first time in weeks received a decent supply of ration packs.

By February 2, the snow began to thaw, causing extensive flooding, and turning the ground into thick mud. A large, but long overdue consignment of rubberized winter overshoes arrived. Although thankful for their eventual arrival, the men were upset by the delay as many serious non-battle-related casualties could have been avoided had the "shoepacks" been more widely available at Bastogne. Ed also recalled the positive effect on morale when a shower unit finally arrived.

Haguenau – No place for heroes

Situated between Schweighouse-sur-Moder and Bischwiller, 25 miles from Strasbourg, Haguenau was and remains one of the largest towns in the region of Bas-Rhin. Straddling the meandering Moder, in 1940 Haguenau was a thriving industrial town with a wartime population of around 18,000, though most of them had fled by February 1945. From Haguenau the Moder twists and turns for around 10 miles in an easterly direction through Drusenheim before filtering into the mighty river Rhine, marking the border with Germany.

Along with a vitally important road network, Haguenau also boasted a major railway terminus and a military airfield was located nearby at Kaltenhouse, which had been captured by the Allies in December 1944.

Over on the enemy-held bank, the massive Haguenau forest swallowed the northern boundaries of the town, while further north the land rose steeply to mark the beginning of the Vosges du Nord mountain range.

At 1330hrs on February 5, Colonel Sink and 2nd Battalion arrived at Harthaussen and established a temporary forward CP with the 313th IR (45th ID), until the Fox could organize his own HQ at nearby Château Walk. The château was located on the southern side of Haguenau along Rue Député Hallez and had been a former German Youth camp. Close to the château was a heavily booby-trapped area of woodland known as the Weitbruch Forest, where engineers worked hard to clear the sector of "Schu mines." These small, wooden-framed, antipersonnel devices were virtually undetectable and had recently caused several serious civilian and military casualties.

At 2200hrs, the 506th took over the MLR from the 313th IR with 1/506 on the left and 2/506 to the right. Over the next five days the 506th remained in defense of Haguenau, conducting vigorous patrolling, both combat and recon, across the Moder while waiting for replacements.

Every rifle company underwent drastic changes to its structure and manpower as the new blood began to arrive at Château Walk, but not all the platoons were affected:

> Because we were pretty much up to strength at that moment in time, I don't recall being sent any new replacements.

In the center of Haguenau, the river – which was now in full flood – was overlooked on both sides by a number of tall, abandoned factory buildings. Ed's platoon was working from a schoolhouse that had been badly damaged by shellfire. Close to the school was a demolished bridge and on the other side of the Moder, 3rd Platoon could easily observe a large house with shuttered windows that they knew to be occupied by several German machine-gun teams. John van Kooijk came to visit for a couple of days. The Dutchman was now working for Captain Alphonse Gion in the IPW team, interrogating German POWs. The Opel Kapitan had finally stopped working on the way to Alsace. Although the old doctor's car had been badly damaged by shellfire in Bastogne it had served 2nd Battalion well, and had seen much use with Dick Winters and Lewis Nixon.

As predicted, the men felt that any cordiality shown by the local population seemed false. Despite this, enough information was gathered by the IPW team to uncover a small group of enemy soldiers who were trying to infiltrate the area dressed as civilians. Ed's CP was under constant observation from a culvert across the river, making any movement in daylight difficult. On the 10th, Sergeant Bill Kiehn, who had taken over 1st Squad after Frank Mellett's death, was buried by tons of concrete when the barn in which he was sleeping was hit by enemy shellfire. Kiehn's death was difficult for Shifty to accept, as they had been very close friends. It was even harder for Paul Rogers and Moe Alley, who tried to save him by clawing at the rubble with their bare hands but could only recover his crushed and battered body. During this time, 3rd Platoon captured a civilian who had crossed the river and John van Kooijk carried out the interrogation. Surprisingly the man turned out to be a coal miner who was just trying to get back to his family in Brumath. It was just like old times for John and Ed, as the civilian showed them a few enemy concentrations and possible CPs across the Moder that were later dealt with by the air force.

On February 12, the 101st area was reorganized and each regiment tasked to defend a sector with a reinforced battalion. H Company was attached to 2nd Battalion and took over the left flank. Spring came early with three days of clear weather and beautiful sunshine. Over the next few days, elements of the 143rd ID began to arrive in preparation to relieve the regiment. A party was held by the officers to celebrate Carwood Lipton's battlefield commission, which became effective on February 16. Lipton, who did not drink, accepted a glass of whiskey without hesitation and then, much to the embarrassment of the others, almost choked on the high-strength liquor.

By February 23, the 506th had started moving out by road to a rear assembly area near Saverne, 50 miles southwest of Haguenau. Forty-eight hours later the regiment moved by truck to the railway station, in preparation for the 200-mile rail journey back to Mourmelon ... finally they were going "home."

Return to Mourmelon – February 26–April 2, 1945

When the division returned to Mourmelon in late February, most of Camp Châlons had been taken over by a field hospital. Medical and support staff were now occupying the permanent barracks that the 101st had so painstakingly repaired before leaving for Bastogne, forcing the regiment to live in a village of pyramidal tents. The battalion underwent several changes to its command structure, the most important of which was Dick Winters' promotion to major, and his officially taking over from Robert Strayer, who had recently replaced Charlie Chase as acting regimental executive officer. Captain Lloyd Cox became 2nd Battalion executive officer and Harry Welsh returned from hospital and became the battalion's intelligence officer.

Looking like he was leading this guy on a leash, Paul Rogers came into my office with a tall skinny lieutenant, carrying his personal records in a packet. "Whose is he then?" I hesitantly inquired. "He's yours – he belongs to you now!" "What d'ya mean, he belongs to me?" "I was told by battalion that he's your new assistant platoon leader." The guy stood there grinning for a moment before speaking. "Hi, I'm Roy Gates, how do you do? Here are my records." After studying the paperwork for a minute or two, I glanced up, "Christ Almighty, you've been a second lieutenant for almost six years ... heck, Gates, 1938 ... you mustn't be worth a damn!" "Yes, sir that's right." We all burst out laughing, "I think I'm gonna like you Roy, welcome to our platoon." With that, I asked Paul to settle "Mr Gates" in. As they were on their way out, I suggested that Roy should stay close to Staff Sergeant Rogers if he knew what was best. Reading further, I saw that Roy wasn't a "Point" man, which was a relief. In fact he'd been a graduate of the flagship Texas A&M Research University, whose officer cadet programme was second to none and his previous posting was with 10th Armored Division so it wasn't all bad.

Over the next few weeks we learned that his promotion during the last couple of years had stalled due to the fact that he'd struck a superior officer, who unfortunately turned out to be the son of a general. Roy's family was extremely wealthy and before the war had sold their successful leisure business to The Disney Corporation. We were also astonished to find out that as a teenager he had studied French in Paris with Ernest Hemingway's son John. Roy being fluent in French was a real bonus for the platoon, because it meant we could now sell our "loot" on the black market in Paris without any problems ... and he was smart enough to let Paul run things when I wasn't around ... yes indeed, Roy Gates turned out to be a great asset and a life-long friend who, when asked, always compared me to a crazed gerbil.

One afternoon as I was driving out the main gate, one of the soldiers looked familiar so I stopped. At first O'Neil Wynne didn't recognize me, but I sure knew him from back home. O'Neil was well known around Norfolk for his brilliant 10-pin bowling skills ... almost a mini-celebrity. "Soldier," I said, "do you know how to salute? Let me see you do that again." He still hadn't clicked. "Come on soldier, that is a terrible salute, put your rifle down and come to attention. What's your name?" "Wynne, sir, Private O'Neil Wynne, sir." "That's a peculiar name, where ya from?" "Oh, Norfolk..." "Really? I've a friend who comes from there by the name of Shames, ever heard of him?" Then the penny dropped. "Aw ... hello Ed, sorry 'bout that. It's great to see you. How've you been?" "I'm doing OK, thanks. Do you fancy a beer?" "Oh come on man, I'm on duty." After a quick chat with the guard commander, I got O'Neil released and we drove into town for a drink. Luckily this time, Strayer wasn't around to fine me $50 for fraternization. After the war, O'Neil turned pro and became the number one duckpin bowler in the country ... what a guy.

Many were granted seven-day leave passes and hundreds of troopers were flown down to the French Riviera each Sunday.

I got a furlough to Cannes and stayed with First Lieutenant John Kelly from D Company and several other officers in the beautiful Carlton Hotel on the seafront. One night Kelly, whose face was all broken up from boxing, got roaring drunk, took off all his clothes and jumped into a fountain. We just couldn't handle him and eventually someone called the MPs, who after a pretty fierce fight, had to physically restrain the crazy bastard on the ground.

That night, minus John, who had been sent back to Mourmelon for a disciplinary hearing, we hit the town for more fun and frolics. We'd just read an article in *Yank* magazine, written by some general complaining about our troops, who, when in convoy, were inclined to call out to women as they passed by. The column had earned this guy the nickname "You Who," which was quite amusing. Anyhow, we were drinking in a club when one of the boys spotted this general walking in with a couple of staff types. Before we could stop him, our buddy stood on the table and started shouting, "You Who, You Who ... I'm a big-arsed bird!" and was immediately arrested for his trouble. After that I figured to heck with socializing and went by myself on a tour to Grasse, the perfume capital of the world, situated about 12 miles outside Cannes. Despite all the arrests, I really enjoyed the break and when I got back there was a letter waiting from my sister Anna. Like I asked, she had visited St Paul's Catholic Church in Portsmouth, Piet van Ganzewinkel's last known address, and discovered that he'd been promoted to Monsignor and moved to Richmond, where she telephoned, and "Father Van," as he was known, came down the next day and read my letter. Father Van was overjoyed to know that his family were all OK, which gave me a wonderful feeling.

A presidential citation

March 15, 1945 was a big day in the history of the 101st Airborne as they were the first complete division ever to be awarded a distinguished unit citation from the President of the United States, Franklin D. Roosevelt. General Eisenhower presented the award "For Extraordinary Heroism" during the defense of the key communications center at Bastogne between December 18 and 27, 1944. The day was bathed in sunshine as Ed and 12,000 other men stood sharply to attention in line along the edge of the airfield as dozens of transport planes buzzed about overhead.

Absent from the podium was Anthony McAuliffe – who had recently been promoted to major general. He and the 103rd Infantry Division were still fighting hard along the Siegfried Line west of Wissembourg in Alsace. Those who were present on the podium alongside "Ike" were SHAEF members of staff Major General Lowell Rooks and Lieutenant General Sir Frederick Morgan. Also included were senior members from the First Allied Airborne Army, Lieutenant General Lewis Brereton and his Chief of Staff, Brigadier General Floyd Parks. As well as the commander of XVIII Airborne Corps, Lieutenant General Matthew B. Ridgeway, there was Major General Paul Williams of IX Troop Carrier Command, Mr Steve Early, the secretary to the White House, Captain Harry Butcher who was Eisenhower's naval aide, and representatives of the Oise Base Section. Next to the stand, adding a touch of glamor was German-born actress and singer Marlene Dietrich who happened to be performing at Mourmelon in a United Services Organizations show.

Speaking via a public address system Eisenhower declared:

You in reserve were hurried forward and told to hold that position. All the elements of battle drama were there. You were cut off and surrounded. Only valor, complete self-confidence in yourselves and in your leaders and a knowledge that you were well-trained and only the determination to win could sustain soldiers under those conditions. You were given a marvelous opportunity and you met every test. You have become a fighting symbol of which all citizens of the United Nations can say to their soldiers today: "We are proud of you." It is my great privilege to say to you here today, to the 101st Airborne Division and all its attached units: "I am awfully proud of you. Just as you are the beginning of a new tradition, you must realize, each of you, that from now on the spotlight will beat on you with particular brilliance."

Whenever you say you are a soldier from the 101st, everybody, whether it is on the street, in the city or in the front lines will expect unusual conduct from you. I know that you will meet every test of the future like you met in Bastogne. Good luck and God be with you.

As the supreme commander stepped back from the microphone, the divisional flag – now adorned with a sky-blue citation ribbon – suddenly fluttered in the breeze. The US Army band struck up a march as the troops began to pass by in review. For almost 70 minutes the olive drab-clad officers and soldiers filed past the podium while Ike, Major General Taylor and the other dignitaries proudly took their salute.

Directly after the parade, it was announced that the Army was introducing a point system, which would ultimately lead to some of the "old timers" like Ed, Paul, and McClung going home. In the meantime, those who had been through Normandy, Holland and Bastogne would be entered into another lottery for a limited number of 30-day furloughs to the USA – which, as previously, Ed didn't win.

On the morning of March 24, the 17th Airborne Division, commanded by Major General William Miley, took off from Mourmelon as part of Operation *Varsity* – to assist Field Marshal Montgomery's 21st Army Group in their crossing of the Rhine (codenamed Operation *Plunder*). The 17th Airborne dropped on the eastern bank at Wesel along with the British 6th Airborne Division, commanded by Major General Eric Bois. Both divisions were part of XVIII Airborne Corps and despite heavy casualties bravely opened the way for the Allies into Germany. In one day the joint force dropped 16,000 men onto one DZ, dwarfing Normandy and Holland – making *Varsity* the largest single airborne assault in military history. By the end of March all four US Armies fighting in Western Europe were east of the Rhine, First and

Ninth Army followed through to encircle and neutralize enemy forces in the Ruhr. With the "Gates of the West" now firmly open, the 101st Airborne Division would go on to provide security and establish military law wherever and whenever required but for now the 506th remained at Mourmelon waiting for its next mission.

The Officers' Mess at Mourmelon had a ballroom on the second floor and the regiment organized a dinner dance with a band just before we were put on standby for the Ruhr. I was instructed to drive to Reims with, I think, Fred Bahlau, who had been recently commissioned, to invite and arrange transportation for the US Army nurses stationed at the hospital. Interestingly, the place had been built after World War I, from money donated by American billionaires Andrew Carnegie and John D. Rockefeller. Fred and I had a ball, just going round talking to all these chicks and once we had their approval a number of trucks were sent out to bring the girls back to camp for the do.

Many of the senior guys kept sending me to the bar to get their drinks ... I didn't mind, it's just the way it is. The party was in full swing when Lieutenant Colonel Strayer passed out in front of Sink. I'd had four or five strong vodka martinis when the colonel asked me in no uncertain terms to remove Strayer. "What shall I do with him, sir?" I inquired, "Anything you like, just get him out of here!" I called over Second Lieutenant Alexander Hamilton who had only recently been posted to E Company's 2nd Platoon. As we carried Strayer out by his hands and feet, Hamilton asked where were we going to put him. I was pretty drunk and feeling slightly mischievous, I suggested we stick him in Bob Sink's tent under the bed.

I heard when Sink awoke the following morning and discovered our little "gift" still fast asleep he kicked Strayer straight out the door and into the street! Thankfully Strayer never found out it was me but it was an opportunity to kind of even the score a little, as it was fair to say that by this stage in the game, I truly hated that man's guts.

12

"RUHR POCKET"
Western Germany, April 3–24, 1945

On April 1, 1945 the 101st Airborne was attached to Major General Ernest Harmon's XXII Corps, part of the Fifteenth Army now under the command of Leonard Gerow.

The advance party left Mourmelon on Saturday, March 31, and was followed two days later by the main body. Consisting of 117 officers and 2,006 enlisted men, the regiment traveled via Maastricht in an impressive convoy of trailer trucks – a distance of some 200 miles. The 506th took over from the 387th Infantry Regiment, 97th Infantry Division, and were deployed south of Düsseldorf, around the town of Nievenheim and the villages of Stürzelberg and Zons, 50 miles east of the border with Holland and Belgium.

Situated on the western tip of the Ruhr Valley, the ancient city of Düsseldorf straddles the Rhine. With a population of some 540,000 people and growing, Düsseldorf had become an important industrial center for the Nazi war machine at the beginning of World War II. But around 60 percent of the city had been destroyed during strategic Allied bombing raids and as a result approximately 200,000 civilians had fled into the surrounding countryside.

Colonel Sink established his regimental CP in the nearby town of Gohr, which became the central hub of operations for the next three weeks. The troops were billeted comfortably in private houses and farms. On the regiment's extreme left flank, bordering the River Erft, were the troops from the 327th GIR. On the right, at Worringen, was the 504th PIR, part of the 82nd Airborne Division. The MLR for the 506th was a roughly 10-mile front along the Rhine that meandered north from Worringen through Himmelgeist to Düsseldorf. The 387th Infantry Regiment handed over its sector to the 506th on April 4, and the 506th's job was to maintain contact between the 327th and 504th and conduct regular recon and combat patrols across the Rhine. In the meantime, the 506th PIR was tasked with maintaining military government within each battalion's own specific area.

All the bridges across the river in the regimental sector had been destroyed, isolating around 5,000 troops from the 176. and 338. Volksgrenadier-Divisions on the eastern bank of the river. Despite these fragmented pockets of resistance, the war was all but over and the German will and means to fight was virtually exhausted. As part of the blocking force, 2/506 took control of the eastern flank while 3rd Battalion was allocated the northern area of the 506th's MLR, tying in with the 327th GIR. As usual the 321st GFA supported the 506th with their 105mm guns.

At the end of March 1945, around 300,000 enemy troops, mostly belonging to Feldmarschall Walter Model's reconstituted Heeresgruppe B (Army Group B), were encircled east of the Rhine along the Ruhr valley. The area, which became known as the "Ruhr Pocket," was almost 80 miles deep and 50 miles wide.

Walter Model was directed to fight for every last inch of German soil. In early March, after failing to destroy the vitally important Ludendorff Bridge that spanned the Rhine at Remagen, Heeresgruppe B found itself outflanked by US ground forces. Due to the tenacity of the US Ninth and Fifteenth Armies the "pocket" was quickly reduced to a 25-mile front bordering the Rhine north from Cologne (Köln) to Düsseldorf. The job of cleansing the western edge of the pocket along the river had been given to units from the Fifteenth Army. Model, who had led the unsuccessful German offensive in the Ardennes, was ordered by Hitler to destroy the factories and turn the region into a fortress. Although he ignored the "scorched earth" directive, Model's attempts at defense ultimately failed when in the middle of April, Heeresgruppe B was split in half by the Allies during their final penetration of the pocket. Personally unwilling to submit to Hitler's instructions, Model discharged his youngest and oldest troops, while informing the remainder to either surrender or attempt a breakout through the encirclement. Berlin denounced Model and his army as traitors and ordered SS units within the pocket to seek revenge on any soldier or civilian refusing to stay and fight.

Despite the chaos on the other side of the river, the first week on the ground was quiet for the 506th, with many troopers still being sent on leave. For the most part, combat activity consisted of patrolling or crossing the Rhine in small boats to assess enemy strength and capture a few prisoners for intelligence purposes. On April 12, 3rd Battalion was relieved by 1/506 and sent to Nievenheim as regimental reserve. Shortly after 1st Battalion took over the MLR, a large-scale raiding party from A Company, comprising seven officers and 125 enlisted men, was sent across the river to destabilize any enemy troops remaining in the area.

John van Kooijk was assisting 2nd Battalion executive officer, Captain Lloyd Cox and HQ Company executive officer First Lieutenant Lee May when Colonel Strayer asked them to interview a Dr Mueller, who had been caught operating a telephone switchboard at the chemical plant in Zons. Dr Mueller was a chemist in his 60s, who had been an officer in World War I, and denied all accusations of spying. A map had been found in the factory showing an area due south of Düsseldorf between Cologne and Neuss. Many places now occupied by the 506th, such as Stürzelberg, Hackenbroich, and Zons, were neatly marked with figures in black and red, denoting what 2nd Battalion thought might be estimated US troop numbers. Eventually John and Captain Gion from the IPW team concluded that Mueller knew nothing and sent him home.

Before leaving, Mueller happened to mention that the owner of the factory was living nearby with his family in an underground shelter. When questioned, the "director" confirmed that the map was in fact his and claimed that it showed statistics pertaining to his workforce from before and during the war. While interviewing the factory owner, the team learned that two German deserters were living on a barge moored opposite the industrial area at Zons. The men were quickly arrested and proved to be an interesting source of information. It is likely that the detailed intelligence provided by these men coupled with other information found in the factory at Zons may well have encouraged Bill Leach, now a major, to personally lead a reconnaissance mission between Benrath and Baumberg.

Between Benrath and Baumberg, the Rhine bends acutely eastwards and it was along the Stürzelberger Strasse near Zons that Leach decided to launch his night mission. On their return trip across the river, the strong currents resulted in Leach and his men paddling straight toward F Company's position. A nervous replacement opened up with a .30 caliber machine gun and killed Major Leach and every man in his boat. Five days later, on April 18, the bodies of Leach and Private First Class Robert Watts were recovered from the river opposite the F Company CP at Stürzelberg.

The authorities had established collection centers at Nievenheim for refugees or displaced persons (DP centers). Many German civilians escaped from their own troops across the Rhine into the US sector and had to be sprayed with delousing powder before being processed. While in the Ruhr, Ed's platoon undertook various tasks including the requisition of private homes for billets. The platoon also conducted a few patrols north of Stuttgart with John van Kooijk, who had his CP in a beautiful villa belonging to the owner of a local textile factory,

Mr Vielhauer. On one patrol during this period they found a number of decomposing American bodies in a nearby wood, probably from the 387th IR, which reminded everyone that the war was by no means over.

On April 16, a liaison party from the 97th ID reported to the regimental CP, confirming that elements of their division had occupied Baumberg on the eastern bank of the river. Shortly afterwards the 506th was informed that elements of the 94th ID would soon be relieving its front-line battalions.

Official contact was made with the US infantry units on the eastern bank by a patrol from the 506th that crossed the river under a white flag. Not long afterwards 1st Battalion and 2nd Battalion were relieved by 1/303 and 2/303 from the 94th ID and sent to Weckhoven, Horrem and Dormagen. The next two days were spent in training, while military control passed to the 94th ID.

Fighting continued in the last pocket of resistance at Düsseldorf until Model committed suicide near Duisburg on April 21. By the end of April around 325,000 German troops had been taken prisoner. On April 21/22, the 506th was transported by truck and rail to Jagsthausen in support of Seventh Army. Three days later, 2/506 made themselves at home in Widdern.

Before leaving the Ruhr, I developed a terrible toothache and our regimental dentist, Dr Samuel "Shifty" Feiler, sent me to Cologne for treatment. I traveled there on an old moped we'd picked up the previous week. When I found the dental van, there must've been about 60 people all waiting in line. I know this was a little out of character but I was in a hurry and drove straight up, parked my bike and walked to the front of the queue. Of course everyone started hollering, asking what the heck I thought I was doing etc., and I snarled back, "Getting my tooth fixed, what do you think I'm doing?" Then this nurse came out and asked me, like I was some sort of schoolboy, to go stand at the back! "Excuse me, but I'm here and I'm next. Listen, my unit is in the process of pulling out and unlike most of these folks I don't have the time to hang around." Hearing all the commotion, the dentist came out and told me that I just couldn't do that sort of thing. "Well, I'm here and I'm telling you that there's nothing you are going to do about it." I mean, except for me, everyone in that line was from the rear echelon. Casually touching my holster, I gave him the "deep six" look, and he immediately backed down. Well, the tooth got fixed but it didn't end there. A week or so later, Sink got a letter from the dental people complaining about my attitude. All the boss could say was, "Not again, Shames, the rear echelon are there to support not hinder us, so in future please, please, please be nicer to them!"

The everlasting truth – Southern Bavaria, April 28–May 3, 1945

By April 22, Regimental HQ had moved to Götzenburg Castle at Jagsthausen in the Heilbronn region – which had been liberated by Seventh Army – situated midway between Würzburg and Stuttgart. A few days later the 506th PIR were transported by train to Ludwigshafen near Heidelberg. During the seemingly endless journey from Gohr, the train stopped at various towns to stock up on coal and water, before finally crossing the Rhine. The regiment was then sent to Ulm on the 25th, where it was attached to VI Corps from Seventh Army, commanded by Major General Lucian Truscott. The mission was not only to protect Truscott's flanks but also help stabilize southwest Bavaria behind Tony McAuliffe's 103rd ID. On April 28, the 506th Battle Group was traveling through Bavaria behind Lieutenant General Alexander Patch's Seventh Army, when they were ordered south toward the medieval walled town of Landsberg am Lech, 40 miles west of the regional capital, Munich. The Germans had established a 15-mile-long stop line, west of the mighty river Lech, from Obermeitinge in the north to Erpfting, 3 miles southwest of Landsberg.

A full 24 hours before the 506th occupied Landsberg, the 12th Armored Division had pushed the enemy forces back across the Lech. As the Germans withdrew they demolished all road and rail bridges behind them. One crossing point remained partially serviceable near Beuerbach at Schwabstadel, but could only be used by infantry. Meanwhile, 4 miles further south, at Kaufering, the engineers were working frantically to build a pontoon crossing for tanks next to the damaged railway bridge. Unfortunately it would not be ready for at least another 48 hours. Later that day (April 27) the 103rd ID, supported by the 10th Armored, attacked the southwestern edge of Landsberg.*

While engaged in combat operations, the troops from Seventh Army started to notice a thick, stifling odor permeating around the town. One by one the 92nd and 101st Cavalry Regiments from Combat Command B, 12th Armored, discovered three slave labor camps designated by the SS as "Kauferings" due to their close proximity to the railhead at Kaufering.

These three facilities were KZ-I, III, and IV, but seven more camps would be discovered. A total of ten labor facilities had been established in the area in June 1944 to house 21,000 slave workers whose job was to build three enormous factories (partially underground) west of the Lech, codenamed "Walnut II" (Walnuss), "Vineyard II" (Weingut), and "Diana II." The factories were built to produce the new twin-engine push-pull Dornier Do335 A-1 "Pfeil" (Arrow) fighter-bomber as well as the Focke Wulf FW190 D9 and the Messerschmitt ME262 jet fighter.

At Kaufering itself, a short distance south of the camp was a rail junction that acted as a central hub for slave labor, with trains continuously arriving from larger camps across the Reich. At this time names such as Auschwitz/Birkenau, Buchenwald, Mauthausen, Flossenbürg, and Dachau were still largely unknown to the advancing Allies but it would not take long for these industrial mega-camps to overshadow the horrors of the smaller facilities such as Landsberg.

---

* Previously the town had played an important role in the development of National Socialism. Adolf Hitler had been imprisoned here in 1923, and while serving a five-year term for "high treason," began to write the first part of *Mein Kampf*, his political directive for the future Nazi state.

By the time US forces arrived, the vast majority of the slave force at Landsberg had already been evacuated eastwards by train or on foot. KZ-IV (Camp 4) at Hurlag was a sick camp, where those no longer able to work were sent to die.

Shortly after dawn on April 27, US soldiers attacking Landsberg noticed a handful of emaciated people emerging from woodland, who informed them about the barracks that were smoldering nearby. Later that morning a small team was sent to investigate and what they found was sickening: over 300 disease-ridden skeletal corpses had been dragged from the huts and dumped in piles at collection points around the camp. Another 40 bodies were gathered between two huts, where they had been doused in fuel and set on fire. Of the 80 neatly arranged sunken barracks, around 12, situated along the edge of the perimeter fence, had been razed to the ground. At one end of the camp, piled high on the edge of a makeshift parade ground, was the bizarre sight of hundreds, maybe even thousands, of filthy overcoats.

Slowly the American troops began to piece together what had happened from survivors. On April 25, with Seventh Army fast approaching, the SS guards were ordered to evacuate all the Kaufering prisoners by foot to Dachau. Those unable to walk from KZ-IV were sent to the railway sidings opposite the camp, where dozens of open boxcars were waiting. Although only a short distance, the walk to the sidings was painfully slow for the decrepit, typhus-ridden prisoners. During the night, dozens collapsed en route to the train. By the morning bodies littered the sidings, as those still living shuffled toward the waiting boxcars.

Shortly after leaving the station, the packed train was tragically attacked by a US squadron of P-47s, killing a number of prisoners. Before reaching Dachau, the train was attacked again and more innocents killed. If that was not bad enough, because of the intense overcrowding at Dachau, 7,000 prisoners, including those from Landsberg, were then forced to march southeast toward Tegernsee. Many were shot during the journey or died from hunger and exhaustion before the guards eventually fled, leaving the survivors to be picked up by the advancing Allies.

By April 27, the 506th PIR had reached a temporary holding area west of Landsberg. The following day, selected personnel from Regimental HQ and E Companies, including Ed Shames and 3rd Platoon were sent to KZ-I to assist the 12th Armored with the humanitarian operation. Situated northwest of Landsberg, close to the underground factories Weingut and Diana II, the semi-abandoned site was made up of around 60 wooden huts. Camp commandant SS-Sturmbannführer Otto Förschner and his staff were nowhere to be found. Förschner had been running the camp for the last three months and had pitilessly tormented the prisoners, who had been predominantly women from Hungary and Lithuania. Around 100 had been left behind suffering from typhoid and the latter stages of malnutrition. The wooden barracks, which had housed the prisoners, were all built into the ground except for the roofs. In one hut they found 20 people, too weak to move, lying in their own excrement on two wide shelves that ran the length of the building on each side of a narrow central walkway.

When the 506th arrived, the gates were open, and some of the prisoners who were able to walk had already made their way into Landsberg looking for food. Members of Regimental HQ Company were detailed to go after the starving inmates and bring them back to camp. Ed Shames saw it all.

Colonel Sink contacted a nearby graves registration unit, who in turn got hold of SHAEF HQ for additional emergency care. Before outside help arrived we did everything in our power to make the survivors comfortable. Most, like me, readily gave up our own food but all it did was send the poor wretches convulsing in agony to the floor.

Most of those Ed encountered outside the barracks were terribly emaciated with horribly blackened mouths.

When the International Red Cross eventually arrived they immediately told us to stop feeding these people because their digestive systems weren't able to cope with our army rations.

Instead the medics set up a high-protein feeding program that primarily contained an easy-to-digest nutritional mixture of raw eggs, milk and sugar.

If we'd have caught the individuals responsible for this hellish place, then I think we would've executed each and every one of those bastards without pity.

One of the survivors had been a member of the Dutch underground until he was captured shortly before the Allied invasion of the Netherlands. The teenager, along with several others, volunteered and was accepted onto the regimental IPW team with John van Kooijk.

Earlier that same morning, in the north, 4th ID had begun to push out from Beurbach. But it would be a further two days before Munich surrendered. Eventually 3rd Battalion moved up behind the 411th IR to invest the southern edge of Landsberg and in doing so came across another camp, KZ-VII; one of the last Kauferings to be discovered. Shortly after KZ-VII was "liberated," 1st and 3rd Battalions, along with Regimental HQ, Service Company, and several others, moved into Landsberg and took control. Upon orders from division the two battalions rounded up as many of the townspeople as possible and escorted them to KZ-IV and a couple of other camps so that they could witness for themselves the atrocities committed by their fellow countrymen.

Meanwhile Ed Shames and E Company returned to 2nd Battalion, who were at Buchloe, 7 miles away to the east. Here, John van Kooijk who had been working alongside Ed with the IPW team, was reassigned to Harry Welsh, who had established his CP in the local town hall.

Dachau – a candle for the dead

On May 2, the regiment moved east toward Munich, which had surrendered two days earlier, to Starnberg. While the 321st GFA transported about 80 Kaufering camp survivors to a German military hospital near Munich, the 506th was given the job of helping process thousands of German soldiers who had surrendered. Many were just sitting around waiting for someone to come along and pick them up.

Before the regiment moved to Miesbach, Bob Sink summoned Ed Shames to discuss the possibility of sending a small team to Dachau, which had been liberated on April 28.

I was asked by Sink to provide him with a personal assessment of the camp that was believed to be a central hub for over 140 subsidiary facilities, including Landsberg. Sink handed me a file containing a few pieces of paper plus an aerial photograph and gave me two days to complete the task. I went back to the platoon, which was now billeted in a nearby barn, and carefully studied the picture and maps before formulating a plan of action. I selected Carl Fenstermaker as my driver/translator and left Roy Gates and Paul Rogers in charge, before heading off at dawn the following morning. Like Gutty and Strohl, Fenstermaker also came from Fogelsville and had recently returned after a spell with the Pathfinders. In fact he'd been directly involved with the resupply missions at Bastogne.

Located about 10 miles northwest of Munich, Dachau was the first camp of its kind to be opened and operated by the Nazi regime, who incarcerated political prisoners, regular criminals, homosexuals, Jehovah's Witnesses, and Roma gypsies there. Developed from a former World War I munitions factory, the "correctional facility" at Dachau was dramatically enlarged by the SS in 1937 using the plentiful supply of prison labor. Thirty-two enormous single-story huts were built in two neat rows on either side of a central roadway. Every block encompassed a set of self-contained barracks, each designed to hold 208 prisoners. The industrial area and railway sidings adjacent to the new camp were converted into a vast training center for the SS. At the same time, SS leader Heinrich Himmler began recruiting personnel to staff hundreds of new labor camps based on the blueprint modeled by his "super facility" at Dachau. Although Dachau was a labor camp rather than a "death camp" like Auschwitz, it possessed a gas chamber and a small crematorium, which was enlarged in 1942.

The prisoners at Dachau were used in local German industry. Those who could no longer work were originally sent by rail to the Hartheim Center near Linz where they were murdered by lethal injection. However, toward the end of 1944 the SS began to use a rifle range and gallows located inside the crematorium compound to kill those deemed unable to continue working. Ed would see evidence of the vile practices carried out at the camp such as the completely unethical medical testing facility. Dr Fritz Hintermayor headed a small medical team that included Dr Klaus Schilling and Dr Bruno Fialkowski. These two physicians were responsible for thousands of malaria experiments conducted on over 1,200 priests who had been imprisoned due to their opposition to the regime. Dr Hans Eisele was in charge of Dachau's surgical department and during the course of the war carried out countless cruel experiments on hundreds of innocent men, women, and children. By the end of April 1945, conditions rapidly deteriorated as more and more prisoners arrived from other camps, including those at Landsberg.

The Jourhaus Gate, where the SS administration also had their offices, was the main entrance to Dachau. Access was via a small bridge across the Würm Canal, which ran down one side of the camp.

On the morning of April 28, 3/157 from the 45th ID reached the outer perimeter of the SS complex at about the same time as the 42nd ID. Ten of the guards had already fled, plus the commandant, SS–Obersturmbannführer Weiter, and the medical staff. The garrison contained around 560 SS troops, who were either recuperating from wounds in the base hospital or attending courses at the training school.

At 1100hrs, after a brief gun battle in which 30 SS soldiers were killed, junior SS officer Heinrich Wicker surrendered to Brigadier General Henning Linden, outside a secondary entrance that led into the camp from the SS compound. As the scale and the purpose of Dachau became apparent, elements of I/157 headed into the SS area where almost immediately they gunned down 122 enemy soldiers who were mostly from the Waffen-SS. While the US forces were moving in, approximately 40 of the guards, who had donned civilian clothing, were also caught and beaten to death with shovels by some of the inmates. Over the next 3 hours, several hundred more SS troops were killed by I Company, while the 42nd ID cleared the area up to the Jourhaus Gate – the main access to the camp.

As Ed and Carl were driving toward Dachau four days after its liberation, they noticed the same disgusting smell that had permeated from Landsberg, but far worse. "The odor reminded me in some odd way of the smell from an industrial paper mill."

The day was getting warmer as Fenstermaker turned off the main road alongside the railway tracks, which had been originally designed to support the nearby munitions factories. Among the open carriages parked in the sidings were 30 abandoned boxcars from KZ-IV at Kaufering and also Buchenwald. The double doors were wide open, so they could see that each carriage contained around 20 corpses, rotting in the morning sun – those killed by the Allied air attacks while the train was en route from Landsberg. Several large piles of clothing lay nearby, left behind by those who had survived the train journey and then force-marched to Tegernsee.

As the two troopers stood motionless surveying the scene, they correctly concluded that this must have been the very last train to arrive. Wiping away tears, Ed and Carl got back in their jeep and drove through the industrial area, past the Kommandantur's HQ, toward a neatly planted row of tall poplar trees either side of the main entrance. They crossed over the bridge outside Dachau's Jourhaus Gate and were stopped at a US checkpoint before being given permission to enter. Ed stole a glance at Carl as they continued ahead through the low archway that opened onto an enormous parade square or *Appellplatz*.

The first thing Ed noticed was the three-story 60ft-high guard tower on the other side of the square. With over 30,000 people on site, the camp was ridiculously overcrowded and many individuals were simply wandering around, devoid of all reason. The men were overwhelmed by the sheer scale of the camp and the suffering it contained, compared with what they had previously seen at Landsberg. Being Jewish, Ed found it unbelievably hard to absorb.

Many of the prisoners were dressed in filthy blue and white striped jackets and pants with blue skullcaps, although others wore civilian clothes with large white crosses painted on their backs because the camp quartermaster had run out of prison clothing.

Over on Ed's right were the main support buildings belonging to the SS, containing kitchen, laundry, showers, and workshops as well as a prewar underground cell system. The large U-shaped structure spanned the entire width of the camp. Upon its roof was emblazoned a message in gigantic white letters, which translated as: "THERE IS ONE PATH TO FREEDOM. ITS MILESTONES ARE OBEDIENCE, HONESTY, CLEANLINESS, SOBRIETY, HARD WORK, DISCIPLINE, SACRIFICE, TRUTHFULNESS & LOVE OF THE FATHERLAND."

Over on the left, Shames and Fenstermaker could see the two rows of wooden barracks partly obscured by smoke emanating from thousands of small cooking fires. Putting the jeep in second gear, the two men slowly drove through the crowds along the central roadway to the far side of the camp where the gas chamber was located.

The piles of naked bodies that were still waiting to be cleared made me feel sick. Carl kept asking, *"Entschuldigung bitte, spricht hier jemand Deutsch?"* [Excuse me, does anyone here speak German?]

As we were moving around I noticed one particular lady whose behavior was quite different from the rest. Like many others she was just skin and bone but she seemed to be making a terrible, penetrating, primeval wailing sound. Eventually we came across a guy who seemed much stronger than the other inmates and who could talk to us in German. The man was from a small village in western Poland, called Zary, near Zagan, close to the German border, where his parents had run a bakery. He went on to say that his family had all been murdered and he'd only survived because of his baking skills, which had been useful to the Germans here in Dachau.

During our conversation with the baker we inquired about the woman who was still shrieking behind us. "Oh her, well, yes, she's a kind of 'show piece' – a trophy for the SS," he replied. "What on earth do you mean by trophy?" "About two years ago she arrived here with her six-year-old daughter. A couple of the guards tried to separate them at the station but she put up quite a struggle before they eventually prised the child away. One of the guards threw the kid to the ground and stamped her to death until the intestines ran from her mouth." Carl and I were almost speechless and just couldn't understand how afterwards the mother could become a "trophy." The baker soon put us right. "Don't you people get it? They used her as an example to others as to what might happen if discipline and obedience weren't observed." Carl was becoming an emotional wreck as he translated all of this crazy stuff to me and the morning just went on and on like that. Totally unbelievable.

The full death toll at Dachau will never be fully known but it is estimated that approximately 28,000 people were murdered by the Nazis at the camp.

The stench and horror of that place will stay with me for as long as I live. I met up with Fenstermaker, and Gutty in Fogelsville at Rod Strohl's house in December 1947, which was sort of a mini-reunion with our wives. During those two days, Carl and I tried to discuss our experience but in the end agreed that what we did and saw at Dachau could never be properly told, as it was much too horrible for anyone to comprehend, let alone understand. Now, 70 years later, I'd like to tell you more but it's buried so deep in my soul that I don't think the rest of the story can ever come out.

13

"LAST STAND"

Berchtesgaden and Austria

On the way back to regiment, Carl and I picked up the platoon on the autobahn. Despite still maintaining military discipline, after what we had just seen, I instructed my boys to loot as much as they wanted but not to take innocent lives. After all I think they'd earned the right, don't you? Paul Rogers selected a small number of private houses around Miesbach as billets. If we found a nice place to stay like this, I simply evicted the owners, didn't care where they went just as long as they cleared out when we told them to. Often when entering a village or "sightseeing" as we called it, I'd go straight to the Burgermeister with a demand that all weapons be brought in for disposal. Anyone found to be hiding anything after the amnesty would be severely dealt with. It was amazing what would turn up alongside the regular military rifles and pistols, such as the most beautiful antique hunting rifles and swords. Of course we helped ourselves to many of these items before handing the rest over to the authorities. I developed a particular interest in the 9mm Luger but each one I acquired had to be in pristine condition or special in some way.

Colonel Sink and the regimental combat team were still in Miesbach when alerted for the move to Obersalzberg and the Austrian border. The authorities had informed General Taylor that they were expecting the Waffen-SS to make a last stand around Hitler's Alpine resort at Berchtesgaden.

Earlier on April 20, Bavarian-born Feldmarschall Albert Kesselring, who had replaced von Runstedt as Commander-in-Chief West, was at his HQ in Motzenhofen near Munich when the order came to defend Obersalzberg, and Heeresgruppen C and G immediately began withdrawing to bolster the "Alpine Fortress."

Favored by Hitler and his ministers, Berchtesgaden was a beautiful town set between three jagged massifs. At 6,017ft, Kehlstein Mountain overlooked Berchtesgaden from the east, while much of the lower features of Baderlehenkopf and Kälberstein protected the western approaches. The fast-flowing river Ache courses through the eastern edge of town before dividing into the Ramsauer and Königssee valleys.

Dominated by the awe-inspiring twin peaks of Watzmann Mountain (8,901ft), the nearby spa resort of Königssee nestles alongside the crystal clear waters of a huge lake, one of the deepest in Germany.

On April 30, when news of Hitler's suicide reached Bavaria, what was left of the Third Reich sought to negotiate with General Eisenhower and his immediate subordinate General Jacob Devers, commanding officer of the US 6th Army Group.

The writing was on the wall when the Allies easily overran what should have been the most heavily defended parts of southern Bavaria. After transferring his HQ to Alm, Kesselring – with permission from Grossadmiral Karl Dönitz, who had been appointed by Hitler as his successor – sent a notice of possible surrender to SHAEF HQ. Despite his foresight, 60-year-old Kesselring was no politician and struggled to organize public security with the regional *Gauleiters* (branch leaders personally selected by the Führer). At a conference in Königssee, those *Gauleiters* who bothered to attend refused to accept the situation and naïvely demanded that the German Army continue to fight "guerrilla style" so that the Nazi Party could maintain some sort of civil order. Propaganda Minister Joseph Goebbels called these guerrilla fighters "Werewolves," but they never really materialized, as most of the German troops who flooded into the Alps simply wanted to surrender and receive a hot meal.

As overall commander, Kesselring insisted that there would be no "fight to the death." To avoid looting, he ordered the *Gauleiters* to hand over any surplus food and clothing to the civilian population. When General der Panzertruppen Hans Röttiger's Heeresgruppe C surrendered on May 2, the Alps were thrown wide open. Two days later negotiations with SHAEF were scheduled to begin at Salzburg. Kesselring sent the commander of 1.Armee, General Hermann Foertsch, and a small delegation to conduct the talks, although everything suggested by Kesselring and his colleagues only really amounted to a series of unworkable demands. During this period, Kesselring made his first personal approach to Eisenhower, who declined any dialogue that did not involve the total surrender of all German forces.

Two weeks earlier, northeast of Berlin, 52-year-old Reichsmarschall Hermann Göring had abandoned his beautiful château, Karinhall, in the Schorfheide Forest. Before leaving Karinhall, Göring sent a long telegram to Hitler, who was furious when he read:

> In view of your decision to remain in the fortress of Berlin, do you agree that I take over at once the total leadership of the Reich, with full freedom of action at home and abroad as your deputy in accordance with your decree of 29th June, 1941. If no reply is received by 10 o'clock tonight, I shall take it for granted that you have lost your freedom of action and will act for the best interests of our country and our people.

Hitler accused Göring of high treason and ordered his immediate arrest. Unaware of Hitler's less than positive reaction, along with hundreds of other leading Nazis, Göring headed to Berchtesgaden. Upon reaching the Alpine fortress, Göring and his staff were taken into custody by the SS based in Obersalzberg, which had just been bombed by the Royal Air Force. Many of the buildings were damaged during the raid, including Hitler's house, known as the Berghof, Göring's holiday home, and the SS caserne. Luckily for Göring, because of the bomb damage to the caserne, the SS were forced to move him further south into Austria. The Reichsmarschall's good fortune continued when he was rescued en route by a small contingent of loyal troops belonging to the Luftwaffe.

Berchtesgaden – May 4–10, 1945

The road from Munich was one of the first autobahns built by the Nazis when they came to power. The motorway also connected Berlin and Nuremberg to Salzburg and Linz in Austria. On the morning of May 4, the 506th PIR were traveling east on the highway toward Siegsdorf behind the US 3rd ID. Civilian wood-burning steam vehicles and an assortment of jeeps and trucks made up the ragtag convoy. A number of amphibious vehicles also known as DUKWs or DUCKs were available in case the regiment came upon any serious water obstacles. Driving down the autobahn the regiment passed a number of dense wooded areas that had been carved out to create dozens of individual makeshift hangars for the Luftwaffe. Reaching Siegsdorf the battle group ran into the back of a massive traffic jam, causing G and I Companies to be sent southeast along a secondary road toward the river Rote Traun at Inzell where unbeknownst to them, the bridge had recently been demolished by the retreating Germans.

Ahead of the 3rd Battalion advance party was Combat Command V, a detachment of the French Division Blindée, which was attached to 3rd ID. Some of Combat Command V's tanks had already made it across the bridge before it was blown, but the rest were now stranded as they had no bridging equipment. The result was havoc. It is somewhat unclear what happened next but it seems likely that a squad from 3rd Platoon, G Company was sent back to scout an alternative route in from the west.

Early on the morning of May 5, the main body arrived at Inzell. It took a while for the engineers to move up the line and – rather ironically – their heavy bridging equipment overbalanced and toppled into the river. When this occurred, Sink decided it would be quicker to use the DUKWs and ordered 3rd Battalion to prepare for the crossing. Everyone was feeling apprehensive at this stage because the French had been encountering small pockets of fanatical Hitler Youth, who did not want to surrender. Because of the increasing delays, Colonel Sink established a temporary CP and sent Bob Strayer, with 1st and 2nd Battalions, back to the autobahn with the intention of reaching Berchtesgaden via Bad Reichenhall – a huge detour of over 50 miles. Ed Shames and 2nd Battalion had not been on the autobahn long before they encountered 3rd ID who they had been behind earlier before turning off the autobahn. The division had been held up yet again for several hours at another sabotaged bridge.

The previous afternoon (May 4), a few miles northwest of Berchtesgaden, Karl Jakob, Obersalzberg's *Landrat*, or district commissioner, had been brokering a "peaceful" surrender at Winkl with elements of 3rd ID, who had been traveling south from Bischofswiesen. In fact Jakob's vehicle was actually stopped at Winkl by a Sherman tank that just happened to contain the commanding officer of 7th IR, Colonel John Heintges, who, contrary to his original mission of capturing Salzburg, ordered Jakob to return with him to Berchtesgaden. Thus 7th IR became the first Allied unit to enter the town. Heintges came in from the north and drove straight to the main square, called Schlossplatz, and parked opposite the unusual twin-spired abbey and the World War I memorial. Here, Heintges began negotiations for the full and unconditional surrender of the Alpine prize.

Before Heintges arrived, east of the river Ache over at Obersalzberg, the SS had set fire to what remained of the Berghof. Situated one and a half miles east of Berchtesgaden, the area of Obersalzberg was the nucleus of Hitler's mountain hideaway. On the left of the steep road leading to Hitler's palatial home was the Gutshof, built as the blueprint for all future German farms. Close by were the beautiful properties belonging to Göring and several Cabinet ministers (known as *Reichleiters*), including Martin Bormann – all of which had been badly damaged during the earlier RAF raid.

On May 5, a message came through from Maxwell Taylor's HQ: "Effective immediately all troops will stand fast on present positions. German Army Group G in this sector has surrendered. No firing on Germans unless fired upon. Notify French units in the vicinity. Full details to be broadcast, will be issued by SHAEF."

The following morning at 1030hrs, Sink and the regimental combat team (less 3rd Battalion who were still mopping up the renegade Hitler Youth soldiers in the Ramsauer valley) with Ed Shames and E Company as spearhead, arrived from Bad Reichenhall, to occupy Berchtesgaden behind 3rd ID.

Colonel Sink quickly established his CP at the Hotel Geiger where a squad from 1st Platoon, F Company was detailed as perimeter guard. The 60mm mortar squad was assigned to secure a tunnel situated less than half a mile northeast of the railway station. Hidden inside the 250-yard-long passageway was a train containing part of Hermann Göring's art collection, which he had sent on ahead before he left Karinhall in April. Another squad from F Company was sent to Obersalzberg to guard the properties belonging to Göring and his chief liaison officer, General der Flieger Karl Bodenschatz. Badly burned during the failed assassination attempt against Hitler, Bodenschatz had been arrested the previous day while recuperating in the military hospital at Bad Reichenhall. While Ben Stapelfeld's men were clearing Bodenschatz's HQ they came across the body of General der Flieger Gustave Kastner-Kirdoff. The 64-year-old senior Luftwaffe staff officer had shot himself in the head before the French arrived. The French troops had already looted Obersalzberg and brought a number of SS and regular soldiers down to the river Ache before cutting their throats and throwing the bodies into the clear blue mountain water.

The 506th was divided up and billeted in various buildings around the resort. Many went to the Berchtesgadener Hof Hotel on the southwestern edge of town. "We took over several plush private homes and slept in comfortable beds with white linen," recalled Ed. On May 7, 1945, the German Army surrendered and the first VE Day of sorts was quietly celebrated. At 0230hrs, Generaloberst Alfred Jodl, the official representative of Karl Dönitz, surrendered to General Eisenhower at his temporary HQ in a schoolhouse at Reims.

The war in Europe was over.

Many of us now had time to reflect on how World War II changed everyone's lives forever – I think the visit to Dachau was the turning point for me. We all grew up fast … it was like a transition, if you like, from one life to another. But to be honest I'd been lucky, especially when so many of my colleagues and friends like Colonel Wolverton, Paul Simrell, George Retan and Joe Madona didn't make it. Since joining 2nd Battalion, I'd rubbed shoulders with a lot of officers, some good, some bad, but none of them came anywhere close to the standard of my three friends … not even remotely. I mean I had a wonderful group of people in 3rd Platoon, one or two, like Shifty, McClung and Paul Rogers were finest I've ever worked with, but at least I was still alive to tell the tale.

The 101st handed out several pamphlets to the troops, such as *A Short Guide to the Bavarian Alps*. Despite being told that certain areas of Obersalzberg were out of bounds many, including Ed, decided that – no matter the restrictions – they could not let the opportunity to visit the Berghof or the Kehlsteinhaus slip through their fingers.

After crossing the bridge over the Ache, there were two granite pillars displaying a banner which read *"Führer, wir danken dir"* ("Führer, we thank you"). The road from here was the Kehlstein Strasse, the gateway to Obersalzberg and the northern face of Kehlstein Mountain. The drive up to Obersalzberg was comparatively short. The road twisted and turned steeply to the ruins of the Berghof and Hotel Züm Turken, passing what remained of Hitler's enormous greenhouse and the shattered SS barracks before turning off toward the famous Kehlsteinhaus or, as it became known to US forces, the "Eagle's Nest."

Designed originally as a private tea and function room for Hitler, the Eagle's Nest was brilliantly engineered into the tip of Kehlstein Mountain. The views across Berchtesgaden from the Kehlsteinhaus northwest to Baderlehenkopf and Kälberstein were world famous, as was the incredible southern vista down the valley toward Königssee and the Watzmann Massif.

Carved into the mountain directly below the Eagle's Nest was an impressive stone archway. Beyond the bronze entrance doors was a long tunnel leading to a circular domed waiting room where a brass-lined elevator (powered by a U-boat engine) climbed vertically 407ft to the nest.

While at the Eagle's Nest, Ed managed to pick up a bottle of Martell Cognac marked with the Führer's initials. "It was the only thing I managed to get my hands on that hadn't been plundered by the French. We eventually opened the bottle nearly two decades later to celebrate my son Steven's Bar Mitzvah. We did, however, liberate a lovely Mercedes touring car from Hitler's garage at the Berghof. The windows were bulletproof and we all took a few potshots with several different caliber weapons but nothing we had could penetrate the glass by more than a quarter of an inch or so." The following day guards were placed at the tunnel entrance to the Eagle's Nest with only field grade officers above the rank of major permitted to pass. Everyone else had to traverse the steep winding path on foot to the top of the mountain.

Peacekeeper – Saalfelden, Austria

Sink received a short note from Maxwell Taylor on May 8 stating:

A German colonel had arrived at the HQ of 36th Infantry Division from Hermann Göring. The colonel has a letter that he is taking to Generals

Devers and Eisenhower. He states that both Göring and Kesselring are present with a small staff just north of Bruck – go get them.

Patrols were sent and roadblocks established but Sink was too late as Brigadier General Robert Stack (deputy commander of 36th ID) was one step ahead, finding Göring and his convoy in Austria at a small village not far from Bruck.

While most of the 506th stayed behind in Berchtesgaden, Shames and 3rd Platoon were among those tasked to find Göring and other high-ranking officials along the Austrian border. The platoon was sent south by Salve Matheson – who had replaced Clarence Hester after Bastogne as regimental S3 – to establish roadblocks on all the main intersections coming in and out of Saalfelden.

Rod Strohl, who was by then a sergeant, and Shifty, had their own separate vehicle checkpoints or VCPs. I was given photographs of wanted Nazis, both military and governmental officials, which was supposed to make it easier for us to identify anyone trying to flee from the country but in most cases they were quite poor quality and of very little use.

This one vehicle tried to run my roadblock and all the occupants were shot by Popeye, who was only following orders. As we were searching the bodies a crowd began to gather round. Within minutes people were crying and getting emotional, especially over one corpse in particular. There was nothing to suggest that this or any other of the men was anyone special, only he did have a passing resemblance to Hitler's deputy, Martin Bormann, who was also rumored to be in the area at that time. Anyhow, we cleared the crowd and then decided to keep the incident amongst ourselves, as the crap would hit the fan if regiment ever got wind of it. So I asked the boys to get rid of the car and ordered some of the villagers to bury the bodies in some nearby woods. We wondered about that guy for years, but now I believe it could never have been Bormann, as nowadays all evidence suggests he most probably died in Berlin.

Over the course of the next few days we took a lot of pistols from everyone we pulled. I mean some of these people had wives or girlfriends with them like they were on some sort of summer vacation. We had our pick of the best Lugers especially those that were pristine or privately customized, the rest were thrown on the pile.

I think it was the following day, May 9 or 10, when a runner arrived at my VCP, "Sir, Sergeant Strohl wants to see you right away. He thinks he's got a German general!" Leaving Roy in charge, I jumped into the Mercedes and drove over to Strohl. As I pulled in, there were two or three cars parked up with about 15 or so Krauts standing around.

Everyone had already been disarmed except this one guy who was still wearing his sidearm. "Sergeant Strohl," I asked, "why on earth has that bastard still got his pistol?" "I tried to take it, cap, but he refused, saying he'd only surrender it to a senior officer." "For Christ's sake Rod, haven't you learned anything? And since when did you start taking orders from the Krauts? I left you in command didn't I? What in the hell do you think you are doin'?"

We still weren't sure who this guy was but when I demanded the pistol, I nearly choked on my coffee when, smiling and in almost perfect English, he politely ordered, "Please address me as 'Sir,' and as of this moment I will not surrender to you or anyone else below the rank of major. Is that clear?" I just couldn't believe what this man was saying! Fighting back I said, "Let me tell you something, sir, do you know what this is?" With that I cocked and pointed my .45 straight at his head and "politely" demanded, "I'm going to give you exactly five seconds in which to remove your sidearm … do you understand me?" He could see the look on my face and suddenly dropped his guard, "Yes, OK, as you wish." Begrudgingly, he slid the petite holster from his belt and handed it over. I was surprised to find that the pistol was an unusual 7.65mm P.Mod 37 semi-auto with wooden grips that had been made under license in Czechoslovakia.

Turning to Rod I ordered, "Sergeant Strohl, take this Kraut and his men in their vehicles back to Regimental HQ please." "You mean by myself, cap?" "Yep, sure. You've got that TSMG, what are you worrying about?" Rod then swore that he'd kill them all if they gave him any trouble! At that moment, of course we still had absolutely no idea of just how important our man really was, which is why I asked, "Now you ain't gonna give my sergeant here any reason to shoot, are you?" The German officer shook his head, and I called Strohl over. "Rod, give me your ammo." Strohl looked at me like I was crazy, "Give me your ammo and drop your magazine – that's an order." Strohl obeyed and I handed it back but now charged with about three rounds. "This is to insure that we don't have any little accidents on the way, is that clear?" "How am I gonna get back, sir?" "Sergeant, you'll have to figure that one out for yourself, won't you?" I was still mad at him for letting that smiling bastard dictate to him, but didn't really want a repeat of what Popeye had done earlier, either.

Strohl successfully escorted his prisoners to Hotel Geiger before General Taylor collected and took them to the Berchtesgadener Hof Hotel, where they were rather ironically given the best rooms in the house.

An hour or two later, a jeep pulled up and as Rod got out, we laughed and I handed him the pistol, still in its holster. "No, no, no, cap, I can't, really. I screwed up so you keep it, please." It was only then that Strohl told me that our "big shot" prisoner was none other than Feldmarschall Albert Kesselring! Probably the most important man in Germany at that moment in time, and his pistol, serial number 44256, was now mine and nobody was gonna take it away from me! Thank goodness Kesselring never called my bluff, because there was no way on earth if I'd shot him, we could've ever covered that one up.[*]

---

[*] It is possible that Kesselring had already begun talks with the authorities and when stopped in Saalfelden by 3rd Platoon, may have been under the impression that his surrender terms were in place. Rod Strohl concurred with Ed's recollection of events, and an earlier wartime photograph shows Kesselring wearing a holster very similar to the one liberated by Shames. Also it is interesting to note that, in a Signal Corps film taken during his handover to Maxwell Taylor Kesselring does not appear to be carrying a sidearm.

Short summer's sun

Initially after the German surrender, the regiment was given control of the southern area of operations assigned to the 101st Airborne Division, and deployed along two glorious steep-sided Alpine river valleys located either side of the Kitzbüheler Alps, which covered a vast area of some 430 square miles. North of the Kitzbüheler was the Glemm valley, with its rugged terrain divided by the river Saalach, along which are the villages of Hinterglemm and Saalbach. Crossing south over the craggy snow-capped peaks, the mountains drop sharply into the more densely populated Pinzgau region and the Salzach valley. At the mouth of these two valleys is Lake Zeller See and the spa town of Zell am See, where the 13th-century Schloss Fischhorn guards the southern end of the lake at Bruck. The 506th was deployed at Zell am See, Bruck, Kaprun, Uttendorf, Stuhlfelden, Saalfelden, Saalbach and further east at Lend. The 3rd Battalion HQ was established in the gorgeous five-star Grand Hotel close to Regimental HQ and Colonel Sink had his CP at Hotel Zell. The Grand had access to a private "regimental beach" and recreation center overlooking the lake, complete with rowing boats and a bar selling subsidized local beers.

After 2nd Battalion moved to Kaprun, my platoon were sent to Saalfelden, where there was a local discharge center. Roy Gates, Paul Rogers and myself took over the doctor's house just around the corner from the railway station. Everyone else was spread around us in a number of very comfortable properties. Although we personally had nothing to do with it, 2/506 was tasked with administering a large displaced persons camp at Kaprun.

At the time there were around 5,000 displaced people living in the area, mainly in the camp set up at Kaprun or another, which was close to Fischhorn Castle.

On May 15, Shifty Powers was one of dozens of soldiers to win a "golden lottery ticket" back to the States. It was like a dream come true. But as the convoy of trucks was transporting the winners to their next destination, the lead vehicle, in which Shifty was riding, struck an oncoming truck on a mountain road and tumbled over the edge. Many of the men in the truck were killed. Shifty was thrown clear, but suffered serious head injuries, a broken pelvis and arm. Although Ed was relieved that Shifty had survived, he considered the accident a tragedy beyond all human comprehension. Shifty would spend months recuperating in various hospitals before he eventually made it home.

A few days later General Taylor addressed the regiment:

We have reached another critical point in our lives and in the life of the division. It is time to face the prospect of future action in the Pacific. This commitment is only probable – not possible.

Taylor then went on to say that the 101st would be going home on January 1, 1946, and that everyone who remained would be entitled to a one-month furlough before being re-formed in North Carolina as "general reserve." Taylor continued:

So the future for most of you low point men at this stage is unknown. I cannot see why a top-notch division like this should be allowed to remain in the States but that is entirely up to General MacArthur. Back home this division tops the hearts of the nation and the eagle patch is recognized everywhere. The American civilians haven't relaxed their efforts because of VE Day and everyone is anxious to see Japan crushed. Those of you with 85 points or more will be leaving soon for America and I will later say goodbye. I am sure that the men from the 506th would earn the same fine reputation on the shores of Japan that you made on the shores of Normandy and the battlefields of Belgium.

Snapshots

Ed has many anecdotes about those surreal weeks in Saalfelden after the German surrender. At Fischhorn Castle approximately 200 silver cups were discovered. These .900-grade fine hammered chalices had originally been designed and produced in Innsbruck, possibly as gifts from Göring, although more likely by the ex-commander of the 37.SS-Freiwilligen-Kavallerie-Division (Volunteer Cavalry Division) Lützow, SS-Standartenführer Waldermar Fegelein, who had been residing at the castle before the Americans arrived. Now working for division, Charlie Chase was billeted at the castle and instructed Fred Bahlau to commission a silversmith in Saalbach to customize around 40 of these dainty vessels by adding a pair of silver jump wings before individually engraving the name and campaigns of every surviving officer, including those like Ed with battlefield commissions, who had taken part in combat operations with the 506th PIR beginning with Normandy. Each chalice cost 210 marks, or the equivalent then to $21.00, and was deducted from the recipient's mess bill.

Man, they were beautiful and made a wonderful souvenir to take home.

Speaking of souvenirs, Roy took an instant liking to a Contax Zeiss camera that I'd recently confiscated from a German officer at one of our roadblocks. I've never seen a person so excited and he was keen to explain to me just how advanced this camera was and then proceeded to take dozens of photographs in low light conditions, without the aid of a flash … in the end it was easier to let him keep it.

One afternoon, that hapless assistant of mine was messing around with his carbine, which I don't think he ever fired, and managed to knock his front tooth out. Right around the corner from where we were living was a dentist who replaced it with a beautiful porcelain crown and gold inlay. The gold came from a couple of coins that we'd recently "liberated." It turned out that dentist had a son, an officer in the Wehrmacht, who was being held in a local prison camp. In return for fixing Roy's tooth, the dentist asked if we could locate his boy and make sure that he was safe. I remember that this kid had been a member of the Austrian Olympic skiing team. Anyhow, not only did we find him but also managed to arrange for his early release, whereupon Roy drove him back to Saalfelden in the Mercedes.

Each rifle company was given complete control of its own specific *Landkreis*, or area. Shortly after settling in, all vehicles that had been liberated over the last few weeks were recalled due to a fuel shortage experienced by Third Army. Most companies were allowed to keep one vehicle, and many individuals just destroyed what they had rather than letting them go to a higher authority.

Roy and I weren't going to let anyone else have the pleasure of our "company car," so with Roy's help – which I always said was his only contribution to the war effort – we pushed our "Berghof Merc" over the edge of the Grossglockner Alpine road south of Bruck and told Sink that it had all been a terrible accident.

Meanwhile, the division began to construct rifle ranges and introduce a regular training program, which consisted of preliminary marksmanship and practice firing of all squad weapons, PT, marches, orientation, reviews, and close order drill. In the afternoons athletics were stressed with regular inter-company competitions, including basketball and baseball, while most, including Ed, waited anxiously to hear if they had accrued sufficient points to go home. At the core of the US Army Demobilization Plan was the point system. Points were awarded for the number of years and months spent overseas, medals, commendations, campaign battle stars, and other factors such as Purple Hearts, Presidential Unit Citation, and even the number of children. The magic figure for being sent home was 85 points. Of course Ed was well above the minimum requirement and immediately began looking forward to his imminent return to the USA and the distinct possibility of demobilization.

On June 28, around 400 men with a minimum of 85 points were alerted for transfer to the 501st PIR, which was to be the first regiment scheduled for deactivation. Shortly afterwards, the regiment began to decrease its area of operations by about 50 percent. Before the regiment left Austria, Colonel Sink gave the "Old Boys" like Ed a moving and heartfelt speech in which he told them of his pride in the 506th and thanked everyone for what they had done for their country over the last two years before saying goodbye and wishing them good luck.

Bar-le-Duc, France – A touch of class

The 506th PIR received orders on July 31 for a move to Auxerre in the Burgundy region of France. Over the next two days the unit moved out by road and rail and by August 4 was established in the crumbling French garrisons of Joigny and Sens. Meanwhile most of the high-point enlisted men had been transferred to the 501st and sent further east to a large three-story barracks at Nancy. The 101st Airborne Division was now the Supreme Headquarters Reserve.

What now remained of 3rd Platoon was posted southeast of Reims to Bar-le-Duc, and I'd just settled into a lovely private house with Roy Gates when we heard that the atomic bomb had been dropped on Hiroshima. We couldn't believe the power of that thing but quickly began to realize that the war in the Pacific had to be over.

Shortly after the second bomb was dropped on Nagasaki, unbeknown to Ed, he and some of the other high-point officers were put on alert for Marseille.

After Nagasaki that was it for me, and right away, I informed Roy that I was going to Paris, who rightly pointed out that we didn't have any passes. "I've got one," I said, and proceeded to open a musette bag filled with around a dozen of my best pistols! "Are you crazy? You mean you're going AWOL?" "Damn right. I'm gonna catch the train this afternoon – you have command. I'll be gone for three or four days, I think I deserve it, don't you? I'm sick of following orders, now I'm gonna do what I wanna do."

Strolling down the Champs-Élysées, I decided to try my luck at the George Cinque, which was and still is one of the finest hotels in Paris. Placing a pristine Luger carefully on the counter, I politely asked the concierge for the best room in the house. It is fair to say that the immaculately dressed Frenchman was a little shocked but quickly responded "Absolutely no problem at all Monsieur, but please give me a few minutes to relocate the current occupants." Before the concierge walked away, I inquired about the California Hotel, which everyone had told me was the best action in town. "Monsieur Shames, the California is right around the corner and is everything you imagined it to be."

After taking a cold shower – there was no hot water – I got cleaned up and decided to try a bit of shopping on the Rue de la Paye before going to the California. I was looking for something nice and special to take back home to Ida, similar in price to the pen she'd sent me while I was in Bastogne. I stopped by this fancy jewelry store right across from the Ritz Hotel. In the window was a woman's watch surrounded by these red, white and blue banners. I had plenty of money and inquired how much the watch was. The jeweler told me that it had no monetary value to speak of, but he would take 50 packets of cigarettes as payment. As I didn't have a large carton of smokes (that usually cost me less than 50 cents each) I told the proprietor that I'd come back tomorrow with a Luger.

Later that evening, I got dressed up and caught a cab to the California. The hotel was full of WACS [Women's Army Corps] and seemed a great spot to chat up a classy lady or two. After forcing my way to the bar I ordered myself a couple of glasses of champagne and a strong vodka martini and soon began to relax – perhaps a little too much. After a few more drinks, I noticed Bob Sink sitting in the corner getting pretty well skinned with a group of officers and decided to go over. Patting Sink on the back a few times, he turned and I said, "Hi, sir, how are you doing?" His response kinda shocked me for a minute, "What in the hell are you doing here, Shames?" "Sir, I'm AWOL and I don't care what you do!" Sink smiled and said, "Get your tail back to base because I've just signed you off and we are looking to send you home tomorrow!" "Are you kidding me?" "No, I wouldn't jerk you around about a thing like that. Go on, get the hell out of here and good luck in Civvy Street!" "But, sir, I'm not sure if I can get a train at this time of night and besides it's over 125 miles back to Bar-le-Duc!" "Ahhh, you'll think of something, Shames, you always do."

Leaving the California, I was in a bit of a flap but when I saw Sink's driver, Wayne Scott, waiting outside in a sedan, things suddenly became much clearer. Wayne had originally been with me in I Company so we knew each other reasonably well. "I'll give you half a dozen Lugers if you take me back to Bar-le-Duc ... right now!" "Scotty" knew Sink would be in the bar most of the night so he didn't need too much convincing. I jumped in and he drove me to the George Cinque before hitting the road. As we were leaving the city, I burst into laughter and said to Scotty, "Do you realize that I had the best room at the best hotel in Paris and never even got to sleep in the damned bed?"

The following morning, I packed my footlocker with all my worldly goods including my chalice and cognac from the Eagle's Nest and a TSMG that I'd acquired which wasn't on my ticket. However, the regiment gave me special dispensation for the remaining Lugers and also Kesselring's pistol. The old timers, like Hayseed, Strohl, Skinny, Gutty, Moe and McClung, had all gone by then, so after saying goodbye to Roy and one or two others, I joined a group of officers and headed for Marseille. On the train, I got talking to a British colonel and spent the rest of the journey down through the Rhone valley trying to put the world to rights. This English guy was commenting on the desperation of people in Europe and especially Czechoslovakia, which he seemed to have had some personal experience of. He'd come to the conclusion, and I was inclined to agree, that however bad the situation might seem, gold would always buy you something to eat and I quoted my mamma's golden rule, "He who has the gold, rules," which he was inclined to agree with.

When we arrived at the port, there were signs everywhere stating that no weapons were allowed on board ship and if caught, perpetrators ran the risk of severe punishment. Although I'd had written permission for the Kraut handguns, that night I still went to bed worrying what I should do with everything else. The next morning, before boarding the SS *Mariposa* for Boston, as nobody would take my trusty old M1, which had been with me since Toccoa, I had to throw it, along with the Thompson, down the nearest latrine! Christ, it was like giving a baby up for adoption or something, I was heartbroken and at the last minute decided to hide my Colt .45 amongst the German handguns stored in my footlocker.

I had my own cabin on the *Mariposa*, which was a liner that used to sail from San Francisco to Hawaii. Nobody checked the footlockers when they came off the ship. I mean, in the end, I could've put anything in there, which was particularly upsetting. I arrived home on September 15, during the Jewish festival of Yom Kippur, which signifies a kind of atonement for the upcoming year – which I always thought ironic! I called my mother to tell her that I had my train ticket and was scheduled to get into Norfolk at a specific time. I always hated it when a train was packed with enlisted men and the only spaces available were reserved for officers. It just seemed so unfair and I never abused the privilege if I could help it. When I arrived in Norfolk, there must have been 40 members of my family waiting, including my mother, brother George, and sisters Simmie and Anna. It was an incredible homecoming and completely unexpected.

14

"AMERITOCRACY"

Life after war

The morning after arriving home, Ed asked his brother George if he could borrow his car to visit Ida, and on the way he stopped off at an ABC liquor store.

Following the repeal of prohibition, Alcoholic Beverage Control Stores were still in operation across several states including Virginia.

When I tried to buy four bottles of whiskey the guy on the checkout asked for my coupons. Standing there in uniform, I just shrugged, "What the hell are you talking about? Ain't got no coupons, I've been away fighting the damn war – where've you been?" When the man told me to go put the bottles back, I leant over, grabbed his necktie, pulled him across the counter and tore into him. The store manager quickly came over, apologized profusely, handed me the booze, and wouldn't take a penny for it. After that I calmed down, shook hands, and made a hasty exit.

Ida's mother answered the door and showed me in, she was very frosty and I wondered what on earth Ida had told her about me. That day, Ida was lying on the couch in the living room with her foot all bandaged up. "It's great to see you my dear, but what on earth is going on with your foot?" "Oh it's nothing, Eddie, just an infected insect bite. When did you get home?" At that moment her sister came in and had a real go at me. I hadn't realized that the family had visitors and she thought it was highly inappropriate that I'd rocked up with four bottles of hard liquor! After Ida told her sister to scram, I began to share my feelings and was shocked to learn that Ida was now engaged to a naval officer called Joseph. On top of this bombshell, it turned out that Ida was also one of the most popular "pen pals" in Tidewater! Before I said goodbye, Ida admitted that at some point she'd sent gifts to all her soldier friends but the gold pen she'd sent me in Bastogne was kinda special … so I knew there had to be more to it.

The next day I telephoned to ask if Ida fancied coming to the Starlight Room in Norfolk with my cousin Sylvia Lichty to celebrate my homecoming. She knew Sylvia very well, so it wasn't like a date or anything, and besides, it would be a fun night out. That evening, when I collected Sylvia, my uncle Abe Winer gave me a bottle of Southern Comfort as a present. Because of the stringent rules in Virginia, clubs weren't allowed to sell wine or liquor but you could bring your own and pay a small "membership fee" whereupon glasses would be provided. The Starlight was on the 6th floor of the Monticello Hotel, and connected by a huge circular staircase. I drank like a fish then and could hold my liquor, but it wasn't quite the same for the girls. By the end of the evening, Ida and Sylvia had got so plastered on the whiskey and Southern Comfort that they slid down the handrails of the staircase, shouting their heads off as we left! Eventually around 1am, I arrived at my mother's and grabbed some tomato juice in a desperate attempt to sober the girls up. When that failed dismally, I figured we'd stop off at a nearby Toddle House, which was a national quick service restaurant chain, to get a few cups of black coffee. By this time it was nearly 2am, and I had to start thinking about getting the girls home!

Once we got back on the road, Ida and Sylvia collapsed in a stupor on the floor of the car, I just couldn't keep them on the seats! Thinking that both sets of parents were gonna kill me, I stopped at Sylvia's first, propped her up against the door, rang the bell and took off. I drove Ida round for another hour or so hoping she'd sober up some more before plucking up the courage to take her home. I didn't wait around and after making sure she was OK, abandoned her on the porch.

The next morning my Aunt Gussie rang to inquire what had happened to Sylvia, and I told her that it must've been something she ate … and luckily she believed me! After that I figured the best form of defense is offense and went over to Ida's and took her out for the day. Shortly afterwards, I learned that my discharge paperwork had been delayed so Fort Monroe couldn't do anything except send my regular salary checks via Western Union. Over the next 45 days, I took Ida out almost every day for either breakfast, lunch or dinner – and sometimes all three!

During my enforced sabbatical, it became obvious that I couldn't keep borrowing George's car, and I started looking around for one of my own. Of course you couldn't get a new automobile from anywhere at that time, so George put me in touch with Bernie Samuels, a used car dealer, who subsequently sold me a big 1941 Buick. Despite being in great condition, the tires were badly worn and couldn't be replaced due to rationing.

Ed rang Shorty Madona's mother Philomena, who was living in Meredith near Hartford, Connecticut.

His sister picked up the phone and when I asked her if it would be possible to visit, she told me she'd call back. The answer was of course "yes" but after making all the arrangements, a few minutes later, she was back on the line with bad news. I wasn't expecting Philomena to change her mind but from what I could gather she couldn't handle something like that. The family knew all about my relationship with Joe from the letters he'd sent home and all these years later, not being able to talk to his mom face to face still bothers me.

Putting the Madona situation behind me, I decided to visit Father Van over in Richmond which was about 100 miles away. During the trip, I was almost driven insane by one of the Buick's tires, which kept puncturing. Out of sheer desperation, I stopped off at the OPA Regional Office, which just happened to be in Richmond.

The Office of Price Administration was a federal agency established during the war to prevent inflation. The OPA were also empowered to issue ration coupons for scarce consumer goods such as gasoline and tires.

Recognizing the eagle patch on my uniform, a lady came over, and commented on how much America owed to the 101st Airborne Division. When I told her that my regiment was about to be disbanded she was horrified. After a while I explained my tire issues but despite being extremely apologetic she couldn't help. Then I really turned on the charm and explained about Father Van and the backstory to meeting his brother in Holland. Good God, as I piled it on, she almost broke down in tears. Before I knew what was happening, she disappeared for a few minutes before returning with enough coupons for me to replace all four of my tires... I just couldn't believe it.

After the tires were fitted, I went over to the church, only to be told by one of the nuns that Father Van had left for Holland a week or so earlier to visit his brother! The sisters then went on to say that ever since the day my sister made contact, they'd all been praying for my safe return, which made me smile.

Shortly before the regiment was officially deactivated at the end of November, I was summoned to Fort Meade, Maryland. While here, Barney Ryan arranged to have my nose fixed at the John Hopkins Hospital in Baltimore – a top research and teaching facility. Barney carried out the operation himself, which erased all trace of the damage left by the Kraut bullet on D-Day. Barney had made a wonderful recovery since being wounded on January 13, and was able to fill in the blanks for me about Joe Madona's last moments.

Not long after the operation, I was assigned to Camp Croft, near Spartanburg, South Carolina. As Croft was officially a separation center,

I figured they were going to discharge me here. I didn't know the camp was also the HQ for a new outfit they were calling the Special Operations Center. After checking in, a colonel by the name of Bush came over. "Glad to have you aboard, Shames." I was totally dumbfounded. "Excuse me, sir, I think you've got the wrong person – I'm waiting to be discharged from the Army!" "Oh, my goodness, I'm so sorry. You don't know, do you?" "Know what, sir?" "Colonel Robert F. Sink is a friend of mine and he has personally recommended you for this job." "Er, what job? I don't understand." "Well we have around 40 recently graduated young officers, all draftees, and you are here to straighten them out. We currently have a company-size cadre and I cannot seem to connect or do anything with them. I'm knocking on 50, and maybe I'm just too old for this sort of thing. I asked for a young officer, with plenty of experience in intelligence and Bob recommended you ... you should be damn proud of that!" "But I don't want to be here, sir, I've got other plans which don't involve staying in the service." "OK, I'll make you a deal. These kids don't seem to give a damn and if you can inject some sort of discipline into them, then I'll see about organizing your discharge papers ... does that sound fair?"

Foolishly I agreed and went over to the Special Ops compound but there was absolutely no one about! Eventually I found the first sergeant, and he told me that some of the kids had gone into town, while the rest were somewhere on the base. I was completely flabbergasted and asked the NCO to call the camp MP HQ and have them send an officer over right away to discuss the situation. In the meantime, I asked the first sergeant to bring me a roster that I could hand over to the MP officer. When the guy arrived, I asked politely if he could round up every one on the list and bring them back to my company HQ, right NOW! In handcuffs if necessary.

It took a while but I got all the kids back. Most were furious when I sent them all into a nearby lecture room for a pep talk. It was just like old times as I made it clear that anyone who didn't shape up over the next week would be thrown into the guardhouse. Suddenly everyone started voicing an opinion. Over the growing noise, I shouted, "Shut up! I don't care how intelligent you are or what your damn rank is – you will obey my word of command and start behaving in an appropriate manner." It took a bit of time but I managed to get everyone onto a routine schedule.

Little did Ed realize but it was to be the start of a career that would span several decades.

One Friday evening two weeks later I was over at the officers' club and after a few martinis decided to call Ida. "Hi babe, how you doin'?" Ida seemed a little cagey with her responses, and then the penny dropped and I realized her fiancé Joseph was there! "OK, now listen, I'm coming over right now, so if you love me, like I love you, then get rid of that son of a gun. I swear you'll never regret it … I swear."

I left immediately and drove 400 miles through the night and arrived at Ida's house around 4:30am, where she was waiting with her mother and father. The situation was difficult, as Joseph was confidently expecting Ida to drive with him to New York State on the Monday, to meet his folks and look for an engagement ring to make things official. Although it was clear that Ida's mother didn't like me, her dad did, but they both needed convincing that I was the right guy for their daughter. Anyhow, things panned out for the best and they insisted I stay. On Sunday after I drove back to Croft, I reminded Colonel Bush that we had a deal and he agreed to start the paperwork for my severance.

Ida and I were married on January 27, 1946 at Bethel Temple in Norfolk. It was a big event and I left with half a bottle of whiskey in one hand and my girl in the other.

With Ida by his side Ed's postwar life had well and truly begun. Nor was it to be without its fair share of adventure as Ed was subsequently recalled to service with "The Company" and this time he did not request any severance papers.

The Muehlebach Hotel

On Wednesday June 5, 1946, around 50 survivors from 3/506 traveled to Missouri to gather at the Muehlebach Hotel in Kansas City to honor Lieutenant Colonel Robert Wolverton's last wishes. On the eve of D-Day, Wolverton had designated the Midwest's most prestigious hotel during his "one year from today" speech, in which he discussed the possibility – if things went well – that everyone would be home by June 1945. Bob's wife Kathleen, who was known as Kay, along with Helen Briggs, an American Red Cross representative to the battalion during the war, arranged the reunion on behalf of her late husband and the 200 men from 3rd Battalion who had lost their lives since that fateful night.

Situated downtown, the ten-story hotel dominated the corner of 12th and Baltimore between the Orpheum and Gayety theatres. The first reunion for the battalion centered on the Muehlebach's beautiful ballroom with its polished wooden floor, enormous mirrors, 25ft-high ceiling and ornate art deco moldings. "We had a sit down banquet followed by a silent vigil." On the Sunday a memorial service was held in a local Presbyterian chapel, where Kay read aloud her husband's pre D-Day prayer. The prayer was followed by an alphabetical roll call of the dead while a bugler played a haunting version of "The Last Post." Choking back the tears, Ed squeezed Ida's hand tightly as Kay read out the names of Joseph P. Madona, Paul L. Simrell and George O. Retan.

Following the deactivation of the 506th PIR on November 30, 1945, many of the men, including Ed, had wondered whether the sacrifice of their friends had been worthwhile. For others it would take 50 years to accept the time spent in Europe as a positive experience. "For me, I don't think the reunion drew a line under anything I did in World War II, it is something that I still struggle with … even today." Joe Gorenc and Don Ross did not make the reunion. Don lost touch with Ed, and it was not until February 2004 that Shames learned what had happened to his bugling prodigy.

I was beside myself to hear his voice again after all these years and as we spoke, I could picture him in my mind just as he was.

After his capture on D–Day, Don had eventually ended up at the Falknov an der Eger prison camp in Czechoslovakia, which was a subunit of the infamous Flossenbürg concentration camp. Forced to break up ice on a frozen river through the worst winter in 50 years, Don suffered severe frostbite to his hands and feet. In early March 1945, with the Allies on the doorstep, Don and his fellow prisoners rose up and disarmed their captors. After leaving the camp, Ross fought with Czech guerrillas for the next two months before joining forces with the Russians, who handed him over to the US 1st Infantry Division in early May. At that time Ross had long hair, a full beard and weighed around 115lbs. Don ended up in Le Havre at Camp Lucky Strike before being shipped home. When he arrived at Newport News (not far from Virginia Beach) at the end of June he was given two months' leave, and the war ended before his furlough expired. Six weeks after Ed and Don were reunited by telephone, Don passed away peacefully at Sutter Lakeside Hospital, California.

Not long after the Muehlebach, Ed attended the first divisional reunion where he was reunited with Buck Taylor, Shifty, Mac and Junior Suerth.

But, due to my rapidly growing commitments with "The Company," this would be the last reunion I attended for many years. Afterwards, we went back to stay with Ida's parents. Don't get me wrong, I mean, their house was really beautiful, we just didn't want to live there. We started renting cheaply for a few months until we found a lovely apartment that cost around $40 per month, which both our families helped to furnish. In December 1946, we decided to take a massive risk and purchase a plot of land for $3,000 in the middle of town. Our folks thought we'd lost our minds as we used up all our savings. By then I was receiving a decent salary from "The Company," and at the end of 1947 we began to look at possible designs for our dream home. We needed roughly $12,000 for the build and furnishings, which of course we didn't have and I wasn't going to sponge off Ida's folks.

My mother suggested I go see Mr Robert Beamon at the National Bank of Commerce, who'd previously had favorable dealings with my dad but that was nearly 20 years ago. It was a typical freezing cold December day when I went downtown to see Mr Beamon. Of course I had no idea that he was now Chairman of the Board! It took some doing but eventually I was shown to his office on the second floor. Beamon's secretary asked if I had an appointment. "No mam, I'm sorry, I don't but my mother, Mrs Shames, said I should see Mr Beamon." After the PA disappeared into his office, Mr Beamon came out. "Are you Edward Shames?" "Yes, sir." "I'm Robert Beamon. How did you get to me?" "My mamma Sadie sent me to see you!"

Mr Beamon continued, "David was your father, right? I saw you in the newspaper a couple of years back – I think it was a story about you being recommended for the Distinguished Service Cross in Normandy…" I explained that Alex Bobuck had probably blocked the citation and the award never went through. "I'm sorry to hear that, but I recognized your surname immediately. I knew your father quite well. So what is it you think you need from me?" "Well, sir, I would like, if it is at all possible, to borrow $12K to build a house on a lot we purchased outright last year." While we were talking Beamon reached into his desk and pulled out a sheet of paper. "Do you have a middle name, Mr Shames?" "Yes sir, I do. It's David, just like my father." With that Mr Beamon wished me luck, said goodbye and asked me to take the folded note downstairs and present it to the main cashier.

The cashier asked, "Do you want to pay for this monthly?" "I don't quite understand. Can you say that again please?" "Well, I'm not sure how this has happened but the chairman of this banking group has personally agreed to give you a loan for $12,000 … does $120 a month sound OK?" Picking myself up, I responded, "I'm not sure we could stretch to that if I'm completely honest with you." "Well, if we added a few more years to the loan then we could get it down to around $60 – can you handle that?" "Yep, that'll be perfect." "If at any time you can afford to pay more then just let us know, OK?" It took me a minute to process what had just happened but whatever business my family had had with Mr Beamon, it most certainly left a lasting impression.

After we built the house, Cliff Irby, the guy I'd hit with the lead pipe back in school, who by now was a wholesale appliance dealer, saved us a fortune by supplying everything we needed, and I mean everything, at less than half price … which was very decent of him. John van Kooijk also realized his dream and stayed with us for around six months. His visit didn't go unnoticed by the press. Despite all the media attention we still found time to sightsee, and Ida and I took him to one of our favorite places, the Outer Banks in North Carolina on the beautiful Atlantic coast, where the Wright Brothers first flew at Kill Devil Hills.

When John van Kooijk's wife died he came to America and was sponsored by Ed to gain US citizenship. John passed away in 1995.

By the early 1950s Ed's postwar career had begun to blossom and despite his busy overseas schedule, Ed still managed to keep in touch with many of his old colleagues like Roy Gates, Buck Taylor, Paul Rogers, Rod Strohl, Gutty, Charlie Chase, Bob Sink, Ben Hiner (who became a dentist), Joe Beyrle, Herb Suerth and Joe Gorenc.

Smartly, Gorenc used the $2,000 that he'd won back in England to set himself up in business as a refrigeration and heating engineer. Tragedy struck in the late 1950s when Joe fell from a chimney and was killed instantly. Just like Bob Sink, Charlie Chase became a three-star lieutenant general. Charlie went on to become the commandant of the Staff College in Norfolk for two years, where I also worked every now and then. At the time Charlie was going through a messy and very painful divorce and he used to come over and stay at our house at least three or four times a week and became part of the family until his untimely death.

Without doubt Ed had an amazing career working for his "outfit," perhaps more so than his work in World War II. Of course much of what he was involved in is still classified but "The Company" has allowed Ed, and sometimes Ida also, to travel the world and experience many different cultures.

All these years later, Ed and Ida are still married, and despite Ida's recent health issues they are still doing their level best to enjoy life to the full.

Although no longer on the active list, I'm still required once a year to qualify on the range to keep my pistol, yep, the same old .45 government automatic that I smuggled back seven decades ago. I often compete with the younger fellows who, using their 9mm Glocks, are fooled into thinking that there is no way that the "old guy" is ever going to hit any target with that "cannon!" Let me tell you now, they very nearly always lose the bet, which is usually a bottle of expensive whiskey.

EPILOGUE

I have no clue where the idea of a foreword originated, but I would like to take this opportunity to introduce a "last word" as a finishing touch. Firstly, I would like the reader to know that I do not consider myself as any kind of "hero," I did my job to the best of my ability, and I firmly believe the men under my command made me what I am. However, I do consider myself a good soldier, who along with many other good soldiers, was exceptionally well trained to accomplish our military missions, and although I'm probably biased, I feel that 3rd Platoon, E Company, 506th Parachute Infantry Regiment, did it better than almost any other unit in the 101st Airborne Division during World War II.

This of course was not by accident but by design and we worked hard in our role when designated by regiment as patrol platoon. My job as leader of 3rd Platoon came my way by accident more than anything else. I truly believe that Colonel Sink assigned me to Captain Nixon (2nd Battalion S3) to help carry the load, as the captain was clearly struggling with chronic alcohol abuse. After realizing that I had no future with Nixon, I petitioned for a transfer to another position and was thrown out of Colonel Strayer's office. It is fair to say that Strayer did not like me, but then again I had little respect for him. Out of desperation, I broke the chain of command rule and asked, without formal permission, to see Colonel Sink.

After being lectured by his adjutant Salve Matheson, I finally got to see Sink, who was not best pleased with what I had done. But to his credit, Sink listened. Although I did not know it at the time, the colonel had just returned from a post-Normandy conference, where an idea had been presented to select and designate a regular rifle platoon, to take on an additional "patrolling" role, and be at the regiment's disposal, whenever and wherever required. Anyhow, to cut a long story short, Sink thought that I might be capable of leading such a platoon and I somewhat ungraciously accepted his offer.

When it finally sank in that I would at some stage be in command of my own platoon, I inquired whom Sink was going to make my assistant. His reply was one that I will never forget, "Shames, I know of no officer in this regiment that would last with you for more than a day, so you are on your own!" At that point in time I didn't know if he was joking or being serious and with that he told me to get the hell out of his office!

Before anything could be formalized, we were put on standby for the invasion of Holland and given less than two days to prepare for the mission. As I was still unassigned, regimental executive officer Colonel Charles Chase temporarily posted me to the regimental S3 department. Directly after the jump at Son, I was assigned to work with the Dutch underground before eventually being posted to 3rd Platoon in October 1944. While on my way to Driel, I bumped into my old buddy from I Company, Shorty Madona, who informed me that word had gone around that a "hard ass" former first sergeant was going to take over E Company's 3rd Platoon and they were determined to show him who was boss! That didn't bode well, but of course, that never bothered me, as I knew the score, and was determined to make a success of it. When I arrived I made it quite clear that I was not there to be loved, but hoped to earn respect and vice versa. It took me a while to get to know the men who – in my humble opinion – turned out to be some of the finest, toughest, sons of bitches in the entire army, and also the smartest.

My platoon sergeant, Amos Taylor, could easily have been an officer, but never had the opportunity, although rather selfishly I'm glad, because he was a huge asset to our platoon. Paul Rogers was one of the finest, if not the finest, soldier I ever met in the US military. If I was half as good a man as him, I'd die happy and most of the other people in my platoon would have said the same.

Up until joining E Company, I'd never met a mortarman like Rod Strohl. His skill with a 60mm mortar was uncanny, usually – as if by magic – within two shots he was on target. Away from the weapon, on patrol, he was always dependable and superbly professional.

Forrest Guth became a very dear friend and after the war I was best man at his wedding. As an armorer, that man could repair almost anything, and was a joy to have around. I had two exceptional patrol scouts, "Shifty" Powers and Earl McClung, who were perfection personified. Both were expert riflemen, both came from a Native American background, and I probably used them far too much because of their exceptional tracking and marksmanship skills.

Walter "Smokey" Gordon was not only incredibly skilled with a machine gun but he was also smart; after the war he became a lawyer. Never a dull moment with him around, no matter how bleak, he always had something to liven up the situation. During Operation *Pegasus 1*, we were in the same boat going across the Rhine. I was terrified that it would all end in disaster, but Smokey came up with some wisecrack that made our entire seven-man team almost implode with muffled laughter.

On the other hand, I could never forget Robert "Popeye" Wynn, who never smiled and was always serious but could be counted on to do his job. He was another guy that I knowingly took advantage of, but as Popeye was such an intuitive soldier, he became imperative to our night patrolling schedule.

I'd also like to mention Herbert Suerth, who came to me as a replacement before Bastogne after being turned down by everyone else. Not because he was unqualified but because he looked about 15 years old. After checking his records, I discovered that he was only a year or two younger than me but he had a great educational background, so I snapped him up. I was convinced that I'd made the right choice, but fate played a hand in that "Junior" as we named him, was in the wrong spot at the wrong time and spent 18 months in hospital after being wounded at Bastogne. Up until quite recently, Herb was president of our association, which rather reluctantly we decided to shut down owing to the inevitable dwindling numbers. He is still a dear friend and even today in October 2014, is still affectionately known to me by his old nickname.

It would be remiss not to mention James "Moe" Alley who, as you will know from this book, holds a special place in my heart and story. Also "Skinny" Sisk, the craziest person I've ever known. Don "Cosmetic" Moone and Joe Lesniewski, who still hated me until the day he died! Joe, I still loved you, despite our differences.

We had three light machine-gun teams in the platoon, all led by Smokey, but I would never hesitate to have Walter Hendrix, aka "Black Jack," or Frank Mellett fill in any job we took on needing heavy firepower. They all knew their stuff. Unfortunately Frank was killed instantly during the final attack on Foy. Frank was so good at his job that he held the rank of non-com in a slot that really called for a Private First Class.

I could go through the entire roster of over forty men and tell you about how good and proud they were to serve in 3rd Platoon of E Company. I think it is fair to say that we were not the most popular group of people, perhaps because we were sometimes over confident, or maybe there was a little jealousy from time to time but that being said we were all proud to have served, and especially with E Company.

I was with 3rd Platoon for 11 months, which was quite unusual under the circumstances. A lot of officers would say that they were just lucky, but those in 3rd Platoon will tell you that maybe luck did play her part, but we worked 24/7 on trying to achieve perfection. We of course never attained perfection, but I think we came damned close. None of us will ever forget one of our key players, Robert McArdle. We called Private "Mac" our supply officer, and above everyone else he was probably the most important man in the platoon. If we needed anything then he would get it and quick. He had a knack that would allow him to find, beg, borrow or steal anything that wasn't nailed down tight! No matter the situation, if either myself, or Paul Rogers, asked for something, seemingly no matter what, it would be instantly "requisitioned" by Mac. I still don't really know Mac's background, but he had a quip for everything and he worshiped Paul Rogers.

All the soldiers I have talked about are the reason why I say that our platoon, was perhaps one of the best trained, with the best soldiers. I have been honored to be able to say I was part of this unit and I think working alongside the members of 3rd Platoon did ultimately make me a better officer.

There are just two things that I am most proud of about my service in the 506th Parachute Infantry Regiment, 101st Airborne Division: my battlefield commission and the fact that the 3rd Platoon brought more men home from the war than any other of the 500 platoons in the division.

I've often wondered why I survived when most of my colleagues did not. Of course no one in the world can answer such a question but I still think about the guys, especially Shorty Madona, practically every day. Although it's been over 70 years since they died, to me it only seems like yesterday and it was a true privilege to know them.

Edward D. Shames
506th Parachute Infantry Regiment, August 1942–September 1945

BIBLIOGRAPHY

Listed below are the works that I have consulted during my research over the last 14 years. To their authors I offer my sincere thanks.

Books and papers

Ambrose, Stephen E., *Band of Brothers* (Simon & Schuster Classic Edition, 2001)

Bando, Mark A., *The 101st Airborne at Normandy* (MBI, 1994)

Bando, Mark A., *101st Airborne: The Screaming Eagles at Normandy* (MBI, 2001)

Baumgardner, Randy, *101st Airborne Division – Screaming Eagles* (Turner Publishing, 2nd Edition, 2001)

Brotherton, Marcus, *Shifty's War, The Authorized Biography of Sergeant Darrell "Shifty" Powers, the Legendary Sharpshooter from the Band of Brothers* (Penguin Books Ltd, 2011)

Burgett, Donald R., *As Eagles Screamed* (Bantam Books, 1979)

Burgett, Donald R., *The Road to Arnhem* (Dell Publishing, 2001)

Day, Roger, *Ramsbury at War* (self-published, 2004)

DeTrez, Michel, *American Warriors* (D-Day Publishing, 1994)

DiCarlo, Hank and Westphal, Alan, *Currahee Scrapbook* (506 PIR, 1945)

Forty, George, *Patton's Third Army at War* (Ian Allan Printing Ltd, 1978)

Gardner, Ian and Day, Roger, *Tonight We Die As Men* (Osprey Publishing, 2009)

Gardner, Ian, *Deliver Us from Darkness* (Osprey Publishing, 2012)

Gardner, Ian, *No Victory in Valhalla* (Osprey Publishing, 2014)

Gutjahr, Major Robert G., *The Role of Jedburgh Teams in Operation Market Garden* (thesis presented to the US Army Command and General Staff College, 1978) c/o Tom Timmermans

Hannah, Harold W., *A Military Interlude, Cornfields to Academia to Parachutes* (self-published, 1999)

Heaps, Leo, *The Grey Goose of Arnhem* (Futura Publications Ltd, 1976)

Höjris, René, *Anthony "NUTS" McAuliffe* (Roger Publishing House, 2004)

Hoyt, Edwin P., *The Invasion Before Normandy* (Robert Hale, 1985)

Kesselring, Albert, *The Memoirs of Field-Marshal Kesselring* (William Kimber, 1974)

Killblane, Richard and McNiece, Jake, *The Filthy Thirteen* (Casemate, 2003)

Koskimaki, George E., *D-Day With the Screaming Eagles* (101st Airborne Division Association, 1970)

Koskimaki, George E., *Hell's Highway* (101st Airborne Division Association, 1989)

Koskimaki, George E., *The Battered Bastards of Bastogne* (Casemate reprint, 2011)

Laurence, Nicole and Léonard, Michel, *Saint-Côme-du-Mont Témoins d'hier* (Eurocibles, 2005)

Levit, Sgt Saul, "The Siege of Bastogne," *Yank Magazine* (1945)

Margry, Karel, *De bevrijding van Eindhoven (The Liberation of Eindhoven)* (September Festival Foundation, 1982)

Marshall, S. L. A., *Night Drop* (Atlantic Monthly Press, 1962)

McAuliffe, Kenneth J. Jr, *NUTS! The Life of Anthony C. McAuliffe* (self-published, 2011)

Mehosky, Ivan Paul, *The Story of a Soldier* (Rutledge Books, Inc., 2001)

Nekrassoff, Philippe R., and Eric Brissard, *Magneville Ce jour Lá* (Park Printing, 2000)

Norton, G. G., *The Red Devils (From Bruneval to the Falklands)* (Leo Cooper, 1984)

Pöppel, Martin, *Heaven & Hell – The War Diary of a German Paratrooper* (Spellmount, 2000)

Ramsey, Winston G. (ed.), *D-Day Then and Now, volumes 1 and 2* (Battle of Britain Prints International Ltd, 1995)

Rapport, Leonard and Northwood, Arthur Jr, *Rendezvous with Destiny* (Infantry Journal Press, 1948)

Ross, Donald C., *He beat the Odds – WW2 Autobiography* (self-published, 2004)

Sigmond, Robert and Van den Bosch, Cees, (ed.) *Escape across the Rhine, Operations 'Pegasus' I and II, October/November 1944* (Airborne Museum Hartenstein, 1999)

Taylor, Thomas H., *The Simple Sounds of Freedom* (Random House, 2002)

Terrify and Destroy: The Story of the 10th Armored Division (The Stars & Stripes, Paris, 1944/45)

Van Hout, Jan, (ed.), *Aangeboden Door De Gemeente Eindhoven, Herinneringen Aan September 1944 (Memories of September 1944 – presented by the Municipality of Eindhoven)* (self-published, 2004)

Webb, Robert, *Freedom Found* (self-published, 2000)

Reports and personal letters

440th Troop Carrier Group After Action Reports, Normandy 1944

436th Troop Carrier Group After Action Reports, Holland 1944

Air Support Requests 101st A/B Division 20–26 September 1944

"Buck" Taylor's letter to Dick Winters (December 14, 1992), c/o Joe Muccia

Eindhoven Fire Brigade Reports 13–19 September (1944), c/o Tom Timmermans

G Co Morning Reports 1942 to 1945, c/o Tim Moore

Headquarters 3rd Bn 506th PIR Combat Report for Neptune (1944), *Utah Beach to Cherbourg June 6–27, 1944,* The Historical Division (US Army World War II)

Headquarters VII Corps Exercise *Tiger* Reports, US National Archives

Headquarters 506th PIR "After Action Report" – Operation "Market" (1944)

Headquarters 506th PIR Citation "Operation Pegasus 1" – Operation "Market" (1944)

Headquarters 506th PIR Statistics: 17–26 September (1944)

Headquarters 506th PIR Unit Journal for Operation "Market" (1944)

Headquarters 506th PIR "After Action Reports" (17 December 1944– August 1945)

Headquarters IX Troop Carrier Command Operation: "Linnet," "Comet" and "Market" (1944)

Interview Notes from War Crimes Investigation Team, October 1945, c/o Gerhard Roletscheck

Memoir of C. Carwood Lipton, "Experience at Bastogne" (April 1990 revised February 1991), c/o Reg Jans

Memoir of John van Kooijk, "Experiences with 2nd Bn, 506th PIR during *Market Garden*, Bastogne, Alsace, Germany and Austria (1990), c/o Joe Muccia

Memorandum to Lieutenant Van Horn from Colonel Sink about Operation *Pegasus 1* (23 August 1945), c/o Joe Muccia

Memoire of Maarten van den Bent "Pegasus I" – Airborne Museum Hartenstein, c/o Daan Viergever

Missing Aircrew Report June 7, 1944, US National Archives, c/o Denis van den Brink

Medical History of Normandy Campaign, 506th PIR Medical Detachment (1944)

Operation Neptune – 506th PIR Regimental Journals May 28, 1944–June 27, 1944 (1944)

Paul Rogers' letter to Walter Gordon (August 2, 1992), c/o Joe Muccia

Participation of the 101st Airborne Division in Exercise *Tiger* (1944), US National Archives

Pegasus Memorial Battlefield Tour Guide, 12 September 2008, c/o Daan Viergever

Personal Letter of Carwood Lipton, c/o Reg Jans

"Shifty" Powers' letter to Stephen Ambrose (May 24, 1992), c/o Joe Muccia

Tactical Operations of the 101st A/B Division 17–27 September (1944)

Tactical Study HQ XVIII Corps Airborne Operation "Market" (1944)

US Army Military History Institute, George E. Koskimaki Collection: personal letters and documents, including 101st Divisional After Action Reports (December 1944), 101st Signal Co, 321st GFA Bn, Troop Carrier and Glider Information.

GLOSSARY

AEB	Airborne Engineer Battalion
AOC	Army Operations Center
AP	armor-piercing
AWOL	absent without leave
BC	battlefield commission
Bn	Battalion
Co	Company
CO	Commanding Officer
CP	command post
CQ	Charge of Quarters
DP	displaced person
DZ	drop zone
FIBUA	Fighting in Built Up Areas
FO	forward observer
GFA	Glider Field Artillery
GIR	Glider Infantry Regiment
ID	Infantry Division
IR	Infantry Regiment
IPW	interrogation of prisoner of war
KP	Knokploegen
LOD	line of defense
LZ	landing zone
MG	machine gun
MLR	main line of resistance
MP	Military Police
NAAFI	Navy, Army and Air Force Institutes
NBS	Nederlandse Binnenlandse Strijdrachten
NCO	Non-commissioned officers
OC	Officer Commanding
OCS	Officer Candidate School

OP	observation post
OPA	Office of Price Administration
OPLR	outpost line of resistance
PIR	Parachute Infantry Regiment
PLF	parachute landing falls
POW	prisoner of war
PT	physical training
PX	postal exchange
RE	Royal Engineers
ROTC	Reserve Officer Training Corps
SHAEF	Supreme Headquarters Allied Expeditionary Force
SOE	Special Operations Executive
SPG	self-propelled gun
TD	tank destroyer
TSMG	Thompson sub-machine gun
USO	United Services Organization
VCP	vehicle checkpoint
WACS	Women's Army Corps
XO	executive officer

INDEX

Praise for *Tonight We Die As Men*

"A product of original research and an important contribution to the literature… An amazingly detailed glimpse into the tragic experiences of this heroic parachute battalion."

Mark Bando, author of *101st Airborne: The Screaming Eagles at Normandy*

"It will be hard to find a better book about a single airborne battalion in World War II… The two British authors take the reader back to Toccoa, Georgia, and the initial training received (some would say endured) by the men of the 506th PIR, commanded by Col. Robert F. Sink, then on to airborne training at Fort Benning and Camp Mackall. They also flesh out the personalities mentioned in the book so that by the time the regiment is in England and preparing for its baptism of fire in Normandy, the reader has developed a fondness for each trooper."

Mason Webb, *World War II History*

"Ian Gardner and Roger Day have set out to tell the story of the 3rd Battalion of the famed 101st Airborne Division 506th Parachute Infantry Regiment. The objective of the battalion was to capture and secure the two wooden bridges built by the Germans over the Douve River east of Carentan, as access to what became known as Utah Beach. Despite the successful achievement of this important objective by the 3rd Battalion, accomplished with heavy losses, the authors found that little had been written about the battalion. In fact, they call the 3rd a 'forgotten battalion,' as opposed to the 2nd Battalion of 'Band of Brothers' fame."

James C. Roberts, *Washington Times*

"The most comprehensive, factual World War II history I have ever read. The reader is given a vivid account of the day to day life of the combat soldier in Europe. I appreciate the fact that I have met some of these men personally and now I am more aware of what they went through to defend our freedom."

Lamar Davis, Stephens County Historical Society, Toccoa, GA

Praise for *Deliver Us From Darkness*

"The experiences of the ordinary soldier and civilian are graphically explained and this book is highly recommended, not just for war historians but particularly as a valuable reminder of the sacrifices made almost seventy years ago, so that we can enjoy our current freedoms."

The Historical Association

"That's the beauty of books like this, not just to tell the larger story but to uncover small acts of heroism … for future generations to read."

The Journal